W9-BZL-685

CURRENT TOPICS IN EARLY CHILDHOOD EDUCATION

VOLUME 1

Current Topics in Early Childhood Education

Volume 1

Editor:
LILIAN G. KATZ

Associate Editors:
Mary Z. Glockner, Sharon T. Goodman, and Mima J. Spencer

ERIC Clearinghouse on Early Childhood Education
University of Illinois

ABLEX PUBLISHING CORPORATION
Norwood, New Jersey

1977

The material in this publication was prepared pursuant to a contract with the National Institute of Education, U.S. Department of Health, Education, and Welfare. Contractors undertaking such projects under government sponsorship are encouraged to express freely their judgment in professional and technical matters. Prior to publication, the manuscript was submitted to the Area Committee for Early Childhood Education at the University of Illinois for critical review and determination of professional competence. This publication has met such standards. Points of view or opinions, however, do not necessarily represent the official view or opinions of either the Area Committee or the National Institute of Education.

Ablex Publishing Corporation
355 Chestnut Street
Norwood, New Jersey 07648

ISBN 0-89391-000-7 ISSN 0363-8332
Printed in the United States of America

Contents

Preface

The nine papers presented in this volume were collected by staff members of the Educational Resources Information Center Clearinghouse on Early Childhood Education at the University of Illinois (ERIC/ECE). The major responsibility of ERIC/ECE, which is funded by the National Institute of Education (Department of Health, Education, and Welfare), is to collect, select, and disseminate information related to the education and development of children. This volume is a collection of informative integrative reviews of primary research and development reports relevant to workers and students in early childhood education.

The papers were originally submitted for publication in a proposed journal, *The Quarterly Review of Early Childhood Education.* However, the process of accumulating the necessary number of high quality manuscripts with which to launch the journal has been slow. As a result, it was decided that these nine papers should be made available in book form.

In the search for manuscripts, the editorial staff and the consulting editors used three major criteria: (1) selected papers should represent a wide range of topics relevant to the development and education of children from the prenatal period through the eighth year of life; (2) papers should serve to integrate, synthesize, and/or criticize research on a topic; and (3) selected papers should offer explications and clarifications of questions, issues, and positions related to the overall state-of-the-art of early childhood education. The papers in the present volume satisfy these three criteria.

Some of the topics are classical ones. Franklin and Biber explore the persistent problems of the relationship between developmental theory and early childhood pedagogy. The papers by DeVries and Kohlberg and Zimiles take up stubborn problems surrounding measurement, evaluation, and the nature of evidence in studying children's development. Asher *et al.* and Bernstein present reviews of two important subtopics in psychosocial development: school friendships and children's concepts of death. Takanishi and Boocock help us put current problems in their historical as well as crosscultural perspectives. The two papers by Lee and Kedar Voivodas and Levitt and Cohen on sex role development and parent involvement point out important emerging concerns in the field of early childhood education.

Current Topics in Early Childhood Education is a series that we hope to publish regularly. Readers' reactions and suggestions will be very welcome.

LILLIAN G. KATZ

CURRENT TOPICS IN EARLY CHILDHOOD EDUCATION

VOLUME 1

1

Psychological Perspectives and Early Childhood Education: Some Relations between Theory and Practice[1]

Margery B. Franklin

Sarah Lawrence College

Barbara Biber

Bank Street College of Education

INTRODUCTION

The aim of this paper is to delineate some of the central issues that confront us, as psychologists and educators, in this period of accelerated application of psychological theory and research to early childhood education.

In the past decade we have seen a rapid growth of programs in early childhood education. Many have arisen as part of an awakened sense of social responsibility, especially the recognition of the urgent need to deal with the plight of children from poor and minority group populations. Some have arisen in response to the demands of middle-class families, especially those where mothers work, for increased care and/or tutelage for their preschool children. Others have developed to serve primarily as "laboratories" for the study of the initial stages of development. Though differing in purpose and pattern, these programs have in common the conviction that the child's experience during the early years has important and enduring effects on his subsequent development, in fact, on all his transactions in the world of people and ideas.

The sources of underlying conceptualizations are many and diverse, but it is clear that a significant proportion reflect the direct impact of interest and

[1]An earlier version of this paper entitled "Issues in the Relation of Psychology to Early Childhood Education" was presented at the President's Symposium, *Interactions Among Theory, Research, and Application in Child Development*, at the meetings of the Society for Research in Child Development, Philadelphia, March 1973.

effort on the part of curriculum developers who draw heavily on aspects of theory and/or research in child development (cf. Parker & Day, 1972). While some programs are eclectic, drawing on an assortment of theoretical precepts, others are based, more or less rigorously, on theory-specific concepts about the nature of psychological development and related appropriate methods of education. Some programs are comprehensive in nature, encompassing the totality of experience and relationships that are planned and provided. Others are circumscribed components inserted into the matrix of a general program. In almost all corners, however, we see a more and more widespread effort to bring the concepts and findings from the academic discipline of child psychology to bear on the education of young children.

The complexities of interrelations between psychological theories and educational ideologies, between the findings of research and the implementation of specific goals in practice are indeed awesome. A number of recent books and articles (Fein & Clark-Stewart, 1973; Kohlberg & Mayer, 1972; Mayer, 1971; Sigel, 1972a) reflect an intensified effort to come to grips with the intricacies of these complex interrelationships. There is, for example, increasing recognition of the question of values inherent in the establishment of any educational program, as well as greater awareness of the sociopolitical implications of intervention programs, originally designed to provide "compensatory" education for children of so-called disadvantaged backgrounds (cf. Bronfenbrenner, 1974; Sigel, 1973). This heightened awareness, expressed in the self-critical reflection evident in the current writings of psychologists and educators, stems no doubt, in part, from the fact that many of the innovative programs in education failed to achieve their stated goals in the time allotted (cf. Ford Foundation, 1972). But another factor, with more positive implications for the future, is the increased interchange between psychologist program developers and educational practitioners that necessarily occurred as more psychologists moved into the heretofore unfamiliar territory of the school and more educators consciously sought psychological-theory bases for curricular planning.

On the contemporary scene we see a diversity of programs reflecting the influence of differing psychological viewpoints. We have seen, also, in the past five or six years, a changing attitude toward the evaluation of outcomes of differing educational programs, a growing mood to reexamine the earlier assumptions and techniques underlying evaluative procedures. The programs included in the Planned Variation Experiment for Head Start and in Project Follow Through provide an extraordinary opportunity to observe the linkage of underlying values, theoretical suppositions, educational goals, and methods of implementation that characterize widely divergent programs in early child education (e.g., Bissell, 1973; Fein & Clark-Stewart, 1973; Maccoby & Zellner, 1970).

In this paper we shall focus on three central currents in the field, undertaking to clarify the differing assumptions on which they are based, the differing ways in which they draw on and utilize psychological concepts, and on the ways in which they therefore involve young children in qualitatively different encounters with people, problems, and ideas in the school setting. We begin by looking at two approaches to early childhood programming which are based quite explicitly on two divergent psychological perspectives: the behavioristic-learning-theory perspective and the Piagetian cognitive-developmental perspective. For our third case we examine in somewhat greater detail a long-established program design recently designated as the developmental-interaction approach (Biber, in press; Shapiro & Biber, 1972). From the perspective of psychological theory this approach represents an integration of cognitive-developmental stage concepts and ego psychology formulations. In the case of the developmental-interaction approach theory has an important place as a basic rationale for practice, but essential elements of this educational design have roots in the progressive education ideology of the John Dewey period.

The final section of the paper is concerned with a summary statement of the issues arising in our discussion of these three central approaches to early childhood education, including a consideration of some of the problems that must be confronted in the task of evaluating effects of differing modes of education.

At the outset we may say that we do not claim to approach our task here as neutrals, as impartial observers, or disinterested bystanders who are simply reporting on the current scene. We speak from the perspective of developmental-interactionists but we have attempted to present alternative views in their own terms.

THE BEHAVIORISTIC-LEARNING THEORY APPROACH

A growing number of programs in early childhood education reflect the direct impact of contemporary behavioristic psychology. These approaches share in common the idea that many basic concepts of other psychologies—concepts like "cognitive structure," "underlying motivation," etc.—are not only vague but superfluous, and may be counterproductive in the context of education where one is presumably directed toward effecting behavior change in an efficient manner. At the core of all behavioristic psychologies lie the precepts that (a) observable behavior or performance constitutes the primary datum for the scientific investigation of learning processes and for approaches to behavior change, and (b) the basic principles of learning are the laws of classical and operant conditioning.[2] In the behavior modification movement, which appears

[2]Kanfer (1973) discusses four "models" of learning within the behavioristic framework, two of which—"modeling or vicarious learning" and "self-regulation"—do not involve the *direct* application of conditioning procedures. While some of the methods currently employed by behavior modifiers cannot be directly derived from the position of any given behaviorist psychologist, it is nonetheless the case that all are variations on a basic theme and rest on commonly held assumptions. For a recent consideration of concepts of reinforcement in behavioristic learning theory, see Bandura (1974).

to be the strongest among behavioristically-oriented approaches to educational programming, emphasis has fallen on the use of operant conditioning techniques as developed in Skinner's work.[3]

The aim of behavior modification is to achieve measurable changes in observable behavior. Fundamentally, this consists of arranging or planning an environment in which the individual will come to produce what are designated as "appropriate responses" or "desirable behaviors," and *not* persist in producing inappropriate or undesirable responses/behaviors. What an individual does—that is, what behavior he engages in, what responses he will come to emit under given circumstances—depends on the consequences of his behavior. Some consequences serve to increase the probability of occurrence of a given behavior, while others serve to diminish it. By definition, "positive reinforcers" are those events which, occurring after a response, increase the probability of the response; "negative reinforcers" are those consequents which diminish it. Theoretically, only careful observation can determine what constitute positive and/or negative reinforcers for a given behavior of a given individual. In practice, however, there is a tendency to assume—prior to such careful observation—that certain occurrences are generally reinforcing and that others are not. For example, the widespread use of M & M candies as a reward for behavior designated desirable by the trainer is based on the assumption that most young children are very fond of candy.[4] Typically, the "shaping of appropriate behavior" consists of bringing a response or behavior "under the control" of a given stimulus or category of stimuli; that is, in getting the person to produce the response when a given stimulus is present and *not* to produce it when the stimulus is not present or when some other stimulus is present. This is achieved through providing reinforcement when, and only when, the response is produced under specified circumstances. Some of the specific techniques employed have been well described by Ackerman (1972), among others.

In the view of behavior-modifiers oriented toward educational programming, any attempt to change or modify behavior in the classroom (which encompasses not only the eradication of "problems" but the process of education in toto) requires: (a) analysis of the present situation in behavioristic terms, (b) specification of the desired behavior changes, and (c) specification of the techniques appropriate to their realization. In line with their conviction that any program must be based on empirically demonstrated "facts" concerning the efficacy of

[3]While Skinner does not want to be regarded as the father of a "theory," the arguments propounded by Reese and Overton (1970), Kohlberg and Mayer (1972), and others support our view that the "functional analysis of behavior" espoused by Skinner, and the behavior modification approach in general, are firmly tied to an underlying model/theory of psychological functioning and development—and as such are not merely "methods" for the analysis of behavior.

[4]Note that unlike some other behaviorist psychologists, the Skinnerian approach does not link the notion of reinforcement to primary or secondary drive reduction.

given techniques, psychologists who advocate the use of behavior modification techniques in the classroom have done a considerable amount of research to validate their claim that the principles of learning derived from Skinnerian studies of pigeons and rats in laboratory settings are applicable to the analysis and modification of classroom behavior. Becker (1973), for example, reviews a number of studies which were designed to show the effects of regulated delivery of social reinforcement. In a typical study, an aggressive and disruptive child was observed first for a period of days during which teachers simply maintained their "ongoing pattern of responding." Then, there was a period of seven days in which "the teachers showered Martha with social reinforcement and desirable material goods [p. 81]," giving her a great deal of attention and affection. During the third phase of the experiment, only Martha's specifically and overtly cooperative behavior was followed by the delivery of social reinforcement. It was in this phase of "contingent reinforcement" and not in the preceding phase that there was a progressive increase in the frequency of Martha's cooperative play. When noncontingent reinforcement was again instituted (as in the second phase), the frequency of cooperative play dropped. These findings are typical of those used to support the position that it is *not* the creation of a generally warm, accepting, supportive, etc., environment that leads to positive behavior change, but only the planned and systematic administration of reinforcement on a contingency basis (i.e., if and only if the child performs behavior X, does he get reinforcement).

Among programs resting on behavioristic precepts are those of Bereiter and Engelmann (1966), Engelmann and Becker (cf. Maccoby & Zellner, 1970), and Bushell 1973). While not rigorously following a specific behavioristic paradigm, Bereiter and Engelmann drew heavily upon the precepts of behaviorism in developing specific teaching techniques for their "academic preschool." More recently, Engelmann and Becker have been sponsors of one of the models for Project Follow Through which in a similar way is based on behavioristic thinking.

Bushell's Behavior Analysis Program (1973)—another of the Follow Through models—represents a systematic attempt to apply contemporary behavior modification methods to classroom programming and management. Like all behavioristically-based programs, Bushell's program involves the systematic, regulated administration of reinforcement as the principle means for teaching children the behaviors considered requisite for success in school. The behaviors at issue encompass a wide range—from appropriate social behavior in the classroom to the acquisition of specific academic skills. As in other such programs, positive reinforcers include candy or other snacks, access to favorite toys, access to favorite activities such as art, recess, and/or listening to stories. And when there is adequate basis for considering it a positive reinforcer, the teacher's attention, or more specifically the teacher's expression of praise, is utilized as a means of controlling behavior (i.e., teacher's praise is a social reinforcer, its delivery contingent on the child's producing an appropriate behavior). Withholding of such reinforcers is the primary means of reducing and ultimately eradicating those behaviors designated as undesirable. For example, the withholding of praise is used as a controlling technique when the teacher, noticing that one child is being inattentive, gives emphatic praise to another child who *is* paying attention. An important feature of Bushell's program is the establishment in some classrooms of a "token economy" where children earn tokens for designated behaviors; these tokens can subsequently be exchanged for desired goods or the privilege of engaging in a desired activity. In Bushell's program, tokens may also be used to buy the right to indulge for a short period of time in undesirable behavior (1968).[5]

Considering the principles of behavioristic psychology as a basis for educational programming involves coming to grips with several related questions. One question, raised by behaviorists themselves, concerns the efficacy of specific procedures for achieving a circumscribed end result (a given behavior or set of behaviors). As we have said, the argument for the efficacy of behavior modification techniques in classroom settings is buttressed by reference to studies designed to demonstrate that the regulation of reinforcement (i.e., the establishment of reinforcement contingencies) is effective in bringing about observable and measurable behavior change. And, indeed, many of the studies cited in the context of such an argument provide strong evidence that aspects of observable behavior can be regulated through such procedures. However, behavioristically-inclined educators show increasing concern with (a) the extent to which a given learned behavior generalizes to situations other than the one in which original training occurred, and (b) whether continuing production of the desired behavior is contingent upon the continued administration of a given reinforcer. This ties into the question of "durability" of behavior change, and to the possibility of "fading out" reinforcers such as candy and toys in preference to social reinforcers such as praise, and perhaps ultimately in preference to self-administered reinforcers (e.g., "Gee, I'm a good kid for doing that!"). On these issues—generalization or transfer, durability, and the substitution of less tangible for more tangible rewards—evidence is not so conclusive (cf. Scriven, 1973). In other words, it is not clear that behavior modification techniques produce behavior changes which transfer readily to new situations and which can be maintained without the regular administration of tangible rewards. Most behavior-modifer-educationalists see these as technical problems to be overcome through improvements in training methods.[6]

[5]Krasner and Krasner (1973) have discussed some of the specific procedures involved in establishing token economies in classroom settings, and review a number of studies aimed at assessing the efficacy of such procedures.

[6]Whether or not one subscribes to this general approach—and clearly, we do not—it must be granted that aspects of these questions can be stated in sufficiently precise terms to be amenable to empirical inquiry in the behaviorist mode: Can the desired behavior be

At this point, it is important to point out that behavior modification is viewed by its proponents as a *technology*; in the context of education, it is aimed at getting the child to perform in whatever ways the program developer (often a psychologist) considers beneficial, desirable, and educationally worthwhile. It is maintained that behavior modification can be put to any one of a variety of uses, geared toward the realization of any educational objective which is stated with sufficient precision and explicitness. This is, of course, consonant with Skinner's contention that on the level of social planning, the techniques of operant conditioning can be as readily used to create a Utopia (namely, Walden Two) as a fascistic state. The technology is purportedly value-free. It is clear, however, that as soon as technology is applied, decisions are being made which involve levels of value judgments. In current discussion among behavior modifiers over the use of punishment, the focus is on efficacy; many maintain that if punishment techniques prove optimally efficient in a given situation, their use is justified (cf. Mahan, 1973). This formulation reflects the assumption that the technology as such is value-free, and precludes questions about wider ranging meanings of giving and receiving punishment in ongoing teaching-learning situations. With regard to decisions about objectives, behaviorist-educators seem to agree that learning should be transferable and durable, and that if at all possible, children should work for rewards like praise rather than for M & Ms. The fact is that anyone setting up an educational program—whether this is a comprehensive program or a circumscribed program component—cannot operate in terms of such limited objectives but is immediately involved in making higher level (and more clearly value-laden) decisions concerning substantive aspects of the educational process. If behavior modification is the value-free technology it claims to be, it cannot provide guidelines here. The technologist-program-developer must seek an advisor who will define objectives, or go beyond his technologist role in establishing goals. An educational programmer is necessarily involved in delineating program objectives which are inherently, if not explicitly, tied to a broader educational ideology; furthermore, there is generally a strong interaction between selection of means and ends.

When we survey current programs in early education which draw on behavioristic psychology, and which generally make use of behavior-modification techniques (including the extension into setting up a token economy), we find that in fact these programs typically reflect adherence to highly traditional conceptions of the goals of education and of appropriate modes of conduct in the classroom, leading to an emphasis—at the preschool level—on circumscribed academic content and socially conforming behavior. The influential programs of Bereiter and Engelmann (1966) and Bushell (1973) stand as prime

---

shaped? Does the behavior transfer? Does the desired behavior last? Is it necessarily contingent on tangible rewards, or can it be brought under the control of less tangible rewards? Since the preparation of this paper, Levine and Fasnacht (1974) have presented a strong critique of token reward procedures, focused in part on questions such as these.

examples here. In our view, children in such classrooms are not only learning the specific skills and modes of conduct which are the "target behaviors" of the program, but are inevitably picking up other messages, learning other things, as well. For example: That learning itself consists primarily in the acquisition of specific items of information, or highly specific procedures to be applied to given materials; that questions have specific answers which are right *or* wrong, and that knowledge of the correct answers (or, more explicitly, giving the correct response) is the path to success; that the path to success (and presumably to feelings of competence or self-worth) involves a straight line to the teacher or other authority who holds the key as to what is right or wrong, and dispenses the goodies when correct answers are forthcoming. If the teacher is not excessively authoritarian, he or she can be perceived as a harmless and pleasant game-player, a source of gratification to the child who makes *discernible* progress in mastering academic skills or controlling his socially unacceptable behavior. It seems that the child who is having difficulties is likely to learn that teachers are people who sometimes dispense punishment and very often leave one in a praiseless limbo to cope alone, people who cannot be counted on in times of need but only when one is "good." One works or behaves properly in order to achieve external rewards, at first tangible rewards like candy and/or the privilege of playing with a favorite toy or engaging in a preferred activity, and perhaps subsequently (if training is successful) to receive praise from some momentarily benevolent authority figure.

It seems to us that this kind of system must inevitably promote a dichotomy between work and play, or—more broadly—between doing something because one *has* to, and doing something because one *wants* to. The hidden assumption of the program developers would seem to be that academic work or acceptable social conduct is not pleasurable in itself (except for the exceptional preschooler who can administer self-reinforcement); the system of dispensing rewards on a contingency basis serves—albeit unintentionally—to communicate this assumption to the children. Of course, there is considerable evidence that certain kinds of academic tasks and social behaviors are indeed difficult and even distasteful to many children. In our view, this should lead to fundamental questions about the appropriateness and value of various learning-teaching situations for children of different ages, rather than to an emphasis on improving methods of shaping behavior. The underlying model for the token economy is the marketplace, where bartering—the buying and selling of goods and services—is the fundamental mode of transaction. We believe that children being educated in classrooms based on this model must be learning that the ethics and modes of human conduct appropriate to the marketplace are appropriate modes for interpersonal interaction in the classroom, and perhaps in the world at large.

While denying that the technology of behavior modification is inherently bound to an underlying educational ideology, some behaviorists have recently stressed that the task of defining educational goals and values is indeed a serious one, demanding critical consideration. In a recent review entitled "Current Behavior Modification in the Classroom: Be Still, Be Quiet, Be Docile," Winett and Winkler (1972) deplore the fact that most current behavior modification programs, including those using a token economy model, reflect—in their choice of target behaviors—adherence to a highly traditional form of education. Their belief that this is a fortuitous rather than a necessary connection is underlined by O'Leary (1972) who argues that behavior modification has, in fact, been used to the ends of "innovative education." In a similar vein, Krasner and Krasner (1973) attempt to show that there is no conflict whatever between the use of behavior modification techniques (as used in a token economy) and the open classroom approach. We suggest, however, that the prevalent pattern is not merely fortuitous: The behavioristic method of technology requires analysis of input and output in discrete units, observable and measurable. (This is, in fact, its strength, particularly in assessing the effects of a given training procedure.) This necessarily leads to a selection of "target behaviors" that can be handled in such terms; it promotes an emphasis on product rather than process; on isolated responses or behaviors rather than on whole patterns within and across time periods; on forms of learning that are readily susceptible to quantitative measurement. Notions like "change in cognitive structure" or "increased self-awareness" must be translated into behavioral terms and are severely distorted, even obliterated, in the process. This is no loss to the behaviorist whose epistomological framework does not require, or indeed allow, such concepts. And, as we suggested above, the circumscribed focus on predetermined "target behaviors"—also stemming from the technological emphasis—is conducive to a neglect of "side effects," that is, the other learning processes that occur in the total context, and that may be equally or more significant in the long run. In any event, behavior modification is by its own claim a technology; as such, it provides a method of "teaching" and sets limits on the kinds of behavior that can be taken as objectives in the educational process, but it provides no positive guidelines or implications with regard to broader objectives or goals. We have argued that the technology itself has value implications and that the sometimes hidden ideology of behavioristically-based programs is closely tied to the view of human nature, learning, and development that is inherent in behavioristic psychology (cf. Kohlberg & Mayer, 1972).

THE PIAGETIAN COGNITIVE-DEVELOPMENTAL APPROACH

The impact of Piagetian theory on the field of early childhood education has been one of the most striking developments of the past decade. Twenty years ago, Piaget was virtually ignored by mainstream American psychologists, and only a small group of educational theorists were concerned with the implications of Piagetian thinking for educational practice. In the past fifteen years or so, profound changes have occurred in the American psychological establishment. While behaviorism is still a strong force, few would deny that its all-powerful position has been weakened as cognitive-developmentalism has achieved greater prominence. Stemming in part from these changes within the academy, there has been an upsurge of interest in explicating the implications of Piaget's thinking for educational programming (Furth, 1970; Overton, 1972; Schwebel & Raph, 1973) and the establishment of total preschool programs that view themselves as based on Piagetian thinking (Kamii, 1972; Kamii & DeVries 1973a; Lavatelli, 1970; Weikart, 1971). The influence of Piagetian formulations is also manifest in program planning within the British Infant School movement and some of the Open Classroom programs here and abroad that have evolved since the publication of the Plowden Report (1967).

Piaget never purported to be an educational theorist and has made clear that genetic epistomology rather than child psychology in a narrower sense is the thrust of his life's work. His own writings on education (1970) are relatively minor, and have only recently become available in America. It is clear that Piaget's work has strong implications for education, but the task of translating Piagetian thinking into educational practice involves considerable interpretation and decision-making. The differences among currently extant "Piaget-derived" curricula reflect the crucial role that curriculum developers play in bridging the gap between psychological theory per se and the specifics of educational practice (cf. Spodek, 1970).

An active organism view lies at the base of Piaget's approach. In this view, the organism is seen as the source of acts rather than a pawn pushed and pulled by the operation of external forces. The understanding and explanation of human behavior cannot be reduced to analysis of external conditions as causative, either in terms of a prior sequence of environmental events or in terms of present situation variables. Rather, one must focus on what the organism brings to the situation and how this enters into or governs his performance. Most important, what the organism brings to the situation is conceptualized in terms of underlying mental structures, rather than in terms of biologically defined proclivities (as in instinct theory), collections of stimulus-response connections, or propensities to emit a given response under given conditions (as in behaviorism). Behavioral data are thus viewed as a basis for making inferences about the nature or status of underlying cognitive structures, not as the primary object or end of analysis. As physiological structures determine the types and range of stimulation to which an organism at any phylogenetic level is sensitive and thus its "effective environment," so psychological structures constitute the equipment through which the human organism "knows" his world, and govern his modes of transaction with the social and physical environment in which he lives. It is not necessary to posit any condition of need or deprivation, or of specific external stimulation as such, to account for the activation of structures. The functioning of structures is inherent to organic life; this is at the nexus of the "active organism" viewpoint. As already implied, the tenet of constructivism is intertwined with the active organism assumption. Basically, constructivism is the view that man creates his knowledge, that knowledge results from the transformation of material that occurs as psychological structures are brought to bear vis-a-vis the "materials" of the world.

Since learning is an active process, and knowledge is constructed rather than "acquired," the child must be provided with an environment which furthers his own natural tendency to act on and with objects, to explore, manipulate, and experiment. He must be allowed, indeed encouraged, to take initiative, to pose problems, and to generate solutions for himself, even when the problems may seem trivial to an adult and/or the solutions may be "wrong" from an adult point of view. The centrality of the organism's activity in his learning or development should not be interpreted to mean that mere physical activity is at issue, any more than the concept of the "active organism" implies an organism that is always moving around. Rather, it has to do with the idea that the child energizes himself in a psychological sense (which may or may not involve overt action, depending on various factors including his stage of development) and directs himself toward the materials of his environment. In infancy, in the sensorimotor period, direct action on objects is in fact important, for the child's schemas or psychological structures are organizations of action patterns which become differentiated, and further coordinated or integrated in the process of motoric activity, as he discovers the properties of objects and achieves some understanding of relationships through active manipulation of various materials. Such direct exploration and handling of objects is also important at the preschool level during the preoperational period, where the child can see the effects of his actions as he handles and arranges materials in varying ways, and thus gains "physical knowledge" from observing the ways in which objects respond to various manipulations (e.g., dropping a crayon and seeing it break; dropping a metal rod and finding that it does not break), and "logico-mathematical knowledge" which is abstracted from the coordinations of actions themselves. However, at the preschool age, the child is already beginning to engage in mental activity where actual overt action may, at least in some cases, be abbreviated or nonobservable as the child carries out internal rather than external actions–a development related to the advent of representational thought.

The traditional approach[7]–so evident in many behavioristically oriented classrooms–of presenting circumscribed content to preschoolers, predetermining right and wrong answers, and reinforcing those which have been designated as "correct" by the teacher or program developer is not only fruitless but may be detrimental as it stifles the tendency of the child to move out into the world,

[7]Not to be confused with the child-centered approach, which has sometimes been designated as "traditional"–perhaps because it has a long history (see section of this paper entitled "The Developmental-Interaction Approach").

to take initiative, to explore and discover for himself, and so may hinder rather than facilitate genuine cognitive advance by making the child relatively passive in relation to the outer world. That such methods work at all would, in Piaget's view, have much more to do with the inherent propensity of the child toward psychological activity, his tendency to create meaning or order out of chaos, than with the specific methods employed.

In speaking of the teacher's role vis a vis the child's learning, Lavatelli (1970) has drawn the following implications for preschool education from the Piagetian framework: "The teacher's role is to stimulate and to guide, not to teach specific responses, not to tell the child the right answer, nor even to tell him when he is wrong. The teacher must have confidence in the child's ability to learn on his own. When he is wrong, she may ask questions or call attention to cues that he has missed so that he has more data to assimilate, but giving him the right answer will not convince the child. He must be convinced by his own actions [p. 48]."

Perhaps the best know—or, shall we say, the most widely assimilated—aspect of Piaget's theory is that which has to do with the four major stages of cognitive development: the sensorimotor, the intuitive or preoperational, the concrete operational, and the formal operational. We cannot undertake here to review or discuss the stage per se; this has been done by Piaget (1950) by Piaget and Inhelder (1969), and by numerous interpreters of Piaget, including those specifically concerned with the educational implications of Piagetian theory (cf. Overton, 1972). We shall confine ourselves to a few general comments, and subsequently discuss how Piagetian stage theory has been used in the Weikart, Lavatelli, and Kamii programs.

Essentially, development is defined in this view as a series of sequential, ordered changes in the cognitive structures that constitute the human organism's learning apparatus. As we have already said, these changes occur as a result of organism-environment interaction. A stage may be characterized as an internally organized or integrated group of cognitive structures. Each stage is built upon the previous one, and in this sense may be said to derive from it; thus, it is not possible to skip a stage in development. At the same time, each generic mode of thought or stage involves a fundamentally new organization into which previous modes are heirarchically integrated, and therefore change is not merely quantitative (as in the behavioristic view) but qualitative. New structures cannot be reduced to (or fully explained by) earlier ones; they exhibit emergent properties.

With regard to education, the broad and yet profound implication of this view is that modes of thought are qualitatively different at various periods in the child's life, that children at different stages of development will therefore interpret and respond to external situations in qualitatively distinct ways, and that relative consolidation of earlier modes of functioning provides the basis for developmentally more advanced modes. It follows that curricula should be "stage appropriate," that is, that various components of the program should be designed with as full an awareness as is possible of the child's modes of functioning. The fact that the generic forms of cognitive structures and the sequence of stages are rooted in biologically-based proclivities (although not explained by them, as we have said before) means that there is some rough correspondence between age and stage. One can expect, for example, that preschool children are utilizing and developing cognitive structures that are profoundly different from those used by seven- and eight-year-olds. Since there is, however, no reason to expect a one-to-one correspondence between age and stage, or indeed that any individual child will show uniform cognitive functioning, teachers must have ways of assessing each child's modes of functioning in order to provide him with an optimal learning environment.

Thus far, we have indicated some of the general implications of Piagetian theory for education in the early years. Clearly, a theory of development is not in itself a theory of education: in the passage from theory to practice, differing interpretations and decisions are made. Now we briefly consider some of the commonalities and differences among three programs that have taken Piagetian theory as a basis for educational programming at the preschool level.

We have said that if one takes seriously the idea that the child is the agent of his own learning (i.e., accepts the active-organism-constructivist premise), then one of the central objectives of preschool education is to help the child become as active a learner as possible, to provide conditions in which his natural powers can be exercised to full advantage. The three programs referred to are all very much concerned with this broad objective. In this connection, they have given careful attention to the types of materials to be included in preschool classrooms, to the kinds of activities that are likely to promote the child's taking an active stance vis a vis the environment, and to the role of the teacher as guide and stimulator rather than as transmitter of information.[8]

Accepting the "active organism" tenet here involves rejection of traditional methods of teaching in which the child is treated as a passive recipient of "knowledge." But acceptance of this tenet does not provide specification of what constitutes the optimal degree of structure and direct instruction in the learning environment, the appropriate balance between relying on the child's self-initiated action and directly stimulating or leading him to engage in given activities. In this regard, there are marked differences among Piaget-based programs, with Lavatelli's program emphasizing structured training sessions on classification, seriation, and number concepts as a supplement to less structured classroom activity, and Kamii (1973b) arguing that genuine learning must occur within a context and so should not be programmed as training sessions at the preschool level. The Weikart program seems to take a middle line here, involving considerable use of relatively circumscribed, structured, teacher-directed activities within the overall program (e.g., the use of specific games to teach color, size, and shape awareness, with the teacher giving directions—"put together the dominoes that are the same color"—and requiring specific kinds of

[8]The objective at issue here is very close to that espoused by the so-called child-centered programs. It is not surprising, therefore, to find that in promoting this objective, Piagetian curriculum developers have drawn on designs for classrooms, aspects of curricula, and methods of teaching developed earlier by those in the child-centered tradition.

activities and verbalizations from the child in response, e.g., arranging items by size, shape, or color and verbalizing the basis for the grouping).

There are considerable differences among these programs in the use of Piagetian stage theory. At the heart of the Weikart program lies a concept of stages in representational functioning as stages of development which draws on Piaget's work (1951) but nonetheless constitutes a radical departure from Piagetian theory as we understand it. In line with Piagetian thinking, Weikart suggests that the young child acts directly on and with objects and then progresses to "representational thought." And within representational thought, Weikart then demarcates the following "stages": (a) the index level of representation in which parts of objects or aspects of situations are taken as indicative of other aspects of the whole (as when the duck's footprints are taken as "representative" of the presence of a duck); (b) the symbol level of representation in which body gesture and other forms (objects, clay models, pictures, etc.) which resemble (or are iconic to) other entities are interpreted as referring to them; and (c) the sign level of representation in which forms—primarily words—which have no intrinsic relation of resemblance to their referents are understood as having a representational, referring function. The distinctions between index, symbol, and sign are Piaget's, but Piaget considers indexical functioning to be prerepresentational, and—more important—he does not draw an alignment between changes in representational functioning and stage-characteristic cognitive structures as Weikart has done. This is not to deny that Piaget has stressed the significance of the advent of "representational thought," occurring toward the close of the sensorimotor period, and the emergence of a symbolic capacity which is intimately related to the child's developing ability to represent nonpresent "reality" to himself. For Piaget, however, stages of cognitive functioning are differentiated in terms of types of mental operations which are ways of organizing experience and not modes of representation. Weikart's scheme would seem to owe more to Bruner's (Bruner, Olver, & Greenfield, 1966) conceptualization of enactive, iconic, and symbolic modes of representation than to Piaget.

In any event, the theoretical emphasis on representational functioning in Weikart's program leads to close consideration, on the implementation level, of the specific types of materials, child-initiated activity (including sociodramatic play), and teacher guidance that are conducive to the consolidation and further growth of the child's representational competence. The aim of the Weikart program would seem to be to facilitate the child's movement toward progressively "higher" levels of representation in relation to the shift from predominantly motoric to predominantly verbal modes of functioning, with attention devoted to the four content areas of classification, seriation, temporal relations, and spatial relations. As indicated, there is a cognitive-stage-theory base here; the focus on representational functioning is consonant with the general cognitive-developmental perspective (Franklin,

1973; Sigel, 1972b). But the program does not attempt to follow Piaget in a rigorous fashion, particularly with regard to its concept of "higher" and "lower" levels of cognitive functioning and the related emphasis on verbalization and language training at what are deemed appropriate junctures. In fact, certain emphases within the program—for example, the emphasis on reinforcing concepts through repetition of their names, on "labeling," "verbal stimulation," and "verbal bombardment"—belie a consistent adherence to the implications of cognitive developmental theory in general.

By contrast, Lavatelli and Kamii not only adhere to the general implications of cognitive stage theory, but draw systematically on Piaget's study of thinking during the preoperational period as a base for curriculum planning. Both programs emphasize the importance of play as an area of activity where the preoperational child spontaneously utilizes and so further develops his myriad, stage-characteristic cognitive capacities. These programs also reflect careful attention to the sequential developments within the specific areas of classification, seriation, number, and space concepts—as Piaget has described them. Lavatelli's program includes as an important component structured training sessions (modeled on the tasks Piaget designed to investigate the development of logical thought), many of them apparently designed to teach concrete operations to the presumably preoperational child. According to Kamii (1973b), this represents a misapplication of Piagetian theory: (a) preoperational children should not be prematurely pushed, through training, toward the concrete operational stage; (b) logical thinking should not be artificially separated from the development of physical knowledge, as occurs when such focused training sessions are established; and (c) classification, seriation, etc., cannot be thought of, and should not be taught, as separate skills, or indeed as skills in any sense of the term.

Kamii seems to have gone more deeply into Piagetian theory as a total system than has Weikart or Lavatelli, and in this process has arrived at a different group of specific objectives with regard to the education of the preschool child. The cognitive objectives of the program concern physical and social as well as logico-mathematical knowledge, at levels appropriate to the preoperational child, and are seen as linked to socioemotional objectives which encompass the encouragement of curiosity, confidence, and creativity. In the most recent formulations by Kamii (1973a,b) and Kamii and DeVries (1973a), it is suggested that these objectives can best be realized in a program design which is very close to that of the child-centered preschool. The difference, supposedly, rests on the more coherent, Piaget-derived, rationale which promises a more systematic approach to understanding and working with young children.

We see, then, that the programs which draw on Piaget differ in the specific use of this theory as a rationale for preschool education but share adherence to general implications of the cognitive-developmental perspective and a focus on promoting cognitive growth in the preschool years. These programs reflect similar values in their explicit effort–on the level of implementation–to foster the child's sense of himself as an autonomous learner, a questioner, an explorer, a problem solver; his sense of the teacher as a guide, helper, and source of useful information rather than an authoritarian figure dispensing praise and blame for right and wrong answers; his sense of school as a democratic social system in which exchange with peers is as highly valued as any other endeavor. In our view, the dramatic contrast with the "hidden message" of behavioristically-oriented programs is evident, and we see this as stemming from fundamentally different educational ideologies which, in turn, are linked to the different views of human nature and functioning underlying the two psychological theories at issue.

In significant ways, the value orientation and therefore the particular learning environments established for children in these Piaget-based programs are similar to those of the "child-centered" programs which owe a great deal, in terms of their origins, to the work of John Dewey as well to the influence of psychodynamic theory (cf. next section). Furthermore, among those who turn to Piagetian theory as a basis for preschool planning, there seems to be increased emphasis on considering the "whole child" rather than on focusing, in a narrower way, on cognitive development per se. Writing on Piaget's theory in relation to education, Overton (1972) has said that "the development of thought is not viewed as a process isolated from the total development of the child, but rather as a process integrated throughout with the child's interests and values, moral feelings, interpersonal emotions, and most generally his personality [p. 95]." In successive formulations of long-range and short-term objectives, Kamii has increasingly stressed the importance of "socioemotional" functioning and development in relationship to cognitive growth. However, the fact remains that Piaget's theory deals to a very large extent with the evolution of *cognitive* structures and provides relatively little of a substantive nature concerning other related aspects of development. One might say that in developing programs which are geared toward the child's total development, Piagetian program planners have gone outside or beyond Piagetian theory, formulating objectives and related modes of implementation which are *consonant* with the Piagetian perspective but not based on Piagetian theory as such. Kohlberg and Mayer (1972), for example, remark that "attainment of Piagetian cognitive stage is a necessary but not sufficient condition for attainment of the parallel ego stage [p. 491]," and suggest that a "general concept of ego development" is important to delineating broad educational objectives. To what extent the Piaget-based programs actually constitute comprehensive programs which have as their focus the "whole child" and take into account the subtleties of socioemotional development cannot be adequately judged from the literature. However, the program descriptions reflect–to varying degrees, to be sure–a rather preponderant emphasis on cognitive functioning as such, and insufficient attention in our view to feelings and fantasy as they reflect and feed into the child's aesthetic as well as his inter- and intrapersonal development.

THE DEVELOPMENTAL-INTERACTION APPROACH

There is a large measure of common ground between the programs based on this approach and those that adhere more exclusively to cognitive theories of development. But the difference between them is crucial to the planning of learning experiences, the teaching strategies, and the nature of the teacher-child relationships. Essentially, proponents of this approach take the position that, while cognitive-developmental theory is a valuable component for the construction of an educational design, it is not, by itself, sufficiently comprehensive to serve as the foundation for the totality of the educative process.

The developmental-interaction approach utilizes two major stage formulations of the developmental sequence: the cognitive-developmental, drawing on Werner (1940, 1957) as much as Piaget, and the framework developed within ego psychology, most specifically by Erikson (1950, 1959). From the perspective of cognitive development the maturation of the child is seen as a series of changing ways of gaining and organizing his knowledge of the universe of things, people, and ideas. In general terms–the world he first knows through his senses and his physical-motor maneuvers is fundamentally altered when he can deal symbolically, through verbal and nonverbal modes, with his experience. During the next period, the preschool years and first primary years, he becomes a primitive conceptualizer, ordering the complexity of his experience by comparing, grouping, classifying, numbering, and postulating causality but the elements of these processes are still much influenced by perceptual factors, coexistence in time and space, and more importantly by a lingering egocentricism in which self-feelings and wishes influence the contours of the child's image of the world. Not until the middle years of childhood does his conceptualizing become more objective, adhering to logical rules so that he can think in categorical terms independent of perceptual attributes, master concepts by delineating constancies in the object world, and deal with multiple classifications as he becomes aware of relativity of class membership of a given item.

In the second formulation, successive stages of development are characterized as generalized affective-social patterns, comprising the whole complex of self-feeling and self-image, of attitudes and images toward others, and of the style of individual functioning in relation to the opportunities and expectations of a given society. In this perspective, these phases of psychosocial development are closely related to phases of psychosexual epigenesis and reflect the basic conflictual nature of the maturing process–both the conflicting impulses within the self and the struggle between self-generated impulses and the demands of reality outside the self. The stages are defined as polarities–alternative resolutions of the basic conflicts. The relative health of these resolutions is determined by the quality of interaction with the salient figures in the child's life and compatibility with cultural ideals. Thus, looking at functional outcomes rather than the particular organically-based conflicts or developmental tasks to be solved in successive stages, the stepping stones to healthy personality development spanning the preschool years have been defined as: a sense of trustfulness in others and trustworthiness in one's self; a sense of autonomy through making choices and exercising control; a sense of initiative expressed in a variety of making, doing, and playing activities in cooperation with others and in an imagined projection of the adult sex role.

Both of these developmental theories assume basic organismic functions which are operative across the life-span, and an invariant sequence of stages in development; in this respect they are "maturational" theories, rooted in metaphors of biological growth. But at the core, they are both interactionist theories, claiming that the development of stage-specific structures and functions, as well as movement from one stage to the next–that is, development itself–occurs as a function of organism-environment interaction, the reciprocal interplay between the organism's propensities and activities and that which impinges on him from outside, the environment.[9] It is a premise of the developmental-interaction view here under discussion that the separation of these major developmental sequences–the cognitive-intellectual and the affective-social–has important heuristic value but that, in utilizing these formulations in connection with educational planning, it is essential to be continuously cognizant of their interdependence in the way children and people actually function. Cognitive-intellectual and affective-social processes are sometimes seen as constituting parallel and partly overlapping systems. This general position–moving toward an integrative formulation–is exemplified in Kohlberg (Kohlberg & Turiel, 1971) discussions of moral development. Thinking in terms of parallel systems can, however, lead to a dichotomous formulation, where changes in one system are seen as primary or causative, even to the extent of constituting the necessary and sufficient conditions for changes in the other (e.g., if cognitive development is proceeding well, the child will naturally have positive feelings of self-worth in other domains). Actually, the loading of curriculum designs is influenced directly or indirectly by the position taken with respect to these theoretical alternatives: the primacy of one system rather than the other or–the third alternative–a genuinely integrative interactionist view (cf. Mayer, 1971).

Integrative formulations appear in other psychological domains. Creativity has been conceived as a synthesis of various modes of intellectual functioning including divergent thinking, transformation processes, sensing ambiguity, perceiving patterns, and "playing" with ideas as well as logical thinking. From

[9] In general, cognitive-developmental theorists have focused on interindividual and cross-cultural commonalities in human functioning, emphasizing universal forms of thought and the universal stage sequence. While recognizing that progression through the stages can be hastened or slowed down by environmental factors, and that there are differences in the extent and use of the cognitive repertoire (and thus in the total adaptational status of the individual), these theorists have not been primarily concerned with variations in cognitive functioning as a function of variations in environment. By contrast, in the sequence of generalized affective-social patterns (Erikson's developmental stages), environmental forces–family, school, subculture–are seen as moving in qualitatively different directions toward contrasting kinds of personality formation.

this viewpoint, creativity depends also on closeness to experiences of the inner life that underly motivation and the affective-social patterns of the personality (Barron, 1969; McKinnon, 1962; Murphy, 1964). In a more clinically oriented schema, the course of ego development is formulated in terms of the interdependency of impulse control and character development, interpersonal style, and conscious preoccupation including self-concept (Loevinger, 1966).

In the realm of educational thinking the thesis of cognitive-affective interaction has taken various complementary forms. In one formulation, emphasis is on the concept that knowledge is bound as cognitive-affective interactions. Competence in creative and communicative use of symbols is regarded as essential to support of the major ego processes; ultimately an integrated orchestration of emotions, skills, knowledge, thoughts, and imagination becomes available for interaction with the environment (Bower, 1967). In a similar context, a theory of instruction points to a loss to the intrinsic learning process when emotional responses aroused by a learning experience are not dealt with openly, shared by the children as a group, channeled toward symbolic, representational expression, and understood as integral counterparts to the cognitive elements (Jones, 1968). The same thesis is developed in a study of play fantasies in children illustrating, for example, how the quality of early representations of the self bespeaks both cognitive achievement in self-differentiation and the sense of a good or bad self established as the outcome of earliest experiences with need, fulfillment, and denial (Gould, 1972).

The developmental-interaction approach, as it has evolved at the Bank Street College of Education over half a century, had its roots in the progressive education movement (Biber, in press).[10] In that era, as in our own, it was expected that innovation in education could correct basic faults in our democratic society. What was needed was a totally different life of learning for children, one that would correct for the conformism and authoritarianism that characterized the Zeitgeist and was reflected in the school. In contrast to "compensatory" programs (which also aim to correct for basic faults through educational innovation) the goals of the earlier experiments embraced educational programs as total ideologies and the children as "whole" individuals (Biber, 1972).

A radically altered learning environment and new instructional strategies and curricula were developed by educators in accord with Dewey's theories of experiential learning. They sought to implement his major tenets: the child learns through his own active involvement and through interaction with the phenomena of things, people, and ideas in his environment; there is a continuous process of "collateral" learning, the formation of attitudes that are both emotional and intellectual and govern the development of basic systems of prefer-

[10]Certain similarities in goals and implementation have been pointed out between the Bank Street approach and the advisory system of the Educational Development Corporation based on the British Infant School movement (Gordon, 1972).

ence and aversion. In Dewey's words (Dewey & Dewey, 1915): "The greatest of all pedagogical fallacies is the notion that a person learns only the particular thing he is studying at the time."

This basic educational ideology was developed and refined over a period of six decades. Changes evolved through informal and formal modes of experimentation and revision, based on the observations and insights of the educators working directly with the children. The outstanding thinkers in this group were Mitchell (1934), Johnson (1928), and Pratt (1948). Among their special curriculum contributions can be mentioned the development of an intentionally comprehensive educational design for the years following infancy, the utilization of spontaneous play as a tool for learning suited to the idiom of early childhood, and a method for the study of environment in which a cognitive search for relationships is the basis for formulating general principles.

Historically, there is a complex relation between what was happening in those years on the educational front and the advances in the knowledge of human functioning represented in the work of developmental psychologists, in psychodynamic formulations, and the principles of preventive mental health. From one perspective, the contribution of these psychological schools of thought can be looked at as a validation of principles derived from an experiential base by educators who observed and theorized as part of their professional function. A more dynamic interpretation is probably closer to the truth. The educators, committed to building educational practice on a rationale of child development research and theory, sought and found in the contributions of these psychologists not only a congruent view but also refreshment and stimulation for further change in practice. The evolution of the developmental-interaction view represents the progressive integration of both these streams of thought and experience.

In the developmental-interaction approach the inseparability of cognitive-affective processes governs the suitability of teaching methods (Biber, 1967). The possible merit of a technique is weighed in terms of multiple possible effects. Thus, learning experiences designed to further cognitive facility are weighed in terms of the simultaneous learning that is going on with respect to self-image, attitudes toward others, work patterns, or general behavioral modes (Dewey, 1938). Practically, this calls for paying close attention to side effects as well as target success in any intentional teaching strategy and, finally, screening both orders of outcome on the basis of preestablished values.

Side effects sometimes supply a positive increment. Thus, in a given story, the teacher may find material for a target in the cognitive domain–mastery of concepts of multiple roles, for example. If she takes time and makes room for one of the children to enlighten the others from her own experience (her father is a fireman), she is simultaneously serving a goal in the noncognitive sphere, namely, to help children establish mutually supporting roles and see each other, as well as the teacher, as sources of information (Biber, Shapiro, & Wickens,

1971). Alternatively, restricted attention to a target goal may have negative outcomes. The teacher who responds to a preschool child's drawing by pointing out a disparity in size relations and pressures the child to adhere more closely to external reality is violating one of the essential processes by which children achieve a strong sense of self–namely, to have their creative products accepted and recognized as the end of an integrative process in which they, as individuals, find symbolic ways of dealing with both the logical and alogical aspects of their experience.

The curriculum design for this approach incorporates the educationally relevant precepts of cognitive-developmental and ego psychology theory. It takes the view that children are basically curious and impelled to make an impact on their environment; that they are equipped with autonomous ego functioning independent of instinctual drives. Learning takes place through action–concrete and conceptual–and interaction with the objects, people, and ideas of the environment (White, 1963). Knowledge is gained and adaptive patterns established through exploration, manipulation, and investigation. Productive, creative use of knowledge is maximized when there is opportunity for representational reinterpretation of experience (Franklin, 1973). The definition and quality of the interpersonal relations–teacher-to-child and child-to-child– affect and are affected by affective-social patterns. Matching curriculum designs and the learning atmosphere to successive developmental stages takes into account both level of cognitive functioning and stage-specific psychosocial characteristics, drives, and conflicts (Biber, 1967). Motivation to learn is regenerated by satisfied curiosity, the pleasures and intrinsic rewards of mastery, identification with teacher figures, and the internalizations of the trusted adults' confidence in the child's competence.

These general precepts about the course and the process of development influence the teacher's perception of the child as an individual. The child is not expected to function consistently at a given developmental level. Earlier forms of thinking, expression, and adaptation continue to appear even when his predominant response patterns have become more advanced. From the viewpoint of creativity, having a varied repertoire, being able to continue to use the more primitive forms is seen as an advantage (Werner, 1957). It is expected that periods of instability are likely to alternate with other periods in which skills, feelings, action patterns support each other and yield highly integrated behavioral outcome (Biber & Franklin, 1967). It is important, therefore, that the teacher can perceive periods of "regression" or "disturbance" when they occur as being, possibly, part of the complex phenomenon of development and not necessarily an expression of emotional disorganization.

The purview of a child's individuality includes, in addition to the behavioral picture, awareness of the inner processes through which self-image evolves. This requires that the teacher differentiate the elements in the learning environment in terms of how they may influence the child's own assessment of his skills, the clarity of his social sex role, his sense of himself as a learner, and his store of courage and know-how for coping with difficulty. The teacher knows and communicates with the child as a particular person. She is aware of his strengths, difficulties, and desires and these are brought into the open. This is made more possible according to the extent to which the teacher has absorbed the precepts of the interaction of cognitive-intellectual and affective-social processes.

Ideally, in these classrooms, as in cognitive-oriented programs, children are actively engaged in exploring their environment and sharing their experiences in an atmosphere where questioning, searching, and problem-solving are encouraged (and there is no embarrassment about not knowing, among children or between children and teachers). The aim is to provide an abundance of experience and encounter, a variety of situations to which the children need to adapt, plenty of alternatives from which to make choices, and an appropriate setup for self-initiated exploratory play. Direct contact with phenomena and people takes priority over the vicarious; the salient situations for learning exist outside the classroom as well as inside.

Here, in contrast to the emphasis on structured lessons which are prominent in most programs in which cognition is the primary focus, the instructional method is weighted toward making maximal use of the children's varied, ongoing experience, as it transpires, as the prime material for stimulating cognitive processes. When it is successful, this method produces a pervasive climate of why, wherefore, and wherefrom kind of thinking. The teacher uses every appropriate opportunity to stimulate differentiated observation and comparison, to encourage the search for causes and origins, to bring the orderly passing of time, the contour of spatial reality, and the transformations of growth to awareness (Biber, Shapiro, & Wickens, 1971). This occurs in innumerable contexts: in recognizing the separate series of landmarks that distinguish different routes to the play roof; in recording the successive weights of the growing gerbil; in using the known sequence of the schedule of activities to predict what is coming; in exploring the building to find where the heat in the radiators comes from.

The teacher uses various ways of stimulating thinking at appropriate moments. She helps elaborate a child's experience through verbal expression, she rephrases a child's expressed thought or action in a way that lifts the level from particularized performance to a more generalized concept; she offers material for analogous thinking; she puts questions that stimulate perceptual and conceptual search maneuvers. In the course of story-reading, she opens up questions for later pursuit that are a little ahead of the childrens' thinking level. In instances of social dilemma, she unravels the elements of difficulty and helps the child compose a possible solution to the problem. She stimulates anticipatory thinking by posing if-then formulations.

As part of the program design the teacher takes initiative from time to time in introducing certain preplanned learning episodes focused on clarifying specific concepts–similarity, difference, size, part-whole, etc.–using objects and events that are experientially familiar to the children. Also, the classroom is so organized–spatially and functionally–that cognitive functions such as sorting, classification, recognition of written symbols are practiced incidental to daily classroom functioning. Structured learning episodes in the realm of cognition during the early years of childhood are only supplementary to the context–embedded methods for stimulating conceptual organization.

In line with the importance attached to cognitive-affective interaction, the program is designed to nurture the intuitive processes, the capacity for feeling and emotion, for reflective as well as goal-directed thinking in order to bring the totality of imaginative, productive functioning to its highest power. One of the established goals, "to increase the range and depth of childrens' sensitivity to the world around them" (Biber, 1967), has aesthetic components as well.

This view dictates the importance of giving expressive activities an important place in the curriculum. The children are provided with ample opportunity, equipment, and encouragement for many forms of symbolic expression, verbal and nonverbal, for reliving experience by representing it in personally meaningful terms, for fantasying as well as reasoning, for synthesizing the subjective and objective aspects of experience. Their activities in this domain are free from any restraints of imposed standards for duplicating reality or adhering consistently to the relations implicit in logical organization.

The method used for stimulating and enriching spontaneous dramatic play of young children has been highly developed in this program. The teacher observes, provides materials or a few extensions of ideas, perhaps takes a passing role in the play temporarily, but she does not teach how to play. This kind of spontaneous play, originating in the self-determined conceptualization and enactment of the children, individually or in small groups, serves a dual function. It is recognized as an important learning mode for this stage of development–a medium for externalizing thought in which the child gains new cognitive mastery over nascent conceptual content. It is equally important as an experience in which the wondering, problem-solving, and conceptualizing of the groping child mind fuses with the wishes, fears, longings for strength, pleasures, and pains of the forming inner self–in other words, a self-initiated creative process in which the child integrates his understanding of objective reality with his personal meanings and feelings.

Still other techniques are involved in supporting the children's interactions with each other and helping them to function as a group. In the way the children's joint play and activities are organized, in the issues considered crucial in settling disputes, in the guidance for how and when to listen and be heard in a group discussion, the teacher establishes mores of social interchange–ones that maximize the children's learning from each other and offer guidelines for the socializing experience of cooperating, helping, consoling, or coping with disagreement and conflict of interest. In this setting, the child finds himself in a learning environment in which he is a major actor, so organized that he can gain a sense of his own competence through the experience of autonomy—selecting, planning, initiating, decision making. His ways of transforming and reconstructing experiences are valued for aesthetic qualities and expression of feeling as well as for evidence of cognitive mastery. There is a wide latitude for varied personal interaction on many levels since the social climate is not rigidly stratified between stronger and weaker, knowing and not knowing, adult and child. The teacher is looked to not only as a guide for penetrating the how and why of the external surround but also as a willing, dependable resource for dealing with fear, loss of direction, anger, or loneliness when there is hurt and with a sense of justice when there is controversy. When it is successful, the child finds strength and pleasure in creating order through his expanding thought processes, from sharing depth of feeling with teachers and children, and from recreating symbolically the meanings—real and fantasied—that are of the greatest moment to him.

As has been indicated earlier, the teacher carries a complex role in the implementation of this ideology. Her interactions with the children cannot be standardized; she has to be sensitive and adaptive to the simultaneity of thinking and feeling processes. As in the cognitive-oriented programs, she needs to be able to assess the level and the pattern of the child's cognitive functioning; here, she needs, equally, to be aware of how stage-specific, social-emotional drives and conflicts are being worked through by the individual child. The teacher seeks to understand and respond to the child's meanings and feelings in whatever way they are communicated. The lack of standardization, like the requirements for awareness and responsivity, makes the teacher's role challenging but often very difficult. Perhaps more than in other programs, successful realization of educational goals depends upon the teacher's ability to take genuine initiative in translating basic precepts into a productive learning environment. The unusually complex requirements of the teacher's role constitute a challenge to teacher education not readily met within the framework of most teacher education programs.

FINAL CONSIDERATIONS

Certain primary questions—they can be called issues since they arouse considerable controversy among proponents of different views—have surfaced in the course of this brief account of three approaches to programming in early childhood education (i.e., the behavioristic-learning-theory approach; the Piagetian-cognitive-developmental approach; and the developmental-interaction approach). A central question is: What place does psychological theory have in relation to educational planning? Since education revolves around modes of guiding and channeling the processes of learning–and, more broadly, development–sound procedure requires that it turn to psychological theory for conceptualization of these processes. But more than "translation" is involved in the application of psychological theory to the educational domain. It is clear that educational practice–at whatever level–involves an ideology concerning a system of values for human functioning, and a strategy of implementation geared toward the achievement of selected goals.

Here we may focus on the question: To what extent does adherence to a given psychological theory as the basis of an educational design restrict the comprehensiveness of the program–the extent to which it provides for the multiple aspects of learning, ego development, and socialization?

Of the three approaches, behavioristic learning theory appears to be the most limiting when applied to education, generating a technology geared to behavioral change in circumscribed areas. The mechanisms involved turn out to be–though presumably without intention–matched to the philosophy and limited goals of traditional education. Specifically, the role of the child to adult, of learner to teacher, inherent in the teaching techniques derived from behavioristic learning theory match the quality of these relationships inherent in traditional educational philosophy.

By contrast, the psychological territory of cognitive-developmental theory is far more extensive. The explanatory concepts in this theory contribute to a complex, internally consistent image of learning and growth, not in terms of behavioral change per se, but with reference to an active organism, constructing knowledge of the world around him through interaction. In its application to education, this theory dictates responsibility for a comprehensive program with specific criteria for suitable environmental input, and for the nature of the interaction between child and adult. Nevertheless, as we have argued, the focus on cognitive processes is a limiting perspective: the sphere of affective-social patterns is not a fully developed aspect of this theory. Even though there has recently been recognition by some curriculum planners of this school that cognitive processes cannot be supported and stimulated without consideration of concomitant social emotional processes, the cognitive-developmental theory does not itself provide guidelines for the design of this aspect of the learning environment.

In passing we may note that application of another perspective–classical Freudian theory–can have and has had a similar restricting effect on the construction of a comprehensive learning environment. In this instance it is the cognitive processes that take a peripheral position in relation to the psychodynamic forces at the center.

The developmental-interaction approach is a "whole" child approach. Educationally, its goals comprise affective-social as well as cognitive aspects of development. The question of priority on (or, whether) which stands at the center and which at the periphery is irrelevant since the primary thesis is that both these domains of psychological functioning are continuously interactive. This view dictates the most comprehensive program planning of a learning environment with specific guidelines as to the variation of learning experience and the consideration of teacher-child interactions both in general overall terms and in the choice of focus in the particular moment-by-moment exchanges between teacher and child.

As has already been indicated, no one developmental theory stands as adequate rationale for this approach. Both cognitive and affective-social theories are a requisite foundation for the enactment of the educational philosophy which shares certain basic values with the cognitive-developmental approach but includes concepts of healthy personality derived from psychodynamic theories.

The reference to two lines of theorizing as a foundation for an educational program brings a question—or issue—to the fore that is especially pertinent to the general implementation of theory in programming. The attempt to draw on multiple theoretical sources sometimes leads to a patchwork—matching parts of educational practice to this or that theory—and this, in fact, characterizes many programs which have not been dealt with in this presentation. By contrast, in the developmental-interaction approach, an integrative theoretical view has been developed which governs overall decision-making as well as the continuous interactional modes. It is in this connection that the important issue of target and side effects has been raised in the previous discussion. The position has been taken that target-focused techniques inevitably have side effects and that limited theoretical foundations, most extreme from the behaviorist point of view, lead to neglect of the totality of input, and, consequently, lack of awareness of the complexity of what is internalized by the child. With all too brief illustrations we have attempted to indicate the implicit decision making going on in a teacher's mind as she shapes her interactions with the children. At this point, perhaps it should be reiterated that excellence in enacting this educational role is not readily come by, and involves a special kind of teacher preparation.

What do we hear as feedback from the psychologists' involvement in education, especially as concerns the problem of evaluation? For many this is a period of "second thoughts" fed from several sources. In recent critiques of what has been lacking in past studies, we see increased awareness of the complexity of dealing with the varied, interdependent processes of classroom life (Messick & Barrows, 1972; Sigel, 1972a; Soar & Soar, 1972). Shapiro (1973) says, "The parameters of variation cannot be simply boxed in with notations of geography and ethnicity. Nevertheless, one finds few, if any, descriptive or analytic accounts of the educational transactions that take place in the schools or centers under study [p. 526]." Reviews of the literature point to a dearth of studies dealing with the components of classroom situations. The plea, in Shulman's words, is that the language of education and the behavioral sciences develops "a set of terms for describing environments that is as articulated, specific and functional as those already possessed for characterizing individuals" (Shulman, 1970).

One effort to do this appears in the study on the impact of school experience by Minuchin *et al.* (1969), which provided full descriptions of four qualitatively different school environments. What we see now is increased attention to the need for developing methods of analyzing learning environments, taking the total complexity into account before initiating specific innovative practices.

The outcomes of innovative programs developed by psychologists have been measured systematically. When outcomes are not in accord with expectations—as has been the case for many preschool and elementary school projects—various post hoc interpretations are offered. It has been said that program differences did not result because teachers did not know how to implement the method, or did not understand the rationale behind it, or—even more seriously—effective use of the method required basic changes in the teacher's attitudes and perception of children and the learning process. In some comparative studies, the quality of teacher functioning and commitment loom large, emerging as more salient than differences in instructional method per se (Weikart, 1969). Sometimes the underlying theoretical rationale is questioned or even indicted in the process of interpreting findings—for example, where one developmental process was considered in isolation without sufficient attention given to questions of interaction. Still another kind of post hoc inference points to the importance of long periods of continuous implementation prior to final assessment of outcomes. This last was one of the prime factors in the establishment of Follow Through as a sequel to Head Start.

When one embarks on reconsideration of causal variables, one also becomes involved in evaluating the evaluation or outcome-measurement process. Recently, there has been considerable criticism of the more standard evaluation techniques (Eisner, 1972; Fein & Clarke-Stewart, 1973; Shapiro, 1973). This cannot be attributed entirely to feedback from psychologists plunging into the applied field of education, but it has had great impetus from the need to face the reality of what looks like failure in many applied programs. Conceivably, the concept and method of evaluation may be obscuring much of what is really happening and, if it is, we have reason to be uncertain where the failure lies—how much in the program and how much in the method of evaluating it. Zimiles (1970) points to the negative influence of inadequate assessment: "When the shortcomings of the evaluations themselves are glossed over and they are mistakenly presented as offering definitive statements regarding the nature of school influence, and the imperfect indices they use to achieve crude assessment themselves become the basis for school planning, then it is time to recognize that they have overstepped their bounds and begun to interfere with the very processes they were intended to support [p. 245]."

Several of the psychologists who have been close to the task of evaluating compensatory programs in early childhood share a common concern. In their view, the test procedures used to evaluate outcomes of programs are inadequate and often misleading. Such methods sample a very narrow range of a program's effects and are therefore best suited to the programs with the most limited goals. The nature of the test situation itself restricts and distorts the extent to which the child's responses are representative of his capabilities in other situations, particularly in the case of the "disadvantaged" child.

Especially with regard to cognition, assessment strategies have been geared toward evaluating knowledge or capacities in a limited sense and have rarely provided sensitive indices of cognitive functioning. While the distinction between capacity per se and its functional significance has been noted for some time, this has not been given prime emphasis in the design of research. Recently, social concerns, developments in cognitive psychology, and a new perspective in cross-cultural study have coalesced in an analysis of the relations between extent of cognitive repertoire and variations in modes of utilization (cf. Cole, Gay, Glick, & Sharp, 1971).

Evaluation would take a quite different perspective if the criterion of optimal cognitive functioning were not so restrictedly defined as the attainment of the highest levels of logical thinking. Alternatively, one turns to Werner's conceptualization of optimal functioning which does not posit displacement of earlier by later, or of primitive by more advanced modes of thinking (Werner, 1957). Instead the movement from lesser to greater maturity is characterized by widening the range of developmentally different operations and thus making available different modes of structuring to be brought into play in any given situation.

These trends support process-oriented evaluation that does not assess outcome at some arbitrary endpoint but engages in an intimate study of programs, documenting what is happening to children in the learning environment where there can be a full sampling of how the child is using his capacities in interaction with what a particular environment offers him. It has been called formative in distinction to summative evaluation (Scriven, 1972).

Perhaps we have come to the point where it is time to reject the all too persistent emphasis on acceleration and replace it with attention to extent of repertoire in both a functional and developmental context. There are clear implications for education as well as evaluation. Cole and Bruner (1972) suggest "The teacher should stop laboring under the impression that he must create new intellectual structures. He should start concentrating on how to get the child to transfer skills he already possesses to the task at hand. . . [p. 176]." To us, it would be preferable to say that the emphasis on abilities per se should give way to helping the child utilize all the modes of structuring his experience that he has achieved developmentally to serve a more varied range of pragmatic and creative ends.

REFERENCES

Ackerman, J. M. *Operant conditioning techniques for the classroom*. Glenview, Ill.: Scott Foresman, 1972.

Bandura, A. Behavior theory and the models of man. *American Psychologist*, 1974, *29*, 816-820.

Barron, F. *Creative person and creative process*. New York: Holt, Rinehart, & Winston, 1969.

Becker, W. C. Applications of behavior principles in typical classrooms. In C. E. Thoresen (Ed.), *Behavior modification in education*. The Seventy-Second Yearbook of the National Society for the Study of Education, Part I. Chicago: University of Chicago Press, 1973.

Bereiter, C., & Engelmann, S. *Teaching disadvantaged children in the preschool*. Englewood Cliffs, N. J.: Prentice-Hall, 1966.

Biber, B. A learning-teaching paradigm integrating intellectual and affective processes. In E. M. Bower & W. G. Hollister (Eds.), *Behavioral science frontiers in education*. New York: Wiley, 1967.

Biber, B. The "whole child," individuality and values in education. In J. R. Squire (Ed.), *A new look at progressive education*, ASCD Yearbook. Washington, D.C.: Association for Supervision and Curriculum Development, 1972.

Biber, B. The developmental-interaction point of view: Bank Street College of Education. In M. C. Day & R. Parker (Eds.), *The preschool in action* (2nd ed.). Boston: Allyn & Bacon, in press.

Biber, B., & Franklin, M. B. The relevance of developmental and psychodynamic concepts to the education of the preschool child. *Journal of the American Academy of Child Psychiatry*, 1967, *6*, 1.

Biber, B., Shapiro, E., & Wickens, D. *Promoting cognitive growth: a developmental-interaction point of view*. Washington, D.C.: National Association for the Education of Young Children, 1971.

Bissell, J. S. Planned variation in Head Start and Follow Through. In J. Stanley (Ed.), *Preschool programs for the disadvantaged*, Vol. II. Baltimore, Md.: Johns Hopkins University Press, 1973.

Bower, D. M. The confluence of the three rivers–ego processes. In E. M. Bower & W. G. Hollister (Eds.). *Behavioral science frontiers in education*. New York: Wiley, 1967.

Bronfenbrenner, U. Developmental research, public policy, and the ecology of childhood. *Child Development*, 1974, *45*, 1-5.

Bruner, J., Olver, R., & Greenfield, P. M. *Studies in cognition*. Cambridge, Mass.: MIT Press, 1966.

Bushell, D. Follow through–A proposal for learning reinforcement. In Papers Accompanying Presentations made at Follow Through Meetings, Kansas City, Missouri, February 1968.

Bushell, D. The behavior analysis classroom. In B. Spodek (Ed.), *Early childhood education*. Englewood Cliffs, N. J.: Prentice-Hall, 1973.

Cole, M., & Bruner, J. S. Preliminaries to a theory of cultural differences. In I. J. Gordon (Ed.), *Early childhood education*. The Seventy-first Yearbook of the National Society for the Study of Education, Part II. Chicago: University of Chicago Press, 1972.

Cole, M., Gay, J., Glick, J. A., & Sharp, D. W. *The cultural context of learning and thinking*. New York: Basic Books, 1971.

Dewey, J., & Dewey, E. *Schools of tomorrow*. New York: Dutton, 1915.

Dewey, J. *Experience and education*. New York: Macmillan, 1963. Original publication 1938.

Eisner, E. W. Emerging models for educational evaluation. *School Review*, August 1972.

Erikson, E. H. *Childhood and society*. New York: Norton, 1950.

Erikson, E. H. Identity and the life cycle. *Psychological Issues*, 1959, *1* (1).

Fein, G. G., & Clarke-Stewart, A. *Day care in context*. New York: Wiley, 1973.

Ford Foundation. *A foundation goes to school*. New York: The Ford Foundation, 1972.

Franklin, M. B. Non-verbal representation in young children: a cognitive perspective. *Young Children*, 1973, *29* (1), 33-53.

Furth, H. *Piaget for teachers*. Englewood Cliffs, N. J.: Prentice-Hall, 1970.

Gordon, I. J. An instructional theory approach to the analysis of selected early childhood programs. In I. J. Gordon (Ed.), *Early childhood education*. The Seventy-first Yearbook of the National Society for the Study of Education, Part II. Chicago: University of Chicago Press, 1972.

Gould, R. *Child studies through fantasy: cognitive-affective patterns in development*. New York: Quadrangle Books, 1972.

Johnson, H. M. *Children in the nursery school*. New York: Agathon Press, 1972. Original publication 1928.

Jones, R. M. *Fantasy and feeling in education*. New York: New York University Press, 1968.

Kamii, C. An application of Piaget's theory to the conceptualization of a preschool curriculum. In R. K. Parker (Ed.), *The preschool in action*. Boston: Allyn & Bacon, 1972.

Kamii, C. Pedagogical principles derived from Piaget's theory: relevance for educational practice. In M. Schwebel & J. Raph (Eds.), *Piaget in the classroom*. New York: Basic Books, 1973. (a)

Kamii, C. Piaget's interactionism and the process of teaching young children. In M. Schwebel & J. Raph (Eds.), *Piaget in the classroom*. New York: Basic Books, 1973. (b)

Kamii, C., & DeVries, R. Piaget-based curricula for early childhood education: the Kamii-DeVries approach. Paper presented at meetings of the Society for Research in Child Development, March 1973. (A later version will appear in Kamii, C., & DeVries, R. Piaget for early education. In M. C. Day & R. Parker (Eds.), *pre school in action* (2nd ed.). Boston: Allyn & Bacon, in press.) (a)

Kamii, C., & DeVries, R. Piaget-based curricula for early childhood education: three different approaches. Paper presented at meetings of the Society for Research in Child Development, March 1973. (b)

Kanfer, F. H. Behavior modification–an overview. In C. E. Thoresen (Ed.), *Behavior modification in education*. The Seventy-Second Yearbook of the National Society for the Study of Education, Part I. Chicago: University of Chicago Press, 1973.

Kohlberg, L., & Mayer, R. Development as the aim of education. *Harvard Educational Review*, November 1972, *42* (4).

Kohlberg, L., & Turiel, E. Moral development and moral education. In G. Lesser (Ed.), *Psychology and educational practice* Chicago: Scott Foresman, 1971.

Krasner, L., & Krasner, M. Token economies and other planned environments. In C. E. Thoresen (Ed.), *Behavior modification in education*. The Seventy-Second Yearbook of the National Society for the Study of Education, Part I. Chicago: University of Chicago Press, 1973.

Lavatelli, C. S. *Piaget's theory applied to an early childhood curriculum*. Boston, Mass.: American Science and Engineering, 1970.

Levine, F. M., & Fasnacht, G. Token rewards may lead to token learning. *American Psychologist*, 1974, *29*, 816-820.

Loevinger, J. The meaning and measurement of ego development. *American Psychologist*, 1966, *21*, 195-206.

Macoby, E. E., & Zellner, M. *Experiments in primary education: aspects of Project Follow Through*. New York: Harcourt Brace Jovanovich, 1970.

Mahan, M. A. Ethics of using punishing consequences to control behavior. Paper presented at meetings of the Society for Research in Child Development, Philadelphia, March 1973.

Mayer, R. S. A comparative analysis of preschool curriculum models. In R. H. Anderson & H. G. Shane (Eds.), *As the twig is bent: readings in early childhood education*. New York: Houghton Mifflin, 1971.

McKinnon, D. W. The nature and nurture of creative talent. *American Psychologist*, 1962, *17* (7), 484-495.

Messick, S., & Barrows, T. S. Strategies for research and evaluation. In I. J. Gordon (Ed.), *Early childhood education*. The Seventy-First Yearbook of the National Society for the Study of Education, Part II. Chicago: University of Chicago Press, 1972.

Minuchin, P., Biber, B., Shapiro, E., & Zimiles, H. *The psychological impact of school experience*. New York: Basic Books, 1969.

Mitchell, L. S. *Young geographers*. New York: Basic Books, 1963. Original publication 1934.

Murphy, G. Non-rational processes in learning. In R. Gross & J. Murphy (Eds.), *The revolution in the schools*. New York: Harcourt, Brace, & World, 1964.

O'Leary, K. D. Behavior modification in the classroom: a rejoinder to Winett and Winkler. *Journal of Applied Behavior Analysis*, 1972, *5*, 505-511.

Overton, W. F. Piaget's theory of intellectual development and progressive education. In J. R. Squire (Ed.), *A new look at progressive education*. ASCD Yearbook. Washington, D.C.: Association for Supervision and Curriculum Development, 1972.

Parker, R. K., & Day, M. C. Comparisons of preschool curricula. In R. K. Parker (Ed.), *The preschool in action*. Boston: Allyn & Bacon, 1972.

Piaget, J. *The psychology of intelligence*. London: Routledge & Paul, 1950.

Piaget, J. *Play, dreams and initation in childhood*. New York: Norton, 1951.

Piaget, J. *The science of education and the psychology of the child*. New York: Orion Press, 1970.

Piaget, J., & Inhelder, B. *The psychology of the child*. New York: Basic Books, 1969.

The Plowden Report. *Children and their primary schools, a report of the Central Advisory Council for education (England)* (Vol. 1). London, England: Her Majesty's Stationery Office, 1967.

Pratt, C. *I learn from children*. New York: Simon & Schuster, 1948.

Reese, H. W., & Overton, W. F. Models of development and theories of development. In L. R. Goulet & P. B. Baltes (Eds.), *Life-span developmental psychology: research and theory*. New York: Academic Press, 1970.

Schwebel, M., & Raph, J. (Eds.), *Piaget in the classroom*. New York: Basic Books, 1973.

Scriven, M. Objectivity and subjectivity in educational research. In L. G. Thomas (Ed.), *Philosophical redirection of educational research*. The Seventy-First Yearbook of the National Society for the Study of Education, Part I. Chicago: University of Chicago Press, 1972.

Scriven, M. The philosophy of behavioral modification. In C. E. Thoresen (Ed.), *Behavior modification in education*. The Seventy-Second Yearbook of the National Society for the Study of Education, Part I. Chicago: University of Chicago Press, 1973.

Shapiro, E. Educational evaluation: rethinking the criteria of competence. *School Review*, August 1973, *81* (4).

Shapiro, E., & Biber, B. The education of young children: a developmental-interaction approach. *Teachers College Record*, September 1972, *74* (1).

Shulman, L. S. Reconstruction of educational research. *Review of Educational Research*, 1970, *40* (3), 371-396.

Sigel, I. E. Developmental theory and preschool education: issues, problems and implications. In I. J. Gordon (Ed.), *Early childhood education*. The Seventy-First Yearbook of the National Society for the Study of Education, Part II. Chicago: University of Chicago Press, 1972. (a)

Sigel, I. E. The distancing hypothesis revisited: an elaboration of a neo-Piagetian view of the development of representational thought. In M. E. Meyer (Ed.), *Cognitive learning*. Bellingham, Wash.: Western Washington State College Press, 1972. (b)

Sigel, I. E. Contributions of psycho-educational intervention programs in understanding of preschool children. Paper presented at Burg Wartenstein Symposium, No. 57, Wenner-Gren Foundation for Anthropological Research, Vienna, Austria, June 1973.

Soar, R. S., & Soar, R. M. An empirical analysis of selected Follow Through programs: an example of a process approach to evaluation. In I. J. Gordon (Ed.), *Early childhood education*. The Seventy-First Yearbook of the National Society for the Study of Education, Part II, Chicago: University of Chicago Press, 1972.

Spodek, B. What are the sources of early childhood curriculum? *Young Children*, 1970, *26* (1), 48-58.

Weikart, D. A comparative study of three preschool curricula. Paper presented at biennial meeting of the Society for Research in Child Development, Santa Monica, California, March 1969.

Weikart, D. P., Rogers, L., Adcock, C., & McClelland, D. *The cognitively oriented curriculum*. Washington, D.C.: National Association for the Education of Young Children, 1971.

Werner, H. *Comparative psychology of mental development*. New York: International University Press, 1957. Original publication 1940.

Werner, H. The concept of development from a comparative and organismic point of view. In D. B. Harris (Ed.), *The concept of development*. Minneapolis: University of Minnesota Press, 1957.

White, R. W. Ego and reality in psychoanalytic theory. *Psychological Issues*, 1963, *3* (3).

Winett, R. A., & Winkler, R. C. Current behavior modification in the classroom: be still, be quiet, be docile. *Journal of Applied Behavior Analysis*, 1972, *5*, 499-504.

Zimiles, H. Has evaluation failed compensatory education? In J. Hellmuth (Ed.), *Disadvantaged child, Vol. 3, Compensatory education: A national debate*. New York: Brunner/Mazel, 1970.

2

Children's Friendships in School Settings

Steven R. Asher

University of Illinois

Sherri L. Oden

University of Rochester

John M. Gottman

Indiana University

INTRODUCTION

As children grow older their social interaction typically increases and their friendships become more stable (Horrocks & Buker, 1951; Parten, 1932; Shure, 1963). Still, there are many children who go through the preschool and elementary school years without friends or with few friends. One study found that 6% of third to sixth graders had no classroom friends and an additional 12% had only one friend (Gronlund, 1959).

The consequences of low acceptance by peers has been extensively documented. Children who are socially isolated are more likely to drop out of school (Ullmann, 1957), be later identified as juvenile delinquents (Roff, Sells, & Golden, 1972), and have mental health problems in later life (Cowen, Pederson, Babijian, Izzo, & Trost, 1973). The consequences of low peer acceptance may be more severe than the consequences of low achievement. In one study (Cowen *et al.*, 1973), extensive data were gathered on third-grade children. Measures included absenteeism, grade point average, IQ scores, achievement test performance, teacher ratings, and peer ratings. Eleven years later the research team examined a community mental health register to learn which of these children were being seen by a mental health professional. Of all the measures taken in third grade the one that best predicted which children would later have emotional problems was peer ratings. Children who were less liked by their peers were more likely to be receiving treatment for mental health problems eleven years later.

This paper reviews research on children's friendships in nursery school and elementary school settings. Since school dominates many of the hours of a child's day, it is obviously an important setting in which to study social as well as academic events. Most of the research on children's friendships reflects this fact. While there is some research on friendships in camps, neighborhood settings, etc., the size of this literature is dwarfed in comparison to what is known about social relationships in school.

In reviewing this research, we have tried to select studies that have implications for educational practice. Most of the studies are rather well designed and well executed. We have not hesitated, however, to include less rigorous research if its conception or findings might stimulate further research or suggest ideas for educational practice.

The first part of the paper is concerned with the influence of enduring personal characteristics on peer relations. In this section we consider some of the stereotypes that affect children's friendships and offer a few suggestions about ways to overcome these biasing factors. Next, we review research on the influence of the school environment on friendships. Classroom and school situation variables affect social interactions and the extent to which children will make friends with one another. In the third section we examine research on the kinds of social skills that are important to achieving peer acceptance. Many children lack friends because they do not have the necessary social skills. Finally, the paper concludes with a discussion of the ways in which children who lack social skills can be taught how to make friends. A number of teaching methods can be quite effective in increasing the social interaction and peer acceptance of formerly isolated children. It *is* possible to have classrooms in which far fewer children are socially isolated!

PERSONAL CHARACTERISTICS AND FRIENDSHIP

Among the determinants of peer acceptance are personal characteristics that are rather enduring. One's name, physical appearance, race, and sex are not easily changed. Yet all of these variables influence friendship selection and peer acceptance.

Names

In every generation, a few first names which were previously uncommon become popular. This is particularly true for girls' names. A recent survey of New York City hospitals (Beadle, 1973) indicated that seven of the ten most popular names given to boys in 1972 were among the ten most popular names given to boys in 1948. However, none of the girls' names appeared on both lists.

But does it make a difference what names children are given? Apparently so. Names like John, Sherri, and Steven are among those common appellations that would seem to minimize social discomfort. On the other hand, names like Frances, Hugo, and Hilda seem to carry with them social risks.

McDavid and Harari (1966) asked a group of 10- to 12-year-old children in a community center to indicate their friends while another group of children, unfamiliar with children in the first group, rated the desirability of the children's names. The correlation between desirability of names and the popularity of children with these names was significant. Children with more desirable names were better liked. In a follow-up study Harari and McDavid (1973) found that teachers were also affected by children's names. Teachers graded student essays lower when those essays were randomly paired with rare, unpopular, and unattractive names.

What accounts for the relationship between names and peer acceptance? One possibility is that the simple unfamiliarity or strangeness of certain names leads people to dislike or avoid their bearers. Perhaps children initially behave differently toward a Herbert than a Bill and in so doing set up a cycle of less positive interaction. An alternative explanation is that parents who lack social skills are more likely to give their children odd names and fail to teach effective social skills. In this case, peers would be reacting more to the child's behavior than to the child's name.

If the unfamiliarity explanation is correct, then teachers could help an oddly-named child to be included by making the child's name more of an "everyday household word." Repeated classroom use may help. Associating the name with a famous person in history, science, music, etc., may also be effective. But if the issue is not the child's name, per se, but the associated lack of social skills, then the child should be helped to learn social skills. Thus, for each child the teacher should assess whether the child's name is the real cause of his social difficulty.

One last word: It is important not to overestimate the importance of names. It is only one of many variables that influence social acceptance. United States Presidents in the twentieth century have included a Theodore, Woodrow, Warren, Clavin, Herbert, Franklin, Dwight, and Lyndon. The last five elected Vice-Presidents have included an Alben, Hubert, and Spiro. It may be that many Americans will vote for a man they would not want as a friend; a more plausible interpretation is that names are not everything.

Physical Attractiveness

In American society there seems to be considerable agreement about who is or is not physically attractive. In one study (Cross & Cross, 1971), seven-, twelve-, and seventeen-year-olds, as well as adults, were shown twelve sets of photographs. Each set contained six faces of a particular race, sex, and age group. Respondents were asked to select from each set the most beautiful face and then were asked to rate the twelve faces that had been selected. Results showed no significant difference in the evaluations of beauty made by different age groups. Even the youngest tested shared the conception of beauty held by older people.

Not only is there consensus about physical attractiveness, but there is a strong tendency for children's friendship selection to be influenced by appearance. Young and Cooper (1944) studied factors that influence popularity among elementary school children. They correlated over 30 variables with social acceptance. The most significant was attractiveness of the child's facial appearance. The better looking children were better liked. An interesting aspect of the results was that when the ratings of attractiveness were made by children the relationship between attractiveness and popularity was stronger than when adults made the ratings. In both cases the raters did not know the children they rated and could not have been influenced by any previous associations with the children.

What accounts for the relationship between physical attractiveness and social acceptance? As with names, the cause of greater attraction is unclear. Perhaps better looking children are responded to more positively and thereby develop more effective social skills. Dion and Bersheid (1974) found that nursery school children attributed more negative social behavior to their less attractive peers.

Adults also tend to respond to physical appearance in judging children. Dion (1972) gave college students a photo of a second grade child along with a description of a behavioral episode. The photo showed either an attractive or less attractive child. The behavioral episode consisted of some unacceptable kind of behavior. After the subjects read the episodes, they were asked, among other questions, to predict how likely the child would be to do the same thing again. The physically attractive child was judged to be less likely to repeat the unacceptable behavior. Furthermore, on a series of six personality ratings the attractive child was judged to be more honest and pleasant than the less attractive child. These findings are striking since the behavior being judged was identical; only physical appearance varied.

One group of children who tend to be considered low in physical attractiveness are the physically disabled. In one study (Richardson, Goodman, Hastorf, & Dornbusch, 1961) ten- and eleven-year-old children from many different social classes, regions, and ethnic backgrounds were found to rank figures of disabled children lower in desirability. Furthermore, the same rank ordering occurred in every sample. From most to least liked they were: the normal child, a child with crutches and brace, a child in a wheelchair, a child with a left hand missing, a child with a facial disfigurement, and finally, an obese child.

Many explanations have been offered to account for people's rejection of the disabled. One view is that the disabled are victimized by an excessive societal value on beauty (Wright, 1960). Undoubtedly, this at least partially explains children's feelings toward the less attractive, in general, and the disabled, in particular. Another interpretation (Wright, 1960) is that the disabled are less liked because they are presumed to be different. N. W. Asher (1975) has found that people attribute different attitudes and personality characteristics to disabled and able-bodied individuals. In another study (N. W. Asher, 1973) she found that the extent to which college students perceived a disabled person as similar did indeed influence their feelings toward the person.

It is plausible that the same trend would be found with children since children are more attracted to those who are attitudinally similar to themselves (Byrne & Griffit, 1966). If children could discover for themselves areas of similarity with a disabled person, friendships might be possible. The emphasis should be on guided discovery. In the studies mentioned, the subject was not told that he or she was similar to the person being rated. The subject discovered the similarity when reading the person's attitude profile. Adults often tell children: "He is really just like you" but it is likely that this message is believed most when children discover similarities for themselves. This line of reasoning suggests that teachers should provide situations in which children can discover their similarities of attitude, personalities, values, etc.

The variable of similarity-dissimilarity can, of course, cut both ways. If, in interactions with disabled persons, able-bodied children discover more differences than similarities, increased rejection rather than acceptance could result. Rejection might occur, for example, in an environment which stressed physical prowess above all other skills or where the disabled child was overprotected, given unnecessary preferential treatment, or prevented from developing skills and interests of value to children.

Race

Racial awareness comes quite early in life. Children three years of age and older are clearly aware of racial labels and can appropriately identify their own racial membership (Clark & Clark, 1947; Durrett & Davy, 1970; Hraba & Grant, 1970).

Children also use race as a criterion for selecting friends. Criswell (1939) asked New York City children in three schools to write down the names of classmates they would like to sit next to. Results indicated that children were significantly more likely to choose friends from among their own race. What is interesting, however, is that children did make a considerable number of cross-race selections. Forty percent of their choices would have been cross-race selections if they had been making choices without regard to race. When we averaged Criswell's results across all schools, the results indicated that approximately 25% of the selections were cross-race. Thus, although there was a tendency to prefer children of one's own race many cross-race friendships did exist.

Some recent evidence shows a similar pattern of results. S. R. Asher (1973) asked fourth- and fifth-grade children in a middle-sized Midwestern city to write down the names of their five best friends. About 40% of the school population was black. Each month from October to April approximately 55 children, randomly selected, were asked to name their five best friends. The results showed that children made fewer cross-race selections than would be expected by chance. Still, approximately 18% of white children's selections and 44% of black children's selections were cross-race.

In another study Shaw (1973) asked fourth-, fifth-, and sixth-grade children in February and in June whom they most preferred to be with. Approximately 80% of the children were white and 20% black. Both blacks and whites overselected members of their own race. Nonetheless, both whites and blacks chose members of the other race. Overall, about 33% of black children's selections were white and 6% of white children's selections were black.

The studies reviewed thus far show less racial bias among children than one might expect given the history of poor race relations in the United States. One possibility is that children might show more racial bias if they were asked not only to name a few friends, but to describe their feelings about each classmate. A child might feel quite positively about a few members of another race while feeling negatively about the majority of opposite-race children. A recent study by Singleton (1974) is relevant to this issue. Third-grade classrooms were surveyed in eleven different schools in a single moderate-sized city. These children had experienced desegregated education throughout their public school careers and school system personnel were interested in the children's race relations.

Children were asked to rate each of their classmates on two scales: how much they like to work with other children in their class and how much they like to play with other children. The scales were constructed so that "1" indicated "I don't like to" and "5" indicated "I like to a lot." The results were that both blacks and whites rated members of their own race higher than members of the other race. This result was statistically significant. As in the Criswell, Asher, and Shaw studies, however, there was considerable cross-race acceptance. For example, on the play item, blacks gave blacks an average rating of 3.58 and whites an average rating of 3.17. Whites gave whites an average rating of 2.96 and blacks a rating of 2.86. Thus, children's cross-race ratings were in reality not very different from their same-race ratings.

Although the interracial picture in the preschool and elementary school years is surprisingly positive, the pattern in high school is less hopeful. In one study of high school students (Silverman & Shaw, 1973) social interaction was observed at a popular meeting place in the school. The school's population was 70% white and 30% black. Of all the interactions observed, those between white and black students averaged below 3%. It may be that the "threat" of interracial dating draws students at this age apart. If so, we need to provide children with models of positive interracial relationships so that their teenage years are not characterized by nearly complete racial separation.

What conditions promote positive or negative relations between children of different races? S. R. Asher (1973) and Shaw (1973), both of whom collected data across the school year, found little systematic change in children's acceptance of members of another race from the beginning to the end of the school year. It is clear from this that contact per se does not guarantee unbiased friendship selections. It is undoubtedly the nature of the interracial experience that influences the extent to which children make friends across ethnic and racial lines.

One critical issue is the extent to which contact leads children of different races to perceive themselves as similar versus dissimilar. There is evidence that white children more positively evaluate black children when they discover them to hold similar attitudes (Insko & Robinson, 1967). To the extent that children share the same social class, values, life-style, level of educational attainment, etc., it is likely that more interracial acceptance will occur. One way that a classroom teacher may be able to increase cross-race friendships is by attending to similarities of interests between black and white children. In one study (S. R. Asher, 1975), fifth-grade children were asked to rate the interest value of a series of 25 pictures. The correlation between black male and white male ratings was strongly significant. The correlation betweeen white females and black females, although lower, was also significant. So within each sex there appeared to be considerable similarity of interest between black and white children. For example, both white males and black males rated basketball and race cars highly. Commonly held interests may provide a basis for bringing together children of different races.

Another factor that contributes to interracial acceptance is parent attitude. Analysis of integration case reports suggests that the school atmosphere is far more positive when parents are supportive rather than opposed to the integration process. Authorities, whether Supreme Court justices, the President, or parents, serve to legitimize certain points of view. There was, for example, a marked increase in pro-integration sentiment after the 1954 Supreme Court decision. If children perceive their parents as supportive of integration they are probably far more likely to make an effort to reach out to children of another race.

Sex

Although racial factors influence friendship choice, the sex of the child is a more important factor. American social scientists, heavily committed to the elimination of racial bias, have sometimes underestimated the extent to which sociometric data contains evidence of the existence of two separate cultures: boys' and girls'. The degree to which children chose same-sex friends can be seen in three of the studies discussed in the previous section.

Criswell (1939) summarized her data with the comment that "cleavage between the sexes was greater than racial cleavage," and that "a given group of boys or girls nearly always preferred classmates of the same sex but different race to those of the same race but different sex [p. 18]." S. R. Asher (1973) found a strong preference in children for friends of the same sex. Approximately 95% of children's friendship choices were same-sex choices and there was little variation from month to month. Singleton (1974) also discovered strong and statistically significant acceptance of same-sex and rejection of opposite-sex children. On her 1-5 play scale, boys rated boys 3.95 and rated girls 2.08. Girls rated girls 3.78 and boys 2.26. Comparison of these results with those presented for race in the previous section indicate the extent to which sex is an important factor in friendship selection.

A study by Challman (1932) indicates the early age at which children exclude members of the opposite sex. He observed 33 nursery school children, recording the names of children who were in the same group. Results of over 200 hours of observation indicated predominantly same-sex grouping even among children between the ages of 27 to 45 months. Only one boy and one girl showed strong preferences for opposite-sex friendships. More recently, Omark and Edelman (1973) observed playground interaction and found that kindergarten, first-, and second-grade children interacted predominantly with members of the same sex.

One very interesting finding is that when cross-sex friendships are formed they tend to be quite unstable. Gronlund (1955) gave two sociometric surveys four months apart. Only 20% of the cross-sex friendship choices made on the first survey were also made on the second survey. In contrast, children's same-sex choices were about three times as stable.

One concomitant of restricted interaction between boys and girls is a sharp differentiation of interests. Even young children show strong sex-typing of interests. Shure (1963), for example, found that four-year-old nursery school boys spent more time in the block area while girls spent time in the art, book, and doll areas. The same study that showed a high degree of cross-race similarity of interests (S. R. Asher, 1975) found that the correlation of boys' and girls' interest ratings was low. Among white children the top five interests of boys and girls were completely different. Among black children only one of the top five interests was common to boys and girls. Finally, there is evidence that children's interests are highly related to traditional sex-role conceptions. Markell and Asher (1974) had judges rate the "masculinity" and "femininity" of 25 pictures. When these ratings were correlated with children's interest in the same pictures, the results showed that boys were more interested in "masculine" pictures and girls were more interested in "feminine" pictures.

It seems likely, then, that in the long run the occurrence of many cross-sex friendships depends upon diminishing sex-role rigidity. If boys and girls were reared to have a wider range of interests and to enjoy a wider range of activities there would probably be many more boy-and-girl friendships. An interesting question is whether educational programs such as "Free to be You and Me" or "Sesame Street" will produce change in children's sex-role concepts and friendship patterns.

In the short run, one way to bring boys and girls together may be to provide common or superordinate goals (Sherif, 1958). In a study by DeVries and Edwards (1974), seventh-grade math classes were organized so that children worked individually in two classes and were rewarded for individual achievement while in two other classes boys and girls were teamed together and children were rewarded according to their team's performance. After the four-week experiment was over, children were asked a number of questions; one of these requested them to list their friends. In the two "no team" classes, the number of children's choices that crossed sex lines was 21 and 17%. In the "team" classes, however, the number of cross-sex choices was 33 and 27%. The findings of this experiment suggest that using superordinate goals may help overcome the social distance between boys and girls.

SITUATIONAL CHARACTERISTICS AND FRIENDSHIP

One way to increase friendships among children is to structure the educational environment so that friendships are likely to develop and endure. Many children may lack friends or have few friends because the environment does not promote friendship. A variety of situational factors which influence friendship will be discussed.

Population Mobility

Although contact alone is not sufficient to create peer acceptance, children who have prolonged contact with the same peers should at least have greater opportunity to form friendships. Following this line of reasoning, researchers have investigated the effect of residential mobility of individual children and school populations in relation to peer acceptance. In a study of individual mobility (Young & Cooper, 1944), the five least and five most accepted children in each of eleven elementary school classrooms were compared on the length of time in the current school and the number of schools previously attended. The most accepted and least accepted children did not differ on either of these measures. More recently, Roistacher (1974) found that the degree of an individual child's mobility had no relationship to the number of peers in school who knew him. Neither study, then, found evidence that the more mobile child is at a social disadvantage. It should be noted, however, that neither study controlled for within-school differences in socioeconomic status or social skill repertoire. If the more mobile children within schools were socioeconomically more advantaged they may have had skills which offset potential disadvantages of mobility. There is evidence, for example, that middle class children are more effective communicators than lower class children (Gottman, Gonso, & Rasmussen, 1975; Heider, 1971).

While individual mobility may not be an important factor, the mobility of an entire school population may well be important. In one study (Roistacher, 1974), four inner city and four suburban schools were compared. The inner city schools had an annual pupil turnover rate of over 35%; in contrast, the turnover rate in the suburban schools averaged below 10%. Eighth-grade boys in each school were asked to indicate those students they knew well. In schools with high turnover fewer children were known by others. Furthermore, these results were obtained even when other differences between the schools, such as income and racial composition, were statistically controlled.

It would seem, then, that children who attend "high turnover" schools have a social disadvantage when it comes to making friends. In this type of environment, it is necessary for the school staff and community to take special steps to bring children in contact with one another. Other environments with high population turnover (e.g., universities, military bases) provide a variety of social activities for integrating new members and building cohesiveness. Perhaps schools could adopt some of their techniques. Having children eat or play with children from different classrooms might help, especially if the teacher made sure that children learned each other's names. It might also help if children could learn about each other's background, where they lived before, their interests, etc. In a high-mobility environment, children, like adults, need to identify characteristics in others that will help them to rapidly build relationships.

Opportunities for Participation

Situations vary in the extent to which they allow people to participate fully in social interaction. For example, if there is a large variety of social roles to be filled and a limited number of potential "actors," more people will get involved. This is the type of situation that exists in smaller schools. Whatever the size of the school, there are a certain number of roles that must be filled (e.g., band member, club member, student council member, etc.). Thus, students who attend small schools should have greater opportunities for participation. Indeed, Gump and Friesen (1964) and Wicker (1969) have found that students in small high schools participated in a wider range of activities and held more positions of responsibility than students in large schools.

Size of classroom also appears to be an important influence on social participation. Dawe (1934) observed teacher-led discussions in kindergartens ranging in size from 14 to 46 children. As one might expect, the average number of comments contributed by each child decreased as size increased. The average child in the 14-person class spoke nearly seven times while children in classes about 30 spoke fewer than two times each. There is, after all, a finite amount of "air time" which must be shared among classroom members.

The higher participation characteristic of small school settings should lead students to be better known by their peers. Interestingly, Roistacher (1974) found that junior high school students in smaller schools knew more fellow students, in absolute numbers, than did students in larger schools. These data should give pause to those who urge consolidation of smaller school districts into large ones. It may be that there are social disadvantages that offset the potential economic or academic advantages to be gained from consolidation.

If participation and responsibility are important determinants of peer acceptance, then increasing participation and responsibility should promote peer acceptance. A study by McClelland and Ratliff (1947) found this to be the case. They worked in a junior high school where a particularly large number of children seemed to have no friends. They decided to intervene in one class of 35 students. On a pretest measure, 12 students received no sociometric choices on any of four sociometric questions. (With whom would you like to go to a show? With whom would you like to study? Whom would you like to have as a guest in your home? With whom would you rather share a secret?)

One part of their intervention consisted of providing isolated children with special classroom roles (e.g., chairman of the hospitality committee who had responsibility for sending cards to sick classroom members). The class was also divided into small groups based on seating rows. Each group had a captain and various activities such as parties and charity drives were conducted by the groups so that individual member participation was increased. Sociometric choices made after this intervention indicated that only two children were still ignored on all four questions. These results, although based on only a single classroom, are promising. Creating new roles which give children a chance to participate may be a powerful way to overcome isolation.

The importance of participating in a visible and valued classroom role is also demonstrated in a study by Chennault (1967). Two isolated children from 16 special education classes were grouped with the two most popular children from the same classes. Each group's task was to produce a skit for their classroom. They met for 15 minutes twice a week for 5 weeks, and then presented their skit to the class. Sociometric ratings taken after this activity indicated that the participating isolated children were more accepted than a control group of isolated children who had not been involved with the skit.

A follow-up study (Rucker & Vincenzo, 1970) shows that maintenance of this type of change is dependent on continued participation. Isolated children from special education classes met with the most popular members of their class for 45 minutes. The group met twice weekly for two weeks to produce a classroom carnival. The group planned events, decorated the room, awarded prizes, etc. A sociometric measure given three days after the carnival indicated that the participating isolated children were far more accepted than the control group of isolated children. However, a follow-up measure taken one month after the carnival showed that these children were no longer more accepted than the control group. Once their participation ceased, the level of peer acceptance they experienced also declined. The same pattern of initial gain followed by long-run decline has also been found by Lilly (1971). These results suggest that isolated children may be unable to maintain relationships which have been situationally nurtured.

Rewarding Social Interaction

One critical situational component is whether children are rewarded or reinforced by the teacher or by peers for engaging in friendship-making behavior. When the environment rewards certain behavior, the likelihood is greater that the behavior will occur again. If rewards are witheld, the behavior is less likely to occur. Children, like adults, are reinforced by approval of their conduct.

The power of reinforcement was demonstrated in a study by Blau and Rafferty (1970). They paired children together to play a game in which a light went on when the children cooperated. One group of children played the game without receiving any reward from the experimenter. In other groups, each time children cooperated they received a ticket redeemable for prizes. After playing, the same children rated how much they liked each other. These ratings indicated that the children rewarded for cooperation regarded each other more highly than children who were not rewarded.

An important point is that reinforcement has to be maintained to some degree if the desired behavior is to continue. One study (Hauserman, Walen, & Behling, 1973) examined the effect of reinforcing black and white first-grade children for sitting with each other in the lunchroom. The study was carried out in a school lunchroom where children usually sat in racially separate groups. The teachers introduced a game in which children drew papers out of a hat. Each paper had the name of one black and one white child and children were told to sit with their "new friend." At the end of the lunch session, children who had carried out this instruction received tickets, redeemable for candy. In the next phase of the experiment, the name drawing was discontinued. Instead, children simply were encouraged to sit with "new friends" and were reinforced if they sat with an interracial group. In the final phase, reinforcement procedures were terminated.

Results of the study indicated an increase of interracial interaction in the lunchroom during the experimental phase. More important, this effect also generalized to a free play session held in the classroom after lunch. Here, too, children engaged in more cross-race interaction. However, once reinforcement procedures were ended, children once again sat with members of their own race. These results demonstrate the power that environmental reward has on children's social interactions.

Success and Failure

Another important situational variable is the extent to which the school helps the child to succeed academically. The cognitive and social areas of development are interrelated. Children who have difficulty with cognitive tasks are also likely to have greater problems in social relationships. This is demonstrated by the finding that low achieving children tend to have fewer friends in school (Gronlund, 1959).

Why might academic progress be related to peer acceptance? One possibility is that success leads children to "feel good" and be more concerned for other children. Isen, Horn, and Rosenhan (1973) performed an experiment in which they arranged for some children to succeed at a game while others failed. After playing the game, children were asked by an adult experimenter to contribute money to buy toys for poor children. When contributions were made without the experimenter watching, the children who had succeeded at the game were more generous than those who had failed. When the contributions were made publicly, the two groups gave similar amounts.

While success leads children to feel good, school failure probably leads many children to be aggressive and unkindly disposed toward their peers. And from available evidence, the aggressive child (Hartup, Glazer, & Charlesworth, 1967), particularly the inappropriately aggressive child (Lesser, 1959), is disliked and rejected.

Such results suggest that environments which provide children with opportunities for feeling successful would simultaneously be promoting positive peer relations. This means first of all that the curriculum should provide children with a chance to succeed. Second, evaluation of student progress should emphasize the child's own rate of progress (Hill, 1972). In environments where children are compared with one another ("grading on a curve"), a certain percentage of children experience failure regardless of their level of performance and rate of progress.

Activities

Observation of classrooms indicates that the type of available activities influences the kinds of social interaction which may occur. A study by Charlesworth and Hartup (1967) was concerned with activities in which children interacted positively with each other. They observed four nursery school classrooms and counted the frequency of four categories of positive social response: giving positive attention and approval, giving affection and personal acceptance, submission (passive acceptance, imitation, allowing another child to play), and token giving (spontaneously giving physical objects such as toys or food). Sixty-five percent of the positive responses given by children occurred in what the authors termed dramatic play activities (housekeeping area, blocks, trucks, puppet play, etc.). In contrast, table activities (puzzles, manipulative table toys, art activities, stories, flannel board, etc.) were less likely to elicit positive social behaviors. Finally, when children were wandering about the room without engaging in any activity, they were also less likely to interact positvely with others.

Another relevant variable is the number of activity resources available. Since limited resources can lead to conflict and aggression, one way to minimize disturbance and keep children "on task" would be to provide lots of available resources. Indeed, evidence exists (Doke & Risley, 1972) that providing children with activity options, increasing the amount of materials, and dismissing children individually (rather than en masse) from one activity to another results in greater participation by children with the materials. Each of these techniques has the effect of increasing the ratio of available materials per child.

But is a high degree of participation with materials totally desirable? A second look suggests that the picture is more complicated. When the children worked with no activity options and were dismissed en masse, it appeared that ". . . children spent more time talking to each other" (Doke & Risley, 1972, p. 416). Since talking can lead to social learning, some nonparticipation with materials may be valuable. Having fewer material resources may be functional in another sense; the conflict and frustration that result provide children with opportunities to learn how to share and cooperate.

SOCIAL SKILLS AND FRIENDSHIP

Many children may lack friends not because the situation is particularly interfering or constraining but because they do not have certain important social skills. Help for these children requires that they be taught necessary social behaviors. In this section we will consider some of the behaviors associated with being liked and having friends.

Responding Positively

One important set of behaviors involves a child's ability to interact positively with others. As children grow older, they are likely to engage in more positive social responses with one another (Charlesworth & Hartup, 1967). The extent to which children behave constructively toward peers seems to be pretty consistent within a single context. Kohn (1966) observed kindergarten children throughout the school year. He found that the degree of positive interaction shown by children in the fall semester correlated with the degree of positive interaction in the spring. One reason for the stability of positive interaction is that children who give a lot of positive responses also tend to receive a lot. For example, Kohn (1966) found a high correlation between the percentage of positive acts made by a child and the percentage of positive acts which others made toward him or her. Charlesworth and Hartup (1967), in their study of nursery school children, found that the number of children to whom a child responded positively was correlated significantly with the number of children who responded positively to him.

From these data we can hypothesize that children who engage in a high degree of positive interaction would also be chosen as friends on a sociometric measure. Studies in which children are asked to name their friends support this hypothesis. For example, Hartup *et al.* (1967) observed social interaction in a nursery school and correlated the type of interaction each child displayed with the number of acceptances and rejections received on a sociometric test. Social behavior was categorized as positive or negative. The first category included giving attention and approval, giving affection and personal acceptance, submitting to another's wishes, and giving things to another. Negative behaviors included noncompliance, interference, derogation, and attack. Peer acceptance and rejection were measured by asking children to identify three children they "especially like" and three they "don't like very much." Results of this study indicated that in both classrooms the number of positive responses a child made toward peers was positively correlated with peer acceptance. Furthermore, children who gave the most negative responses to peers were the most rejected. It seems, then, that children, who lack friends tend not to positively reinforce interpersonal contact.

In teaching a child to be more socially effective with peers, it is necessary to develop those behaviors that will be perceived by a child's peers as positive. These behaviors may vary across settings. Gottman, Gonso, and Rasmussen (1975) correlated social interaction patterns with peer acceptance in third- and fourth-grade classrooms. One-half of the classrooms were in a middle class school and one-half were in a working class school. As in the Hartup *et al.* (1967) study, the frequency of positive and negative social interactions was recorded. However, the observation categories were extended to include verbal and nonverbal behavior. The results indicated that the children who were liked in the middle class school were those who engaged in positive verbal interaction. In the working class school, the most liked children were those who engaged in positive nonverbal interaction. Middle class children who engaged in positive nonverbal behavior actually tended to be more disliked. These data imply that it is important for children to learn what types of behavior are reinforcing to other children. A child must learn to "psych out" the environment to figure out what kinds of behavior will lead to acceptance or rejection.

Communicating Accurately

Another skill that appears to be important is the ability to communicate accurately with another person. In one study (Rubin, 1972) children played a communication game in which a speaker described unusually shaped patterns to a listener. Data were also collected on children's three friendship play choices. The correlation between having friends and doing well on the patterns communication task was strongly significant in kindergarten and second grades. The correlations were nonsignificant in fourth and sixth grades. A more recent study (Gottman, Gonso, & Rasmussen, 1975) also found a relationship between having friends and communicating effectively.

Why might poorer communicators be less liked? One reason, perhaps, is that it is not very reinforcing or personally validating to be with someone who cannot express his ideas clearly and who may not be an especially good listener either. Another reason is that effective collaboration, whether it be in play or at work, depends on two people having a common idea of what they are about. The child who communicates poorly may also be playing or working at cross-purposes with peers.

Whatever the reason, it is important to identify possible reasons for poor communication performance. Some children may communicate poorly because they have less adequate vocabularies. Kingsley (1971) found that kindergarten children who did poorly on a communication task had more limited vocabulary. Second, some children may not recognize that effective communication often involves making fine distinctions. Asher and Parke (1975) found that young children can communicate as effectively as older children if fine distinctions are not required but do poorly when fine distinctions are required. Third, some children may not be considering the listener's perspective when communicating with another person. In one study (Flavell, Botkin, Fry, Wright, & Jarvis, 1968), elementary school children taught a game to a listener who was either sighted or blind. The children gave rather useful information to the sighted person but far less useful information when the listener was blind. For example, they would say "Put this piece here"; or "Take the red one and put it next to the blue one." This type of behavior suggests that the children were not thinking about the listener's point of view.

Research is needed on whether teaching children to be more accurate communicators increases their acceptance by other children. There is evidence that communication skills can be improved through practice or teaching (Chandler, Greenspan, & Barenboim, 1974). One study (Gottman, Gonso, & Schuler, in press) included sociometric measures and found that isolated children who were taught to be better communicators were more accepted by their classmates. No firm conclusion can be drawn since communication skill training was only one of a number of interventions with the children. Still, the results suggest that future exploration is warranted. If an isolated child is also a poor communicator, it could help to teach communication skills.

Being Expert

One way for a child to gain peer acceptance is to be very good at something valued by other children. For example, being a competent athlete is likely to be a social asset. McCraw and Tolbert (1953) compared the sociometric status of junior high school boys with their athletic ability. They measured sociometric status by asking boys to indicate the three children they liked best in their class, grade level, and school. From these ratings a total status score was derived for each individual. Athletic ability was measured by an index composed of performance on the 50-yard dash, the standing broad jump, and the softball distance throw. At each grade level and in each class, the correlation between athletic ability and being liked was significant.

One group of children who are relatively lacking in expertise are the retarded. A study by Goodman, Gottlieb, and Harrison (1972) found that elementary school children expressed less liking for a sample of educably mentally retarded children from their school than for a sample of nonretarded children. Furthermore, there was evidence that increased contact through integrated classrooms led to increased *rejection* of the retarded. The retarded children in integrated classrooms were more rejected as potential friends. A follow-up study by Gottlieb and Budoff (1973) also found rejection of the retarded as friends and provided additional evidence that increased contact between retarded and nonretarded may lead to increased rejection. In a school with no interior walls, retarded children were more rejected than in a school with walls and segregated classrooms. As long as people judge others by their abilities, increased contact with those who are relatively less expert may lead to less rather than more acceptance.

How might the retarded be more successfully integrated with the nonretarded? The hypothesis that expertness is a critical determinant of peer acceptance suggests that activities should be emphasized in which the retarded have a chance to perform at or near the same level as nonretarded children. There are many areas in which EMR children are nearly indistinguishable from "normal" children. For example, they are likely to be more competent on the playground than in the classroom. Gottlieb (1971) found that children in Norway express more positive attitudes about playing with retarded children than working with them. It is likely that the same is true for American children.

If expertness is an important determinant of being liked, not just for the retarded, but for all children, then it should be possible to improve the status of an isolated child by making an existing talent more visible to the class. For example, while working in a third-grade class, two of the authors had an isolated child plan, with two other children, a puppet show which was presented to the class. Follow-up data indicated that the child gained a friend. If a child lacks skills valued by the group, it should be possible to increase his acceptance by teaching him a valued skill. For example, in a classroom where children emphasize athletics, teaching an isolated child to play a better game of basketball should increase his acceptance into the group. Although we know of no formal research that has evaluated the effectiveness of either of these strategies, many teachers report positive results from their own experience. It remains for researchers to evaluate what may be an effective practice.

Initiating a Relationship

It is conceivable that some children are positively responsive, effective communicators, and expert in certain areas but still lack friends. One possibility is that they may not know how to go about making a friend. In one study (Gottman, Gonso & Rasmussen, 1975), third- and fourth-grade children were asked individually to pretend that the experimenter was a new child in school and that he or she wanted to make friends. The children's responses were scored according to whether they offered a greeting, asked the "new child" for information (e.g., "Where do you live?"), attempted to include (e.g., "Wanna come over to my house sometime?"), or gave information (e.g., "My favorite sport is basketball."). In addition to participating in this role play, the children were asked to name their best friends. Children who were chosen as a friend by six or more peers were found to be much more skillful on the "new friend" role-play than children who received five choices or less.

TEACHING SOCIAL SKILLS

If children have few friends because they lack effective social behaviors, then teaching social skills can be helpful. In this section we will review research on teaching friendship-making behavior to isolated children. Our focus is on teaching strategies that have practical value for the nursery school or elementary school classroom.

Shaping

Shaping uses positive reinforcement to change behavior gradually. The first step is to wait until the child's behavior somewhat approximates the behavior to be learned and then give the child a reinforcer. As the child's behavior further approaches the desired behavior, he or she is again reinforced. This shaping process continues until the new behavior is learned. One of the first studies to demonstrate the effects of shaping on an isolated child's behavior was done by Allen, Hart, Buell, Harris, and Wolf (1964). Their subject was Ann, a four-year-old nursery school child, who, after six weeks of school, was isolated from other children and engaged in a variety of behaviors to gain the teachers' attention. The study began with a five-day baseline period in which Ann's behavior was observed but no attempts were made to change her behavior. During this baseline period, Ann was observed to interact approximately 10% of the time with peers and approximately 40% of the time with teachers.

In the next phase of the study, the teacher reinforced Ann by giving her attention as she interacted with other children. At first, she was reinforced for standing close to another child or playing beside another child. Later, she was reinforced only for direct interaction. The researchers discovered that direct comments to Ann such as "Ann, you are making dinner for the whole family" had the effect of leading Ann away from the children into interaction with the teacher. Reinforcing statements that focused on Ann as a member of a group (e.g., "You three girls have a cozy house! Here are some more cups, Ann, for your tea party.") were quite successful; interaction with adults fell below 20% and interaction with children increased to about 60%.

Then the procedure was reversed. Ann was reinforced for being alone or interacting with teachers and ignored when she interacted with peers. Her behavior returned to the baseline level. This reversal to her previously isolated situation indicates the power of the teacher's attention. Ann's behavior was strongly influenced by what she was reinforced for doing. As a final test, the teachers once again reinforced Ann only for interacting with children. As before, her time spent interacting with children increased and her time with adults decreased.

What happens to isolated children weeks after reinforcement procedures are terminated? A study by O'Connor (1972) is relevant. Eight isolated children were reinforced for making social contact. The amount of time they spent in social interaction dramatically increased. However, when reinforcement was terminated their behavior reverted back to the baseline level. The failure to produce longer lasting effects is somewhat surprising. One might think that isolated children would find it reinforcing to be with other children and that the experience of being included by others would adequately sustain the new behavior. Perhaps the isolated children were socially unskilled and other children found them unpleasant to be with.

One approach to the problem of maintaining change is to gradually decrease or fade out the reinforcement rather than abruptly terminate it. A case study (Coats, 1967, reported in Baer & Wolf, 1970) with a four-year-old child found that when the teacher gradually decreased the frequency of reinforcing the child's social behavior the behavior lasted. Perhaps the gradual decrease in reinforcement gave the isolated child more time to learn and practice social skills. In this case, over a period of time his peers would begin to reinforce the child for social interaction. They would take over, as it were, the reinforcing function.

The studies considered here have been primarily concerned with increasing a child's tendency to approach other children. How do you teach an isolated child what to do once he approaches his peers? One method would be to shape appropriate behavior by reinforcing closer and closer approximations of the desired behavior. This approach might be inefficient for teaching complex social skills; one could wait a long time for even an approximation of the appropriate behavior to occur. The next two teaching strategies to be discussed are more direct and possibly more efficient. Modeling and coaching can provide children with rules or general strategies of social interaction. These rules can guide the child's behavior so that he is reinforcing to be with.

Modeling

One way to learn something is to watch someone do it. In every culture a tremendous amount of information is transmitted from one generation to the next. Much of this information is acquired through observation. Children watch their parents shave, hunt, get up early for work, cook, make a bed, ride a bike, read, etc. By watching they learn. There has been a growing interest in using observational methods to change the behavior of children. Just as watching an aggressive model can lead children to be more aggressive (Bandura, Ross, & Ross, 1961), models may serve more positive functions. For example, children have been found to imitate models who reflect thoughtfully on a problem (Ridberg, Parke, & Hetherington, 1971), contribute to charity (Rosenhan & White, 1967), and express moral judgments characteristic of older children (Turiel, 1966).

If children learn by observing others, then an isolated child's social involvement could be increased by showing him a model of a socially effective person. O'Connor (1969) identified socially isolated children in nine nursery school classes by using a combination of teacher nominations and direct behavioral observation. Half of the isolated children saw a social interaction modeling film; the other half, the control group, saw a film about dolphins. The modeling film, 23 minutes long, consisted of 11 episodes in which a child entered a group of other children. The situations were graduated from low threat (sharing a book or toy with two other children) to high threat (joining a group of children who were gleefully tossing play equipment around the room). The model was always well received by the children (e.g., offered a toy, talked to, smiled at, etc.). A narrator described the action as it occurred in order to call children's attention to the relevant behaviors. For example, in one sequence the narrator says "Now another child comes up close to watch. She wants to play, too. She waits for them to see her. Now she gets a chair and she sits down with them so they will play with her. She starts to do what they are doing so they will want to play with her. . ."

After seeing the film, each child returned to the classroom where postfilm observations were immediately made. Results showed that the social interaction of children in the modeling group greatly increased. In fact, they were interacting somewhat more frequently then a sample of nonisolated children. The control group that watched the dolphin film did not change at all. These are impressive results, particularly in the light of the brief nature of the "therapy."

But does it last? A second study by O'Connor (1972) is relevant. Again, isolated children were selected from nursery school classrooms. One group of children saw the modeling film. As in the previous study, the behavior of the children following the film was as interactive as that of the nonisolated children. In addition, follow-up observations were made weeks after the film. The children who saw the modeling film continued to interact with their peers. Another study using the modeling film observed children one month after exposure to the film model and also found that social interaction continued at a high level (Evers & Schwarz, 1973).

One intriguing issue left unresolved by this research is why isolated children learn from O'Connor's film models but have not learned from the real-life peer models who are in their classes. Nearly every class has highly popular children who are also socially quite skillful. One possible explanation is that the film narrator draws the children's attention to appropriate social details that they otherwise miss. Perhaps in the flow of events in the real world the isolated child fails to attend to significant elements of the popular child's behavior.

This analysis suggests that making the peer model's presence explicit could have positive results. A study of disruptive behavior by Csapo (1972) is suggestive. She paired six emotionally disturbed children with six peers who were exemplars of classroom decorum. The disturbed children sat next to their classmate model and were told to watch the model and do what he was doing so that he could learn how to get along better in class. Observations indicated that all six disruptive children improved their behavior dramatically. Follow-up data were collected for ten days after the intervention was concluded and the six children continued their socially appropriate behavior.

Coaching

The development of language is a significant advance in a child's educational potential. Once children comprehend language, they can acquire new social behavior through direct instruction. Teachers and peers can become coaches who verbally transmit rules of social behavior. As we are using it here, coaching has a number of components. First, the child is provided with a rule or standard of behavior. In simple terms he is told what he should do. Second, the child has opportunities to rehearse or practice the behavior. Finally, there are opportunities for feedback in which the child's performance is discussed and suggestions for improvements made. The studies we will review here use at least two of these three components.

Studies of assertiveness training with college students can be used to illustrate coaching. McFall and Twentyman (1973) were interested in teaching assertive behaviors to unassertive people. As part of the training, the trainee was confronted with a series of simulated, or role-play, situations which typically pose difficulty for unassertive people (e.g., saying "no" to an illegitimate request). In each situation the trainee was given verbal instructions on how best to handle the situation. Coaching was found to be effective in improving assertive behavior in the training situation and in a real-life situation. Of particular interest was the finding that trainees who had a chance to rehearse or practice the new behavior improved more than those whose training did not include opportunities for practice.

Coaching can also be effective with young children. Using verbal reasoning techniques appears to be one of the best ways to insure that children internalize rules of social behavior. For example, studies of child-rearing methods suggest that verbal reasoning leads to more prosocial behavior by the child than physical punishment (e.g., Hoffman & Saltzstein, 1967). More recently, Parke (1970) has found that punishment, when it is administered, is more effective if accompanied by a verbal rationale. Parke suggested that rationales might include various kinds of information such as descriptions of consequences of behavior, examples of acceptable behavior, and explicit instructions on what to do in specific situations.

These types of rationales were provided in a study by Chittenden (1942). A critical situation for young children is one in which there are limited play resources (e.g., two children and one toy). Chittenden chose this situation and sought to teach children to take turns with materials, divide or share the materials where possible, or play cooperatively with the materials. She selected 19 nursery school children whose play with others included a high proportion of dominating behavior and a low proportion of cooperation. Ten of these children received training in how to play cooperatively with others; the other nine children served as the control group.

Chittenden's training situation was ingenious. Each child was introduced to two dolls named "Sandy" and "Mandy." In a series of situations, the dolls confronted the problem of how to play with a single toy. Sometimes they were unsuccessful and their interaction ended in a fight. At other times they were successful and they took turns, shared, or played cooperatively. Eleven training sessions were held. In the first session Sandy and Mandy were introduced; and in the next ten sessions the dolls faced a series of limited resource situations. Chittenden provides scripts for each of the sessions that could be used to repeat her training. Briefly, the first sessions served to teach the children to discriminate unhappy outcomes such as fighting, anger, etc., from happy outcomes such as sharing, having a good time, etc. In later sessions, the dolls sometimes played successfully, thereby modeling appropriate behavior. At other times they fought and the experimenter-teacher and child discussed possible ways of resolving conflicts the dolls faced. In still later sessions the child was asked to show the dolls what they could do to play more successfully. For example, after Sandy and Mandy fought over who was to use some toy cars the experimenter-teacher asked "What would you do? Show them what to do." These situations provided tests of the child's understanding.

More than a week after training, the children were observed in a real-life play situation. The results showed that the trained children had significantly decreased in their amount of dominating behavior. They also increased in cooperative behavior but the increase was not statistically significant. The control group children showed little change in their behavior from pre- to posttest.

A more recent coaching study by Zahavi (1973) has also obtained impressive results. She selected eight nursery school children who had been the most aggressive during six hours of observation over a two-week period. The head teacher, who was highly regarded by the children, met individually with four of the eight children for approximately fifteen minutes. The meeting consisted of three phases. First, the teacher explained to each child that hitting others causes harm; second, that the other children would not like the child if he hit them and that hitting does not solve the problem; and third, the child was asked to think of alternative behaviors to hitting such as sharing or taking turns. At each phase, the teacher asked the child questions so that he would participate in formulating these concepts. Six hours of follow-up observation conducted during the two weeks after training indicated that two of the four children greatly decreased their amount of aggressive activity. Furthermore, the decrease in aggression was accompanied by an increase in positive behaviors. The four control group children did not change. Next, these four children were coached by the teacher. Observations made one week later indicated that three of these four children dramatically changed their behavior. These results are quite impressive in the light of the short coaching session held by the teacher. They provide testimony to the way a teacher can verbally guide the behavior of even very young children.

Neither of these studies measured sociometric progress so there is no way of knowing whether children gained friends as a result of their change in behavior. Two recent coaching studies have included measures of friendship. In one (Gottman, Gonso, & Schuler, in press), "low-friend" children from a single third-grade classroom were selected. Two of the children received training and two were control subjects. The training consisted of modeling and coaching in which the child saw a video tape of a girl entering a group of peers. The video tape was discussed and the "low-friend" child role-played situations in which she was a new child in class and wanted to make friends. After this role play the child was taught to be a more effective communicator. The emphasis of the training was on thinking of the listener's perspective when talking to another person.

Results of this study indicated that the two coached children were rated more highly by peers while the two control children received ratings quite similar to their earlier ones. Observation in class suggested that none of the children increased their frequency of interaction. However, the two coached children changed in the kind of children they interacted with. One girl sought out more popular children and the other interacted more with other "low-friend" children. Apparently the training affected children's selection strategies.

In another coaching and friendship study (Oden & Asher, 1975) three "low-friend" children in eleven different third- and fourth-grade classrooms were identified based on sociometric measures. One of the three was coached. This child, in five separate sessions, played a game with a classmate. Each session the child played with a different classmate. Before playing, the child was advised on how to have the most fun. The coach suggested such things as participating fully, cooperating, communicating, and showing interest in the other person. The child was asked to think of examples for each of these categories. After playing the game the coach asked the child "how it went" and the child discussed his experience in terms of issues such as participation, cooperation, communication, and showing interest. One of the other three "low-friend" children in each classroom participated in the same number of play sessions but received no coaching. The remaining "low-friend" child from the classroom came out of the room with a classmate, received no coaching, and played a game alone.

The experiment lasted for four weeks. About five days later the children were once again asked to indicate how much they liked to play with and work with the other children in the class and to name their friends. The results were encouraging. On the "play with" measure the coached children received a significantly higher rating; the rating of the children who were paired but did not receive coaching actually went down slightly; and the rating of children who played alone did not change. On the "work with" rating and the naming of friends measure the results were generally in the same direction but not significant.

In summary, it appears from a number of studies that coaching can improve children's social skills and lead to increased peer acceptance. Given the capacity of children to learn from verbal instruction and the opportunity to practice, a teacher would be wise to include coaching as a method for helping socially isolated children.

SUMMARY

We have considered some of the characteristics that are associated with having friends. It is important to keep in mind that children who lack friends may do so for different reasons. Social relationships are affected by the child's personal characteristics, varied aspects of the situation, and the child's social skills. With careful observation and informal "experimenting," it should be possible to infer the reasons for a particular child's social difficulty.

If a child's personal characteristics seem to be distracting from his or her friendship-making capability, emphasis could be placed on the child's similarity to other children such as having a common interest or goal. If the situation seems to be constraining peer relationships, there are a number of classroom features that could be changed. Introducing opportunities for children to participate in activities, rewarding social interaction, facilitating success experiences, and providing socially conducive activities can make a difference. Research to date suggests that it is important to maintain changes in the situation if friendships are to continue. If children lack friends due to limited social skills, a variety of teaching methods can be used. Shaping, modeling, and coaching have been found to improve the social interaction of isolated children. The results are particularly encouraging given the short-term nature of the "treatment" employed in most training research.

In terms of teaching social skills there are two areas, in particular, that we need to know more about. First, do the effects of social skill training last? To date, there have been no long-term follow-up studies. Results gathered about one month after training are encouraging, but there is a need for more longitudinal information. A formerly isolated child may need the psychological equivalent of "booster shots."

Second, we need to know which changes in social behavior lead to increased peer acceptance. For example, in shaping and modeling studies, the proportion of time children spend interacting with peers increases. Typically, however, no sociometric data are gathered, so it is impossible to say whether increased friendships result. For example, it is hard to know how the other children are perceiving the new behavior. It is possible that a formerly isolated child's classmates are thinking: "What a kid! He used to be by himself all the time; now he's always hanging around." The attention of the teacher and researcher should, therefore, be directed toward changes in both behavior *and* sociometric status.

Although we need to know more about how friendships develop and how they can be facilitated, we do know enough right now to improve the social relationships of children. The best strategy may be to use multiple methods of teaching social skills. The combined effects of shaping, modeling, and coaching would probably be more effective than any single technique alone. Finally, it would probably be best to consider situational variables when teaching social skills. Children need a suitable environment in which to practice newly developing abilities.

REFERENCES

Allen, K. E., Hart, B., Buell, J. S., Harris, F. R., & Wolf, M. M. Effects of social reinforcement of isolate behavior of a nursery school child. *Child Development*, 1964, *35*, 511-518.

Asher, N. W. Manipulating attraction toward the disabled: An application of the similarity-attraction model. *Rehabilitation Psychology*, 1973, *20*, 156-164.

Asher, N. W. Social stereotyping of the physically handicapped. Submitted for publication, 1975.

Asher, S. R. The influence of race and sex on children's sociometric choices across the school year. Unpublished manuscript, University of Illinois, 1973.

Asher, S. R. The effect of interest on reading comprehension of black children and white children. Unpublished manuscript. University of Illinois. 1975.

Asher, S. R., & Parke, R. D. Influence of sampling and comparison processes on the development of communication effectiveness. *Journal of Educational Psychology*, 1975, *67*, 64-75.

Baer, D. M., & Wolf, M. M. Recent examples of behavior modification in preschool settings. In C. Neuringer & J. L. Michael (Eds.), *Behavior modification in clinical psychology*. New York: Appleton-Century-Crofts, 1970.

Bandura, A., Ross, D., & Ross, S. A. Transmission of aggression through imitation of aggressive models. *Journal of Abnormal and Social Psychology*, 1961, *63*, 575-582.

Beadle, M. The game of the name. *N. Y. Times Magazine*, October 21, 1973, pp. 38-39, 120-126, 128-130.

Blau, B., & Rafferty, J. Changes in friendship status as a function of reinforcement. *Child Development*, 1970, *41*, 113-121.

Byrne, D., & Griffit, W. A developmental investigation of the law of attraction. *Journal of Personality and Social Psychology*, 1966, *4*, 699-702.

Challman, R. C. Factors influencing friendships among preschool children. *Child Development*, 1932, *3*, 146-158.

Chandler, M. J., Greenspan, S., & Barenboim, C. Assessment and training of role-taking and referential communication skills in institutionalized emotionally disturbed children. *Developmental Psychology*, 1974, *10*, 546-553.

Charlesworth, R., & Hartup, W. W. Positive social reinforcement in the nursery school peer group. *Child Development*, 1967, *38*, 993-1003.

Chennault, M. Improving the social acceptance of unpopular educable mentally retarded pupils in special classes. *American Journal of Mental Deficiency*, 1967, *72*, 455-458.

Chittenden, G. F. An experimental study in measuring and modifying assertive behavior in young children. *Monographs of the Society for Research in Child Development*, 1942, *7*, No. 1 (Serial No. 31).

Clark, K. B., & Clark, M. K. Racial identification and racial preference in Negro children. In T. Newcomb & E. Hartley (Eds.), *Readings in social psychology*. New York: Holt, 1947.

Cowen, E. L., Pederson, A., Babijian, H., Izzo, L. D., & Trost, M. A. Long-term follow-up of early detected vulnerable children. *Journal of Consulting and Clinical Psychology*, 1973, *41*, 438-446.

Criswell, J. H. A sociometric study of race cleavage in the classroom. *Archives of Psychology*, 1939, No. 235, 1-82.

Cross, J. F., & Cross, J. Age, sex, race, and the perception of facial beauty. *Developmental Psychology*, 1971, *5*, 433-439.

Csapo, M. Peer models reverse the "one bad apple spoils the barrel" theory. *Teaching Exceptional Children*, 1972, *5*, 20-24.

Dawe, H. C. The influence of size of kindergarten upon performance. *Child Development*, 1934, *5*, 295-303.

DeVries, D. L. & Edwards, K. J. Student teams and learning games: Their effects on cross-race and cross-sex interaction. *Journal of Educational Psychology*, 1974, *66*, 741-749.

Dion, K. K. Physical attractiveness and evaluation of children's transgressions. *Journal of Personality and Social Psychology*, 1972, *24*, 207-213.

Dion, K. K., & Berscheid, E. Physical attractiveness and peer acceptance among children. *Sociometry*, 1974, *37*, 1-12.

Doke, L. A., & Risley, T. R. The organization of day-care environments: Required vs. optional activities. *Journal of Applied Behavior Analysis*, 1972, *5*, 405-420.

Durrett, M. E., & Davy, A. J. Racial awareness in young Mexican-American, Negro, and Anglo children. *Young Children*, 1970, *26*, 16-24.

Evers, W. L., & Schwarz, J. C. Modifying social withdrawal in pre-schoolers: The effects of filmed modeling and teacher praise. *Journal of Abnormal Child Psychology*, 1973, *1*, 248-256.

Flavell, J. H., Botkin, P. T., Fry, C. L., Wright, J. W., & Jarvis, P. E. *The development of role-taking and communication skills in children*. New York: Wiley, 1968.

Goodman, H., Gottlieb, J., & Harrison, R. H. Social acceptance of EMRs integrated into a nongraded elementary school. *American Journal of Mental Deficiency*, 1972, *76*, 412-417.

Gottlieb, J. Attitudes of Norwegian children toward the retarded in relation to sex and situational context. *American Journal of Mental Deficiency*, 1971, *75*, 635-639.

Gottlieb, J., & Budoff, M. Social acceptability of retarded children in nongraded schools differing in architecture. *American Journal of Mental Deficiency*, 1973, *78*, 15-19.

Gottman, J., Gonso, J., & Rasmussen, B. Social interaction, social competence and friendship in children. *Child Development*, 1975, *46*, 709-718.

Gottman, J., Gonso, J., & Schuler, P. Teaching social skills to isolated children. *Journal of Abnormal Child Psychology*, in press.

Gronlund, N. E. The relative stability of classroom social status with unweighted and weighted sociometric choices. *Journal of Educational Psychology*, 1955, *46*, 345-354.

Gronlund, N. E. *Sociometry in the classroom*. New York: Harper, 1959.

Gump, P. V., & Friesen, W. V. Participation in nonclass settings. In R. G. Barker & P. V. Gump (Eds.), *Big school, small school: High school size and student behavior*. Stanford, Calif.: Stanford University Press, 1964.

Harari, H., & McDavid, J. W. Name stereotyping and teachers' expectations. *Journal of Educational Psychology*, 1973, *65*, 222-225.

Hartup, W. W., Glazer, J. A., & Charlesworth, R. Peer reinforcement and sociometric status. *Child Development*, 1967, *38*, 1017-1024.

Hauserman, N., Walen, S. R., & Behling, M. Reinforced racial integration in the first grade: A study in generalization. *Journal of Applied Behavior Analysis*, 1973, *6*, 193-200.

Heider, E. R. Style and accuracy of verbal communication within and between social classes. *Journal of Personality and Social Psychology*, 1971, *18*, 33-47.

Hill, K. T. Anxiety in the evaluative context. In W. W. Hartup (Ed.), *The young child: Reviews of research*, Vol. 2. Washington, D. C.: National Association for the Education of Young Children, 1972.

Hoffman, M. L., & Saltzstein, H. D. Parent discipline and the child's moral development. *Journal of Personality and Social Psychology*, 1967, *5*, 45-57.

Horrocks, J. E., & Buker, M. E. A study of the friendship fluctuations of preadolescents. *The Journal of Genetic Psychology*, 1951, *78*, 131-144.

Hraba, J., & Grant, G. Black is beautiful: A reexamination of racial preference and identification. *Journal of Personality and Social Psychology*, 1970, *16*, 398-402.

Insko, C. A., & Robinson, J. E. Belief similarity versus race as determinants of reactions to Negroes by southern white adolescents: A further test of Rokeach's theory. *Journal of Personality and Social Psychology*, 1967, *7*, 216-221.

Isen, A. M., Horn, N., & Rosenhan, D. L. Effects of success and failure on children's generosity. *Journal of Personality and Social Psychology*, 1973, *27*, 239-247.

Kingsley, P. Relationship between egocentrism and children's communication. Paper presented at the biennial meeting of the Society for Research in Child Development, Minneapolis, 1971.

Kohn, M. The child as a determinant of his peers' approach to him. *The Journal of Genetic Psychology*, 1966, *109*, 91-100.

Lesser, G. S. The relationships between various forms of aggression and popularity among lower-class children. *Journal of Educational Psychology*, 1959, *50*, 20-25.

Lilly, M. S. Improving social acceptance of low sociometric status, low achieving students. *Exceptional Children*, 1971, *37*, 341-347.

Markell, R. A., & Asher, S. R. The relationship of children's interests to perceived masculinity and femininity. Paper presented at the annual meeting of the American Educational Research Association, Chicago, 1974.

McClelland, F. M., & Ratliff, J. A. The use of sociometry as an aid in promoting social adjustment in a ninth grade home-room. *Sociometry*, 1947, *19*, 147-153.

McCraw, L. W., & Tolbert, J. W. Sociometric status and athletic ability of junior high school boys. *The Research Quarterly*, 1953, *24*, 72-80.

McDavid, J. W., & Harari, H. Stereotyping of names and popularity in grade-school children. *Child Development*, 1966, *37*, 453-459.

McFall, R. M., & Twentyman, C. T. Four experiments in the relative contributions of rehearsal, modeling, and coaching to assertiveness training. *Journal of Abnormal Psychology*, 1973, *81*, 199-218.

O'Connor, R. D. Modification of social withdrawal through symbolic modeling. *Journal of Applied Behavior Analysis*, 1969, *2*, 15-22.

O'Connor, R. D. Relative efficacy of modeling, shaping, and the combined procedures for modification of social withdrawal. *Journal of Abnormal Psychology*, 1972, *79*, 327-334.

Oden, S. L., & Asher, S. R. Coaching children in social skills for friendship making. Paper presented at the biennial meeting of the Society for Research in Child Development. Denver, 1975.

Omark, D. R., & Edelman, M. S. A developmental study of group formation in children. Paper presented at the annual meeting of the American Educational Research Association, New Orleans, 1973.

Parke, R. D. The role of punishment in the socialization process. In R. A. Hoppe, G. A. Milton, & E. C. Simmel (Eds.), *Early experiences and the processes of socialization.* New York: Academic Press, 1970.

Parten, M. B. Social participation among preschool children. *Journal of Abnormal and Social Psychology,* 1932, *27*, 243-269.

Richardson, S. A., Goodman, N., Hastorf, A. H., & Dornbusch, S. A. Cultural uniformity in reaction to physical disabilities. *American Sociological Review*, 1961, *26*, 241-247.

Ridberg, E. H., Parke, R. D., & Hetherington, E. M. Modification of impulsive and reflective cognitive styles through observation of film-mediated models. *Developmental Psychology*, 1971, *5*, 369-377.

Roff, M., Sells, S. B., & Golden, M. M. *Social adjustment and personality development in children*. Minneapolis: University of Minnesota Press, 1972.

Roistacher, R. C. A microeconomic model of sociometric choice. *Sociometry*, 1974, *37*, 219-238.

Rosenhan, D., & White, G. W. Observation and rehearsal as determinants of prosocial behavior. *Journal of Personality and Social Psychology*, 1967, *5*, 424-431.

Rubin, K. H. Relationship between egocentric communication and popularity among peers. *Developmental Psychology*, 1972, *7*, 364.

Rucker, C. N., & Vincenzo, F. M. Maintaining social acceptance gains made by mentally retarded children. *Exceptional Children*, 1970, *36*, 679-680.

Shaw, M. E. Changes in sociometric choices following forced integration of an elementary school. *Journal of Social Issues*, 1973, *29*, 143-157.

Sherif, M. Superordinate goals in the resolution of intergroup conflicts. *American Journal of Sociology*, 1958, *63*, 349-356.

Shure, M. B. Psychological ecology of a nursery school. *Child Development*, 1963, *34*, 979-992.

Silverman, I., & Shaw, M. E. Effects of sudden mass desegregation on interracial interaction and attitudes in one southern city. *Journal of Social Issues*, 1973, *29*, 133-142.

Singleton, L. *The effects of sex and race on children's sociometric choices for play and work.* Urbana, Illinois: University of Illinois, 1974. (Eric Document Reproduction Service No. ED 100520.)

Turiel, E. An experimental test of the sequentiality of the developmental stages in the child's moral judgements. *Journal of Personality and Social Psychology*, 1966, *3*, 611-618.

Ullmann, C. A. Teachers, peers and tests as predictors of adjustment. *Journal of Educational Psychology*, 1957, *48*, 257-267.

Wicker, A. Cognitive complexity, school size, and participation in school behavior settings: A test of the frequency of interaction hypothesis. *Journal of Educational Psychology*, 1969, *60*, 200-203.

Wright, B. A. *Physical disability–A psychological approach*. New York: Harper & Row, 1960.

Young, L. L., & Cooper, D. H. Some factors associated with popularity. *Journal of Educational Psychology*, 1944, *35*, 513-535.

Zahavi, S. Aggression-control. Unpublished master's thesis, University of Illinois, 1973.

3

A Radical and Regressive Solution to the Problem of Evaluation[1]

Herbert Zimiles

Bank Street College of Education

The irony of the title of this presentation stems from my observation that the more our current efforts to evaluate educational programs strive for relevance, the more invalid they become. Having reluctantly come to this conclusion, I propose that we radically change our methodological framework for evaluation. Let us examine the case for this proposal.

When Project Head Start was instituted, thereby vastly expanding preschool education, it was accompanied by a mandate to evaluate its effectiveness. The implication was that the program would stand or fall by this evaluation.

The evaluation of Head Start seemed precisely the situation which required the kind of comprehensive evaluation we at Bank Street College had been advocating and had begun to put into practice. One of the guiding principles of our work has been the conception of schools as psychological fields, as environments which significantly influence children's psychological development—cognitive, affective, and social—rather than as mere training grounds for academic skills. Our book, *The Psychological Impact of School Experience* (Minuchin, Biber, Shapiro, & Zimiles, 1969), reports the results of an effort to implement and test this point of view by systematic and empirical evaluation. The research was an intensive study of nine-year-old children who were attending very different kinds of schools. We examined the way in which these different educational experiences had affected the children's self-awareness, interpersonal skills, problem-solving patterns, group behavior, and other aspects of psychological functioning that relate to human development.

[1]Adapted from a paper presented at the Minnesota Round Table in Early Childhood Education, Wayzata, Minnesota, June 8-9, 1973.

The evaluation of Head Start, however, took a quite different and more traditional turn. The first evaluation studies were conducted by psychometricians whose main concern was for the experimental design of the study. Few of the existing instruments had been standardized for use with young children, and since a quantitative evaluation requires a standardized test, the Stanford-Binet was almost automatically selected as the instrument to be used to evaluate the effectiveness of Head Start. Much more attention was given to problems of sampling, the designation of proper control groups, and appropriate methods of statistical analysis of the data. Nevertheless, questions inevitably arose regarding the relevance of Stanford-Binet items for an evaluation of the impact of preschool education, and the search was on for intellectual measures whose content was closer to the teaching and learning which actually went on in preschool and which more accurately reflected the cultural values of the population under study. As a result, the priorities of standardization and quantification in the evaluation instruments were lowered and the criterion of content relevance was raised to a more central position.

The concept of relevance gradually broadened, and became increasingly sophisticated. Other measures of intellectual aptitude or achievement were added. Then a more significant change occurred. Largely under the impetus of the Piagetian rebirth, many investigators began to emphasize that preschool should be fostering the ability to think and function effectively on problem-solving tasks. The argument emphasized that preschools, especially those attempting to provide compensatory education, should be less concerned with training children to achieve specific skills or to learn specific academic content and more concerned with fostering cognitive growth—now that Piaget and Bruner and others had helped clarify what we meant by cognitive growth. Accordingly, evaluators were admonished to revise their assessment procedures still further and focus on measures of cognitive process as well as cognitive achievement.

Each adjustment which defined criteria in greater breadth seemed to represent important progress; it meant that evaluators were beginning to see the fallibility of their simplistic criteria and that educators of young children were coming to grips with the fact that they were not merely concerned with training children to learn specific tasks. Program innovations such as the introduction of a "Piagetian curriculum" virtually dictated that evaluation criteria be defined in terms of cognitive process variables.

The next move forward, not surprisingly, was to extend the definition of educational objectives and evaluation criteria beyond the cognitive realm. The fact that many psychologists found this new domain an alien one is revealed by the reference to it as "noncognitive." Thus, although the social and affective criteria were defined by exclusion, they were at least beginning to be regarded as essential elements in a comprehensive evaluation battery.

Now, after less than a decade of intensive efforts to evaluate Head Start and the new programs in open education, two major advances have occurred: (1) educational objectives are being defined in terms of developmental processes rather than discrete products; and (2) the content of evaluation studies has been extended to include affective and social as well as cognitive processes.

While this amazing progress is to be applauded, one wonders how much advance in educational evaluation has actually been made. My own reservations are based on several considerations. Perhaps the most obvious concern is that when we examine the array of measures radiating from IQ and achievement tests to tests of cognitive processes and then to tests of social functioning and personality, we find a concomitant decline in validity. In attempting to measure cognitive processes rather than products, our use of problem-solving situations as opposed to conventional test items leads to a marked reduction in the amount of cognitive behavior sampled, because it takes much more time to assess problem-solving behavior. While problem-solving tasks, on the surface, seem amenable to extensive analysis of qualitative features of performance, in reality, only a small number of behavioral characteristics can be categorized reliably. The net effect of introducing such new methods of assessment is to reduce the variability of scores, an outcome which adversely affects both reliability and validity of measurement. Thus, problem-solving techniques have limited potential for yielding highly differentiating quantitative data, as compared with the wide range of scores and the high reliability of multiple-itemed intellectual aptitude tests which sample many domains. Personality measures are, of course, even less useful; at best, they have a degree of construct validity that cannot be understood in quantitative terms. It is hard to conceive of a single personality test which has the psychometric credentials to serve as a criterion measure in an educational evaluation.

Another disappointing note is that an increase in the breadth of assessment has not always been accompanied by a shift from product to process orientation. While conservation and other Piagetian cognitive attributes are replacing the learning of the alphabet in so-called innovative programs, such programs still seem just as concerned with training as those of the past. Conservation skills have merely replaced more traditional content in what remains a very traditional form of education. If children are to be drilled and trained, perhaps it would be better to train them in something that seems useful to them, something which has face validity. Piaget uses the conservation paradigm, among others, to illustrate a mode and level of cognitive functioning. Whether or not a child conserves number may be quite revealing about his level of cognitive development, but it is not at all clear that a child who is trained to conserve is very different from one who has not been so trained.

If the recent reform in evaluation methodology has been distorted by many of those who have adopted a Piagetian approach, even greater errors of judgment have been committed in the name of personality assessment. I have received urgent phone calls asking for a good personality measure to be included in an evaluation battery in the same way that distributors are phoned by storekeepers regarding a new line of items they want included on their shelves. The fact that personality measurement remains one of the great unsolved problems of more than 50 years of research activity seems not to have penetrated to those new converts who have suddenly recognized the value of comprehensive, developmental approaches to education. Their indiscriminate enthusiasm is not accompanied by an appreciation of the conceptual and methodological complexities involved in working with personality data. There is, therefore, every reason to be pessimistic about prospects for devising personality measures good enough to be used in large-scale evaluation studies. I have begun to believe that we have made an error in not taking Gordon Allport's (1937) call for idiographic measurement of personality more seriously. One of the problems with personality measurement is that different traits are salient in different ways for different children (or adults). Across-the-board measurement of a particular trait generates a hodgepodge of data. The data gathered from those for whom the trait is salient may be quite informative, but the data obtained from the remainder may have little or no functional significance.

During the days when we were struggling with the problem of evaluating Head Start, we were thwarted in our efforts to get Head Start teachers to tell us what their main objectives were and to describe how they proposed to achieve them. The lack of readiness of educators to contribute to a substantial formulation of educational methods and goals has hampered evaluation studies. Finally, at the end of the school year, we turned to some articulate teachers in the Early Childhood Center which Bank Street College was then operating in a poverty area, and asked them to run down the list of children in their class, indicating for each child the areas of greatest growth during the preschool year. In almost every instance, these teachers singled out for consideration a facet of the child's personality or social behavior that had dominated his functioning in school and that had undergone change in response to their method of working with the child. But the attributes and context varied for each child. There was no question in the minds of the teachers who provided these data regarding the central role played by personality factors in the school lives of these young children, but it would have been impossible to capture the points they were making through the systematic application of a particular personality scale or inventory. Each child manifested a distinctive configuration of personality and social characteristics.

Another problem, well known to everyone but just as widely ignored, that bedevils those who seek a more relevant and comprehensive evaluation of school programs is the fact that a good deal of educational intervention is expected to have future rather than immediate impact. Yet evaluation research is so dominated by a mechanistic, push-pull outlook that we have learned to pretend that whatever findings show up immediately constitute the essential impact of an educational program. Such a perspective invites a narrow and superficial approach to education.

For all these reasons, none of them new, I cannot celebrate the long overdue move toward more relevant and more comprehensive evaluation. I have indicated that there are limits to the degree to which such goals can be attained and have observed that some of the notions of relevance and comprehensiveness have been misunderstood and distorted, thereby threatening to discredit the approach as a whole. I have also noted that comprehensive evaluation is severely limited unless we are willing to assess the long-term impact of educational programs.

This very pessimistic analysis does not imply that the efforts described should be discontinued. We will not solve these important problems unless we continue to work at them. I can think of no more challenging research for a developmental psychologist than that of attempting to analyze the events of a preschool classroom in terms of their potential influence on the participating children, and then to devise an assessment of the children's characteristics which are hypothesized as being influenced. However, such work cannot and should not carry the label—or the burden—of evaluation because its findings, by definition, lack the infallibility and definitiveness we automatically associate with evaluation. When negative results are obtained they are much more likely to reflect the methodological weaknesses of the study than the failure of the educational program. The people working on such studies should not be constrained by the design requirements of evaluation, nor should they be required to carry the psychological and political burden of determining whether a program will stand or fall on the basis of a clearly inadequate study. Without the pressures of serving as an evaluator, researchers are likely to be less defensive and more critical of their work and therefore freer to change and improve it.

If the evaluation of the impact of educational programs on children is to be discontinued because such evaluations are either too incomplete or, when they strive for comprehensiveness, invalid, then how shall programs be evaluated? The alternative plan proposed here simply entails *systematic and comprehensive evaluation of the child's psychological school environment, to be followed by a theoretical analysis of the potential impact of his school experience.* This would entail a shift in emphasis from the assessment of impact on children to the assessment of the antecedent condition, the classroom environment. Even those evaluation procedures which follow the current mode of focusing on the impact of the program on the children are increasingly calling for a detailed description of the school environment. Their interest is primarily in more clearly defining the independent variable of an evaluation study. Many evaluation studies have reported outcome data on participating children without knowing with any degree of certainty or detail what was the nature of the program whose impact was being documented. Indeed, some evaluators make a virtue of such ignorance by claiming that they are unbiased by any prior exposure to the program whose impact they assess. During one of our evaluation studies of Project Head Start, we observed that many of the children whom we had extensively tested had attended only infrequently the Head Start program whose impact we were struggling to measure. It is equally absurd to assess the impact of a program without considering the content of the program. Yet, most evaluators select their assessment instruments without firsthand knowledge of the program's method of operation. Apparently, evaluators view their task as a fishing expedition in strange waters; they cast the best nets available and hope for a good catch. The way in which the dependent variables that are being measured by the evaluation instruments are described makes it seem as though the measures have been chosen on the basis of a theoretical analysis of the actual educational phenomena to be evaluated, but in reality the measures are selected on the basis of convenience, availability, and a superficial judgment of relevance. As matters now stand, when one preschool program is reported as having "scored higher" in evaluation than another, my main conclusion is that the content of the arbitrarily chosen evaluation criteria more closely matched the transactions that took place in one program than the other.

Our inability to measure the impact of a program precisely or comprehensively is understandable in the light of existing methodological limitations, but these limitations do not apply to the task of conceptualizing and describing the program itself. Those who initiate and operate a program should be able to describe what they are doing and what they are trying to accomplish. The task of describing and recording classroom interaction is of a very different order of magnitude from that of attempting to measure how a child's psychic organization and functioning has been affected by experiencing such an environment. It is a paradox that we have the responsibility and the capacity to describe and record the essential character of an educational program, yet do not do so; and at the same time, we do not know how to assess the impact of a complex set of experiences on the psychological functioning of a developing child, yet we persist in trying to do so.

But where are we in our evaluation if we simply document the nature of the program as it occurs but are unready to assess its impact on the participating children? We must carry our analysis of the program one step further. Just as it is the obligation of a program initiator and director to describe the nature of his program, so is it his responsibility to justify its usefulness on the basis of some specified conceptual framework. Any set of actions directed toward care and development of children is based upon an explicit or implicit set of propositions regarding the consequences of the proposed activities. Without a rational basis for its operation, a program does not deserve to be implemented.

Most educators operate on a largely intuitive level. Their conceptual framework is more implicit than explicit. The form of evaluation I am advocating requires that this framework become explicit. One of the greatest obstacles to progress in early childhood education is that formulation of the nature of the young child and his development is incomplete, as is a conceptual scheme for educational programming in relation to our understanding of the child. If such an articulated theoretical framework existed, both in relation to the child and to an educational program for him, it should be possible to arrive at a set of procedures for describing and recording educational environments and for analyzing such environments in terms of their potential impact on the participating children. Thus, we need a system that codifies observations of the adult models to which a child is exposed in school, the emotional climate of the classroom, the nature of the activities he experiences, the kinds of stimulation he receives, the values transmitted, and other related facets of the school environment that are likely to affect his development. In my view, this is the essence of educational evaluation and until we become better able to assess the impact of programs on children, *our primary method of evaluating early childhood education programs should be to describe in great detail what they consist of and how they operate, and then hypothesize, on the basis of our theoretical framework, how a given program will affect children.* While such a speculative approach to evaluation may lack the apparent advantages of current, preferred, empirical methods for validating a program, we are deluding ourselves, wasting time and effort, and misinterpreting data and thereby subverting educational planning by continuing to ignore the glaring deficiencies of empirical methods of evaluating educational impact and neglecting those activities of observation and theoretical analysis that are needed to shore up our conceptual framework for program planning. We need to observe children and programs much more than we do and we need to deal actively with the obligation to articulate and elaborate our conceptual framework. One of the reasons why assessment of impact has not progressed is the poverty of our thinking about children and programs. The more articulate we become about children and programs, the sharper and more effective will be our thinking about the assessment of impact. As already emphasized, I am not suggesting that efforts to assess impact should cease; on the contrary, they should expand, but not under the aegis of evaluation.

While the procedural changes I am recommending may seem radical, they are not at all new, but simply describe how we now function most of the time. The proposition is that these procedures become codified. Most institutions and activities are evaluated in the fashion recommended here. We have very little systematic, experimentally controlled data regarding the efficacy of any of our most important activities or institutions. We do not know if going to a museum or library or concert really makes a difference nor do we have sound evidence regarding the value of taking a trip to Europe; yet we ungrudgingly spend large sums of money on such ventures. If we are selecting a camp for our child, we do not ask for data informing us about the average swimming speed improvement, nor would we be very much influenced by such data were it available.

4

A Crosscultural Analysis of the Child Care System

Sarane Spence Boocock

Russell Sage Foundation

THE ROLE OF THE CHILD

How a society treats its children depends upon its views of what children are like, as well as upon what is perceived as necessary for the smooth functioning of the society itself. As one historical observer put it: "Children can be thought of as vessels to be filled, animals to be restrained, plants to be encouraged, or simply as adults in the process of becoming" (Larrabee, 1960, p. 199). Aries' classic study, *Centuries of Childhood*, makes clear that our current views have not always been the prevailing ones, even in Western culture. Indeed, the very notion of childhood as a meaningful distinct phase in the life cycle is a relatively recent conceptualization.

A review of various periods of American history reveals important changes in the view of the child. In the early days of our country, all able-bodied persons constituted a much-needed source of labor, and each additional child born into a family represented an additional hand with the harvest or an insurance of future support for a parent. If parents did not have an immediate need for the child's labor, there was usually a relative or acquaintance who did. In a society in which idleness was a sin, the ideal model of childrearing included a period of apprenticeship or indentured labor, a system involving at least a quasi-legal contract between a child's parents and the head of the household in which he was placed. The child would be taught the craft or trade of his "employer" and would receive room and board in return for assisting in the workshop and home. (His duties often included caring for the younger children of the household.) Apprenticeship contracts often stipulated behavioral requirements, for example, it would be agreed that the apprentice would not dance, play cards, gamble, or engage in any other kinds of activities which would reflect unfavorably upon his employer (Handlin & Handlin, 1971; Hawes, 1971).

With the growth of industrialized cities in the post-Civil War period came the first recognition of the special needs of children. Accounts of the periods include descriptions of swarms of unattended, often homeless, children roaming the streets of New York and other cities. Some were fully employed. (*The Newsboy, Ragged Dick*, and other best-selling novels of the period romanticized the adventures and ultimate worldly success of newspaper and shoeshine boys.) But many more children survived by begging and stealing (Hawes, 1971, p. 191). It was, indeed, the visibility of homeless, mistreated, and delinquent children, along with the new framework and set of analytical tools of defining social problems provided by the rise of social science in the United States, which led to child labor laws, compulsory school attendance, and the creation of agencies and institutions devoted to the protection of children (e.g., the Children's Aid Society, the Society for the Prevention of Cruelty to Children, and juvenile courts). Children's needs, however, were still subordinated to those of adults and of society as a whole.

Throughout the twentieth century, the elaboration of childhood as a special period has continued unabated. Perhaps the time of greatest child-centeredness in this country was during the two decades following the end of World War II. Among the special characteristics of this period was the proliferation of experts and expertise on child development and child-rearing (as epitomized by the ubiquitous Dr. Spock, whose basic handbook, *Baby and Child Care*, continues to be a best seller). The literature of this period has certain common themes.

1. Children need the devoted and full-time attention of their biological mothers. Otherwise they will suffer from "deprivation" and their later emotional growth will be stunted. As Bowlby, the most influential proponent of the theory, has put it: "when deprived of maternal care, the child's development is almost always retarded—physically, intellectually and socially" (Bowlby, 1952, p. 15).

2. The first five years of life are also the time of greatest cognitive growth, a finding emerging from the influential work of Piaget and leading to everything from the current emphasis upon pressure for preschool education to the growing market for educational toys, books, and kits telling parents how to teach their babies to read.

3. Children are fun. An analysis of publications of the Children's Bureau over several decades has shown the emergence of a "fun morality" which argues that not only are parents supposed to provide for their children's physical and emotional needs, but they are also supposed to enjoy the process (Wolfenstein, 1951).

A second characteristic of this period of child-centeredness was the separation of children and childhood from the workaday life of the larger society. Children in America, like those in urbanized Scandinavia and England, are not expected to make any real contribution to the working of the community. In contrast, kibbutz children in Israel tend gardens and animals from a very early age, and elementary schoolchildren in Jerusalem took on such community responsibilities as mail delivery and garbage collection during the Six Day War (de Shalit, 1970). In mainland China, children in elementary school workshops turn out machine components for buses and other heavy equipment, and all schoolchildren spend 1½ months a year in some form of productive labor (Committee of Concerned Asian Scholars, 1972; Munro, 1971).

The past decade has witnessed a counter trend away from the childcenteredness of the 1950s and early 1960s. Not only is there accumulating evidence that many American children are not being adequately cared for, but there are also indications of a general devaluation of children and child rearing.

It is clear that the traditional reasons for wanting children–that is, for economic reasons or to extend the family line or family name–have all but disappeared in modern secularized societies. It has been argued that as children have lost their economic and familial value to parents, they have become more valued in a qualitative sense, as they provide adults with personal experiences and pleasure of a unique sort (Berelson, 1972). Evaluation of this argument requires an understanding of some very complex demographic trends as well as weighing of what little survey data are available on the subject. It does seem that there is less desire for children among Americans than in the past and that those who do want to have children want fewer of them (see, e.g., Campbell, 1969; Kahn, 1973).

While much of the information necessary to assess the system of child care in this country has not been systematically collected and analyzed, there are a number of empirical indicators of child neglect and abuse. Among the more disturbing kinds of evidence are the widespread incidence of physical abuse, increasing rates of illegitimacy, and increases in the number of children without adult supervision for long periods of time.

Some 60,000 cases of child abuse a year are reported in the United States, though it is felt that many cases, especially in middle- and upper-class homes, go unreported. A 1964 study of California children concluded that about 20,000 were in need of protective services. A study in Denver, Colorado, showed that in a sample year, approximately 100 cases of serious physical abuse were referred monthly to the Welfare Department for services (Zalba, 1971). Hospital emergency room studies indicate that possibly 10% of children who are treated for accidents are actually victims of maltreatment (Day Care Council of New York, 1972, p. 7). A survey of New York City children concluded that at least 1% of the deaths of children under six were caused by parental abuse, and some pediatricians interviewed believed that "if the true statistics were known, child abuse would be the most common cause of death in children" (Day Care Council of New York, 1972, p .8).

The rates of out-of-wedlock births have increased in the United States, especially among the youngest females of childbearing age, at the same time that legal abortion is becoming increasingly available (White House Conference on Children, 1970, p. 54). An especially disturbing trend in pacesetting areas of the country such as southern California is the increase in multiple pregnancies among unmarried high school girls, more of whom elect to keep their babies than was formerly the case among unmarried mothers (Cottman, 1971). Illegitimacy per se does not guarantee inadequate care. However, except in the few societies in which concerted efforts have been made to remove the stigma of illegitimacy and to assure that all children have access to necessary services (e.g., Sweden–see Linner, 1967), children of unmarried mothers too often spend the first years of life in settings characterized by uninformed and desultory care.

Many children who escape physical abuse suffer from serious neglect. Indicators of neglect take a variety of forms. There have been increases in the number of divorce cases in which *neither* parent wants custody of the children (Otto, 1973). There are clues that many children ostensibly in the care of their own parents are, in fact, left without care for long periods of time. This kind of information is difficult to obtain, since few parents will willingly admit that they leave their young children unattended. (A 1966 Swedish study found some 3,000 children under seven years of age left unsupervised while their parents were at work, Roby, 1973, p. 308.) In this country, testimony at recent federal and state hearings, including statements by working-class women who left preschoolers unattended in locked apartments because they feared losing their jobs if they stayed home with them (California Commission on the Status of Women, 1968), indicates that the number of young children left alone or in the care of only-slightly-older children runs, on any given day, into the hundreds of thousands.

What constitutes child neglect is still not clearly defined. While preschool children left alone in an apartment while their parents are at work are obvious cases of neglect, more general (if subtle) trends suggest that our entire society may be becoming less child-oriented. Time studies indicate that American parents spend less time in child care than they did in the past and spend less time than parents in other countries for which time data are available (Robinson & Converse, 1972). Ironically, American women are spending more time than ever on household matters, but large amounts of this time are devoted to the care and repair of "time-saving" appliances and to the shopping that is an important component of the consumption-oriented society. Moreover, a large chunk of many mothers' "child-care" time is spent in chauffering their children, an activity hardly conducive to satisfying parent-child interaction. It has been estimated that even nongainfully employed mothers may spend as little as 15 or 20 minutes a day in actual communication with their preschool children and that many children have no other daily meaningful contact with adults.

Part of the apparent increases in child abuse and neglect may be due to fuller reporting and to changes in the law. For example, changes in the libel laws make it less risky for pediatricians, social workers, and neighbors to report cases of possible child abuse. Recent work by historians also suggests that mistreatment of children may have been even more widespread in the past, in the United States and elsewhere. Moreover, there can be honest differences of opinion in a pluralistic society about the best way to care for young children. Granting all of these possible qualifications, it still seems clear that (a) the problems of American children are, if anything, still underreported (partly because children rarely earn income and pay taxes, cannot vote, have few legal rights, and are thus in a sense invisible); and that (b) the insufficiency of adequate care for young children has reached crisis proportions and constitutes a major policy issue for our society.

While the care of young children is not totally satisfactory in any society, the present child care dilemma seems to be the result of a combination of social trends unique to modern industrialized societies, of which the following seems to be the major ones:

1. *Changes in the structure of households.* There have been several recent studies (Aries, 1962; Hunt, 1970; Laslett, 1972) which indicate that households used to be considerably larger and were characterized by a greater diffusion of responsibility in certain key respects, in particular the sharing of child care by a greater number of persons. The three-generation model that we tend to romanticize today was never as common as most people think, partly because, until recent times, few people lived long enough to form long-term three-generation groups. Also, with the exception of a few atypical periods in history, the aged have normally been considered a burden to their young relatives. Moreover, the three-generation family, where it did exist (e.g., among the wealthy in pre-Communist China), was a stifling environment for many of its members, especially for females and the young. Households of the past *were* more likely to contain apprentices, servants, and other persons not necessarily related by blood, and the male head of the household was likely to be at home for longer periods of time, since his work was often in or near the home. Thus, while homes in the past were not consciously organized for the care of young children, economics and other family functions did necessitate an organization in which some family members were usually available to share in looking after little children.

2. *Changes in sex roles which downgrade parenthood and child rearing.* One of the recent trends that is affecting children's lives is the changing view of society in regard to the adult role. The caretaker role traditionally assigned to the mother is now in competition with other adult roles. The effect upon

children of the women's liberation movement with its emphasis upon careers also underscores the interrelatedness of the role system involved in chid care.

3. *Loss of child care options outside the family.* Several recent studies (Hunt, 1970, for example) suggest that a surprising number of children in the past were reared or spent large amounts of time with adults other than their natural parents. In wealthy families in both Europe and the Orient, the pattern from medieval times until well into the eighteenth century was a kind of exchange of children, such that children at a very early age were sent to live with another family, whom they "served" until adulthood. The American apprenticeship system has already been mentioned. The custom of sending off unwanted children to farms on the western frontier, originally a largely within-family arrangement, was continued on a nonfamilial basis by nineteenth century reformers and organizations–for example, Charles Loring Brace's "placing-out" system, one of the programs of the New York Children's Aid Society which he founded (Hawes, 1971, Chapter 5). It may be that with the closing of the frontier, the decrease in the proportion of the population engaged in farming, and the enactment of compulsory education and child labor laws, the difficulties of raising children have simply become more visible.

4. *A serious imbalance in the supply and demand for child care.* This seems to be one of the largest unrecognized problems in modern societies. During the past year, I have observed day care centers and nursery schools in the United States, Sweden, and Israel. In each country, some of my visits were on registration days (often for enrollment a year in advance). In every case, all places were filled within a few hours of the opening of registration. Mothers often waited in line throughout the preceeding night in hopes of ensuring a place for their children, and directors were confronted with pleading and often tearful or hysterical women, begging them to allow their children to be enrolled. Day care administrators, government officials, and researchers I talked with agreed that any new facilities opened within the next few years would be immediately filled and would still not meet the current demand. While no country seems to have accurate figures on the exact number of children in need of care or the exact number and type of places available, the most responsible estimates in Sweden (Rosengren, 1973) and the U.S. (Featherstone, 1970; Roby, 1973) indicate that places at centers or homes with any kind of governmental licensing or approval are available for no more than 20% of the children who need them (i.e., whose parents are gainfully employed). This figure does not even include families who would like and possibly use day care if it were available, including large numbers of women who would prefer to work but have no one to look after their children. Of the nations reviewed in Roby's recent volume on child care (1973), only in the Soviet Union did the observer encounter no families who were having difficulty in enrolling children in a preschool program and no waiting lists for such schools.

5. *The costliness of children.* Raising children has always been hard work. What is different now is that the costs have gone up steeply (relative to the rewards) and that parents and potential parents have more, and often more attractive, options for investment of their time and energies. Some elaboration of these two points:

The American child no longer represents an economic asset to the family. According to a recent study, the cost of raising one child in the U.S. to age 18 is estimated to be $34,464 ($98,361 if one adds a college education and an estimate of the wages the mother "lost" by taking care of a child instead of holding a paying job).

In no society that I know of has child care ever paid well, in money or esteem. The care of young children is an extremely time-consuming and difficult job. In fact, women will often take the blandest kind of office work for pay that is only a little more than they need to hire someone else to look after their children.

Birth rates have fluctuated considerably during the past half century. Until recently, they have been correlated with business conditions and the state of the economy, with the lowest rates (until 1972) occurring during the depression and the highest during the affluent decade-and-a-half following World War II. The steep decline during the past few years was, however, unprecedented and unpredicted.

A distinctive feature of the very recent decline in the birth rate is that the decreased desire for children cuts across all subgroups of American women (Kahn, 1973):

> In a motley nation, one finds an unusual homogeneity of attitude among women against big families, and, for all anyone can tell, this may be their permanent position, and business cycles be hanged—for the desire to reduce family sizes has clearly been shared by all fertile women, whatever their region, education, age, race, or color. It may be especially significant that the birthrate for poor and near-poor women—who, with less education and less access to reliable contraceptives and to abortions, might be expected to lag behind their better-situated sisters—has actually been going down the fastest [pp. 151-152].

Crosscultural comparisons are difficult to make, since birth and fertility rates are affected by a variety of factors including population policies, labor force and other economic trends, marriage and family laws, and the number and proportion of people of marriageable and childbearing ages. While declining sharply, the U.S. birth rate has still not dropped as far as Sweden's, which was the world's lowest for several years after World War II (Leijon, 1968). Sweden has a current fertility rate of only 1.7 children per family. Sweden also has one of the world's lowest marriage rates. Because so many Swedish children are born out-of-wedlock or to parents who marry after pregnancy or birth of a child, Sweden has developed a national policy that no child shall be deprived of legal rights or social benefits because of the circumstances of his birth (in fact, children of single or unmarried parents are given preference in state-subsidized day care programs).

Israel has a higher birth rate than Sweden or the United States, as might be expected in a society which has a great need for people to settle, develop, and defend an underdeveloped land surrounded by enemies. In fact, in 1968 a special council was established in the Demographic Center, in the Prime Minister's office, to evolve a policy and services aimed at reversing the declining birth rate which had begun in Israel in the 1950's (Harman, 1969). By contrast, China is in the midst of a massive nationwide effort to reduce the birth rate, by encouraging later marriages and smaller families and by providing abortions, sterilizations, and vasectomies on demand (Orleans, 1971).

What these comparisons indicate is that birth and fertility rates reflect a society's attitudes toward children, as well as its need for them. For a more detailed discussion of the reasons for which children may be valued and the methodological issues involved in measuring the value of children, see Hoffman and Hoffman (1973). In addition, research now being conducted by James Fawcett, in which couples in six Asian countries will be interviewed about their perceived value of their children, should give new insights into crosscultural differences in attitudes and beliefs about childbearing and childrearing.

THE ROLE OF THE PARENT

It is difficult to construct an image of the "traditional" role of the parent unbiased by opinions about what family life *should* be like. Historical analysis suggests that the American parent role has been characterized, on the one hand, by virtually total responsibility for the care and supervision of children, and, on the other hand, by relatively limited authority.

> Only when a child reached age six did society at large take a major hand by insisting that he attend school and by providing schools at the taxpayers' expense. What happens to the child the rest of the time is his parents' business. Society intervenes only if he is severely abused or neglected or runs afoul of the law [Schultze, Fried, Rivlin, & Teeters, 1972, p. 253].

European visitors to America in the eighteenth and nineteenth centuries noted not only that American children had a position of relative equality and a say in family affairs that would have been unthinkable in Europe, but that American parents "... give very little advice to their children and let them learn for themselves" (from Rousiers *La Vie Americaine*, quoted in Sorel, 1950, p. 89).

However, until recently, Americans have at least given lip service to the cliche that the presence of children strengthens the family. Now that central assumption seems to be in question. Data gathered during the last two decades shows rather consistently that the presence of children has a negative, rather than a positive, effect upon the husband-wife relationship. Members of childless marriages report greater marital satisfaction than those with children, among marriages with children, the greater the number of children, the lower the satisfaction reported by the parents; and on a variety of marital satisfaction indices, satisfaction drops sharply with the birth of the first child, sinks even lower during the school years, and goes up markedly only after the exit of the last child. (For a discussion of studies on the effects of children upon marriage, see Bernard, 1972, Chapter 4. Senn and Hartford, 1968, provide a more descriptive account of the stress experienced by young parents with their first born.)

Many young people growing up today have little opportunity to experience the tasks of parenthood before they actually take on the role. With our small nuclear families and increasingly age-segregated residential communities, adolescents and young adults have few opportunities to observe young children or to communicate regularly with older persons with extensive parenting experience. In Sweden, both boys and girls, beginning in the elementary school years, have classes in sex education, home maintenance, child care, and the dynamics of family life (Linner, 1967). American schools offer little in the way of practical education in subjects relevant to family life. What preparation for parenthood exists during pregnancy is dependent upon the initiative of the parents-to-be and is largely confined to reading and informal consultation with friends. As Rossi (1967) points out, the most concrete action most parents-to-be take is to prepare the baby's room. While new parents receive much advice from "experts" on every aspect of child development and care, the very existence of so much expertise may discourage rather than reassure the new parent, since it sets such a high level of expectations for their role performance.

Certainly the self-development which is an important component of an individualistic society is at variance with the constant attention and the frequent selflessness often required in the nurturance of babies and young children. Likewise, the youthfulness and glamour so valued for both sexes in America are inconsistent with childrearing. Childless adults have more time to devote to their self-development in general and to their appearance in particular, and they can be rather vague about their age. The presence of growing children not only takes away time that could be devoted to one's personal development and interests, but is a constant reminder of the passing of time and one's own youth. Among the findings of the Detroit Area Study is the fact that proportionately more women in the 1970s than in the 1950s said that companionship with husband was the most valuable part of marriage (60% in 1971; compared to 48% in 1955); while fewer said their prime motive in marriage was the chance to have children (from 26% in 1955 to 13% in 1971; Duncan, Schuman, & Duncan, 1973, p. 8).

Parenthood may also bring to the surface unresolved, and even unrecognized, conflicts about the appropriate roles of men and women. However much in principle the couple may value equality of the sexes, the arrival of a child means that someone must be available 24 hours a day to care for it. It seems unlikely that prevailing difficulties in the relationships between men and women in our society will be resolved until questions concerning both the value of children and the locus of responsibility for their routine care and supervision are acknowledged and resolved.

The Mother

Among the most significant and most discussed changes of the past decade are the changes in women's lives, including the rebirth of feminism in the women's liberation movement. The most obvious and thoroughly documented aspect of these changes is the rising propensity of women to work outside the home. The number of American women in the labor force goes up every time a survey is taken, and during the past decade the rates of participation of mothers have increased more rapidly than the rates for women in general. In 1970, the mothers of nearly 26 million children under 18 years of age were in the labor force. Almost 6 million of these children were under six, that is, below regular school age and requiring some kind of care in their mother's absence. By contrast, ten years earlier, mothers of 15.7 million children under 18 were in the labor force, of whom about 4 million were below school age. Mothers of pre-school-age children are less likely to be in the labor force than those of school-age children: in 1970, a third of all mothers with at least one child under six were in the labor force, compared with about half of the mothers whose children were 6 to 17 years old. However, labor force participation rates of mothers of preschoolers have *increased* more rapidly in the last decade, up 60% as compared with 20% for mothers of school-age children (Waldman & Gover, 1971, p. 19). Survey data also indicate that many American mothers not now working would do so if they could find someone to take care of their children. Thus, we seem to be on our way to a society in which most women, including the mothers of young children, will be employed outside the home.

The trend toward employment outside the home and less than full-time commitment to motherhood seems to be an international one, although the rates and patterns of the increase vary from one society to another. In Sweden, there has been a substantial increase in the number of married women employed outside the home, from 30% in 1960 to 53% in 1973. Having young children is apparently less of an impediment to the employment of women in Sweden, since more than half of the mothers who work have at least one child under age seven (the school entrance age).

In Israel, women constitute about 50% of the total labor force, a higher proportion than in the United States; but a smaller proportion of Israeli than American women work outside the home—30% of all Jewish women, about 25% of married Jewish women, and a very small but rapidly increasing proportion of the Arab women. As in the U.S. labor force, participation is related both to the age of children and the size of the family (*Statistical Abstract of Israel*, 1970).

For economic and ideological reasons, the rate of employment of women is generally higher in communist than in capitalistic societies. Women constitute approximately half of the labor force in the Soviet Union, and the labor force participation of women ages 20 to 50 is approximately 85% (Roby, 1973, p. 388). Reliable empirical data on the employment of women in mainland China are unavailable, although recent visitors observed virtually no women devoting themselves solely to housework and care of their own children. The strong ideological thrust of Maoism toward the full development and use of "womenpower," changes in the marriage law (which have, in turn, produced basic changes in family structure), and a vigorous national program of birth control have altered the roles of parents and children in very basic ways.

In any country, the desire to work seems to be related to a woman's educational background and occupational qualifications. In the few countries which allow working mothers to take a paid leave for up to three years after the birth of a child, women with higher qualifications, better jobs, and higher salaries are much less likely to use the grants. In Hungary, for example, only 30.2% of the mothers with college education, as compared with 73.8% of the women with primary education, have used the grants (Roby, 1973, p. 355). In other words, if a society gave women a real choice between working outside the home or staying home to care for young children, one would predict that the women who would choose the latter would more likely be those of the lower socioeconomic levels, who could obtain only the more menial kinds of jobs; while women who had the qualifications for interesting and well-paying work would prefer outside employment to full-time child care.

The effect of mothers' employment upon their children has been heatedly debated. Some Swedish studies find no substantial or consistent differences in either school achievement or social adjustment between children whose mothers work outside the home and those who do not, although there are apparently more problems if the mother has to work for economic reasons than if she is working because of "professional enthusiasm" (Leijon, 1968, p. 98). In an analysis of the available American research, Hoffman (1963) indicates that there is no unequivocal evidence that outside employment of mothers affects children favorably or unfavorably. Bernard (1972) appears to agree:

> So many other factors enter into the picture—social class, full-time versus part-time employment, age and sex of the child, and the mother's attitude toward the employment—that the impact of employment per se is lost in the shuffle [p. 78].

One of the most important by-products of the women's liberation movement is that many women no longer feel that they should be solely responsible for the day-to-day care of young children—or even that they should be "naturally" interested in children. It may be pertinent to note here that the care of young children has always been allocated to persons with relatively low positions in the society—to slaves and domestic servants, to persons in "nonproductive" years or categories (such as girls and older persons who have retired from "real" work in the society), and to women. Thus one of the consequences of the consciousness-raising aspects of the women's liberation movement is that as women come to think more highly of themselves, they will be less willing to perform the tasks in society that carry less weight and prestige, including the more tedious aspects of child care.

The Father

The role of the father has received relatively little attention in sociological and child development literature. The most recent full-length sociological analysis (Benson, 1968) notes that the father role links the family with the larger society, and has been the embodiment within the family of the social control function. Komarovsky's (1971) study of unemployed blue collar workers showed how the loss of a man's job led to the decline of his position vis-a-vis his wife and children.

Benson also points out the distinction between biological and social fatherhood, noting that these two function have not always been filled by the same man. The latter was a social invention which has taken a variety of forms in different societies. Children have been raised in the home of their mother's relatives, and have been provided for by their uncles, stepfathers, and older brothers, as well as by their biological fathers. Benson concludes that: "The biological father, the progenitor, is not as important as the social or nurturant father precisely because the latter has a family role to play after conception" (Benson, 1968, p. 44).

One of the problems in the United States and other industrialized societies is that the social father role is not being filled in many families by the biological father or any other male. In 1970, 7 million American children under age 14 (over 10% of all children in that age category) were being raised in families in which the father was absent (White House Conference on Children, 1970, pp. 22, 141); and while some of these children undoubtedly have meaningful relationships with men other than their biological fathers, there is also evidence that many of them do not. Studies of lower class "streetcorner" men, such as Liebow's *Talley's Corner* (1966) and Hannerz's *Soulside* (1969), show how peripheral these men are to the lives of the children they have fathered. Nor do the mother's boyfriends, who pass through the ghetto homes in which the children are reared, normally develop father-like relationships with them.

While there have been some recent pleas for a "return to fatherhood" in this country, it is not possible, with currently available research, to conclude whether fatherhood actually was a more fully developed role in the past. It is true that households and communities in which a man's work was typically in or near his home allowed a father to be in contact with his children more often during the normal course of a workday than in our present metropolitan areas where the place of work is usually at a distance from the home. However, the distance imposed by the more authoritarian character of the father role in the past may have outweighed the advantages gained by mere physical proximity. It should also be noted that the call for greater activation of the father role can be differently interpreted. Men urging a "return to fatherhood" are usually expressing nostalgia for the undisputed authority of the male head of the household attributed to the traditional families of the past. Women, on the other hand, are usually asking not for a return to a form of family life perceived by them as oppressive for both women and children but rather: (a) for men to show more interest in and affection for young children; and (b) for a more equitable distribution of the more onerous duties involved in caring for them.

There is little evidence of a strong trend toward male caretakers of young children. The few well-publicized cases of "paternity leave," in which fathers have won the right to spend more time at home caring for their children without the loss of their jobs or their fringe benefits, have so far been limited to a few occupations, such as teaching, that allow relatively flexible working schedules. Scandinavian corporations and agencies which allow men to work less than full time in order to share domestic responsibilities with their wives report that few men have so far taken advantage of the opportunity (interviews with Siv Thorsell, Anita Soderlund). Although it is now Swedish policy to recruit men into day care center positions, in the few centers where I observed any men at all, there was usually only one, and he was usually a conscientious objector or an older man who was for some reason unemployed. (Of course the Swedish policy is so new that it is unfair to draw conclusions about its success.) I observed no men in any of the day care centers or kibbutz children's homes I visited in Israel, and some of the Israeli men I questioned actually recoiled at the notion that men might work in such places. Komarovsky's current studies of American college men indicate that while many give lip service to the general principle of equality and liberation for women, most assume that *their* future wives will stay home with the children during their preschool years and later on, if they go to work, arrange their working schedules around the children's school hours. "Though they were willing to aid their wives in varying degrees, they frequently excluded specific tasks, for instance, 'not the laundry,' 'not the cleaning,' 'not the diapers,' and so on" (Komarovsky, 1973, p. 879).

In a recent paper, entitled "Why Men Don't Rear Children," Polatnick argues that it is so obviously to most men's advantage to keep things the way they have always been that it is doubtful if men will change the way they play the father role in the absence of revolutionary changes in the structure of our society. "Of course, children are not just a handy excuse to keep women out of the job market. Most people—male and female—want to have them, and somebody has to rear them. Men naturally prefer that women do it, so that having children need not interfere with their own occupational pursuits. . . Where outright forbidding of the wife to work is no longer effective, the continued allocation of child-rearing responsibility to women accomplishes the same end. . . " (Polatnick, 1973, p. 64).

To summarize, the ideology concerning the role of the father does seem to be changing in modern industrialized societies, but there is still a large gap between the rhetoric of a more active, equalitarian role and the actual behavior of men in the role. Nor do we have the institutional arrangements which would allow–and motivate–men to change their role behavior. Furthermore, whether or not one views the relationships between men and women as "political," there is a clear conflict of interest between the sexes with regard to the allocation of child care responsibilities.

THE ROLE OF THE CARETAKER

Besides the child's own parents, caretakers may be relatives, friends, professional nurses, teachers, and other child care specialists, or persons without special training who do the work for pay. The caretaking setting may be in or outside the child's home; and, if outside, may range from a large center with a director and specialized staff to another home where a single individual looks after one or more children not her own.

Before discussing the kinds of people who have filled caretaker roles, something should be said about the nature of the activities involved in caring for young children. First, child care is an activity that requires full-time availability but not full-time attention and action (except for emergency situations such as when the child is seriously ill or has some serious behavior problem). In this sense, the role is akin to that of an intern or resident "on call" in a hospital. He must be there all the time and prepared for whatever cases may come in during his hours on call; but the typical shift alternates between periods of intense activity and periods when nothing is happening.

As Nelson and Krashinsky (1972) have pointed out in their economic analysis:

> As long as other activities are going on in the household–cleaning, cooking, or specialized activity for sale on the market like working on the family farm–the extra time cost of having children around is less than it would be for an organization specializing in child care. Besides time, the space needed for child care often is costless in the home where it is needed anyway (for sleeping, cooking, etc.) [p. 3].

A second characteristic of child care is its routine nature. While the creative aspects of childrearing are often emphasized by early childhood experts, a relatively small amount of time is actually spent in "developmental" activities such as reading to children, helping them to enjoy nature, working with arts and crafts, etc. Even in programs designed specifically to enhance children's intellectual and social development, "instruction" is often limited to brief periods of 15 or 20 minutes a day as in the home intervention program developed at Hebrew University Center for Research in Education of the Disadvantaged (Lombard, 1971). Much more time is spent in feeding, bathing, diapering, keeping the child from injuring himself (and patching him when he does). In addition, there are laundry, food preparation, and other "support" housekeeping tasks that multiply when children are present.

Third, while much of the work of child care is routine and can be combined with some other kinds of activities, there is a definite limit on the number of young children any adult can look after. The usual standard of U.S. Federal and state regulatory agencies is a ratio of one adult to every five children which gives some idea of the sheer numbers of child care workers required.

Given the special qualities of caretaking, what kinds of persons have been allocated to this role? Anthropological studies show that caretakers have been of all ages (including children only slightly older than those in their charge), both sexes, and occupying many positions (Mead & Wolfenstein, 1955). Grandparents are the most common caretakers in some societies. The "babushka" has played an important role in Russian society, where three-generation households are still common. Indeed, a concern of some students of Russian society is that, as Russian women gain more education and work experience, they become less willing to stay home and care for grandchildren, which will mean that child care in the home will soon no longer be a viable alternative to state nurseries and kindergartens (Jacoby, 1971). Although statistics on mainland China are still largely unavailable, recent visitors estimate that more than half the children aged 18 months to three years are cared for by a grandparent, and the proportion is considerably higher in rural communes where child care centers are few and their facilities very inadequate (Sidel, 1972; Printz, 1973). In all countries studied, unmarried girls provide a major source of child care, whether they work irregularly as sitters in different homes (as in America) or full-time as in the Bruderhof and other utopian communities where virtually all married women hold jobs outside the home (Zablocki, 1971, pp. 122 ff).

Perhaps the most specialized child care is provided in Israeli kibbutzim, where children live with small groups of their age peers in a series of children's homes, each with its own kitchen, bedrooms, bathing facilities, and at certain age levels, classroom. Each children's house is under the direction of a *metapelet,* or nurse, who has been chosen by the community because of her interest and ability to work with a particular age level, who has received specialized training at colleges operated by the kibbutz federations, and who cares for successive "generations" of children of the same age level. *Metapelets* are themselves members of the kibbutz, and like virtually all adult female members, are usually wives and mothers. *Metapelets* are assisted by other women from the community, who have also chosen this work from among the types of jobs available to the women of the kibbutz (Bettelheim, 1969; Spiro, 1965; personal interviews with kibbutz members).

One of the most interesting experiments in group caretaking of infants and young children is now in process at the Synanon communities in the United States, where children live in a series of children's homes, and are cared for by adult members who have chosen this kind of work, as in the kibbutz. Unlike the kibbutz, however, the parents' day-to-day involvement in the life of the child is not a crucial component of the caretaking system. While many mothers visit the children's home each day, there is no segment of the day which children regularly spend with their parents, and many children do not see their parents at all for weeks or even longer. Each caretaker's position is filled by a *pair* of individuals who alternate in performing the role. Workers in the children's homes generally work ten hours a day for seven days, after which they have seven days off during which time the role is filled by their "partner." (Interview with Elizabeth Missakian.)

The one characteristic which the caretakers of young children in most societies share is their relatively low social status. Moreover, in all of the societies I studied, the younger the children with whom the caretaker works, the lower the pay.

Even in the Israeli kibbutz, where, in my opinion, children are more valued and enjoyed, and where more of the community's capital and energies are invested in their care and education than in any place I have observed, working with children is still considered inferior to "productive labor." Moreover, although the ideology and literature on the kibbutz movement still stresses equality between the sexes, empirical data on kibbutzim work and committee assignments indicate an increasing sex-role differentiation: men are assigned to the secretariat and the more powerful committees, and women to education, health, and parents committees and to jobs in the children's home, schools, and communal kitchens and laundries (Gerson, 1971; Talmon, 1972).

The high birthrate characteristic of the more established kibbutzim and the males' continued refusal to work in jobs related to child care means that women are doing this kind of work most of the time. Candid informants admit that adult women are the most discontented people in kibbutzim today, and that they are believed to be the driving force behind most families who decide to leave kibbutzim (interviews with Yehudah Paz, Beni Katz-Nelson, and kibbutz members).

In the United States, as in other societies, child caretakers have been drawn largely from the societal subgroups with the least status and power. Until recent years, the major burden of child care was assumed by mothers and by female servants (when mothers could afford them).[1] Many women have also depended upon help and advice from female relatives and neighbors, although the extent

[1] In 1900, nearly half of all working women were domestic servants or farmhands. By 1960, the proportion had dropped to one-tenth, and by 1970 to less than four percent (Kahn, 1973, pp. 156-157).

and nature of this caretaking has not, as far as I know, been systematically studied.

A portion of the child care services formerly performed by maids were taken on by the babysitter, an American social invention also. Informal investigation indicates that, during the last two decades, the majority of American children (whether or not their mothers were employed outside the home) have been cared for by babysitters, and that more American adolescents earn money from babysitting than from any other kind of job. However, there are no comprehensive empirical data on how many babysitters there are, who they are, what they do, and what they earn. We do not know either to what extent babysitting provides young people with anticipatory socialization for parenthood. What can be noted about the role is that it is usually a minor one: almost anyone can be a babysitter, and most babysitting is done as a part-time means of earning money rather than as a "real" job requiring any special preparation.

Group care of children has been available on a small scale for over a century. The first U.S. day nursery was opened in Boston in 1838 to provide care for the children of seamen's wives and widows. By the end of the nineteenth century, there were about 175 day nurseries in various parts of the country, mostly operated by settlement houses and other charitable organizations for the children of poor working mothers. A later development was the nursery school, which was also clearly distinguishable from the day nursery by its clientele (mostly middle- and upper-class and relatively well educated), its emphasis upon education and development, and its shorter hours (usually about three hours a day,) which meant that it was not a feasible form of care for employed mothers. In fact, many nursery schools were "cooperative," with some or all of the mothers serving as part-time caretakers. (For a brief history of group child care in America, see Roby, 1973, Chapter 10.)

The first extensive American experience with group care was during World War II, when the Lanham Act provided 51 million dollars for 3,000 local day-care centers in labor shortage areas, and the Kaiser Corporation alone cared for 3,800 children in 24-hours-a-day centers located in company plants (Roby, 1973, Chapter 14; Grotberg, 1972, pp. 78-79).

However, the prevailing attitude in this country has always been that group care of children is unnatural, if not actually harmful, and that the good mother stays at home. Socioeconomic conditions in the late 1940s and 1950s supported this stay-at-home philosophy: neither government nor industry was recruiting more female employees; domestic service as an occupation was disappearing; and economic affluence allowed the majority of the big new families to be supported by the husband's income. By the 1960s, this philosophy was already changing and mothers were entering the labor force in large numbers.

A study by the Child Welfare League estimated that in 1965 almost a million children under 14 (of whom 7,000 were under age 6) were left on their own while their parents were at work; another million were left in the care of older brothers and sisters under 16 or relatives over 65 (Child Welfare League, 1969, p. 3).

All surveys of the day care facilities in this country show that the capacity is far less than the need. According to a 1967 survey by the Child Welfare League, there were 34,700 licensed facilities, with a capacity for 475,200 children. Of these facilities, 10,400 were day care centers, with space for 393,300 children (an average of 37.8 children per center); the remaining were 24,300 licensed family day care homes, with places for 81,900 children (an average of 3.4 children per home). More recent estimates, based upon March 1971 data from the U.S. Department of Health, Education and Welfare, indicate that there has been a substantial increase in the number of places for children in licensed centers and homes, but that the 905,000 places now available are still not close to the estimated several million children who need some kind of day care service (Women's Bureau, 1973, p. 2). Although there are no reliable statistics, all day care researchers agree that there are more places in unlicensed day care than in licensed homes and centers. Roby feels that "private child-minding" is a bigger "industry" than anyone imagines, and she estimates that more than half of the American children under six are now cared for in some kind of regular arrangement (at least part time). She also estimates that as many as 90% of all parents would use organized child care regularly if it were available at reasonable cost, in a convenient location, and open a sufficient number of hours. Given the shortage of licensed centers and homes, there is no question, then, that the majority of children, whether their parents are working outside the home or not, are cared for by babysitters, neighbors, or in unlicensed family care homes.

While day care in the United States is thus primarily a home-based, informal operation, two trends should be noted. One is a trend toward care outside the home in general and toward group care in particular. The second trend is that day care is evolving from a nonmonetized to a monetized arrangement. A 1965 survey (Low & Spindler, 1968) estimated that only 21% of the arrangements for care of children under 14 and 34% for children under six involved a money payment. Although figures for the 1970s have not yet been published, the analysis of the economics of child care in the Roby (1973) volume points out that:

> . . . paid child care is becoming more and more the norm. The steady increase in the percentage of mothers with children under eighteen who work outside the home at once increases the demand for care and reduces the nonmonetized supply of day care. The extended family has vanished; for instance, only 4 percent of Massachusetts homes with children under six have any nonparental adult living in the home. Teenagers spend time with teenagers. Thus child care is becoming increasingly monetized [p. 99].

The shift toward more formalized and commercialized forms of child care means that large organizations outside the home will be increasingly involved in providing care. One likely result of this commercialization is that there will be increased efforts to upgrade and professionalize the caretaker. The median salary for teachers in U.S. centers is $358 a month, less than the average wage of the center's full-time clerical workers. Not surprisingly, the role is still filled mainly by women for whom the salary is supplemental income rather than the main source of family support. As might be expected, the rate of staff turnover is unusually high. Some centers report turnover rates of 100% a year (Chapman & Lazar, 1971, p. 45).

Additional insight into the American situation may be gained by looking at caretaking patterns in other societies which are grappling with the consequences of major increases in the number of employed mothers. The most comprehensive data available are from Sweden. A recent report contained computations of "excess enrollments" in preschools (percentages of children actually attending preschools beyond the number of legitimate places available). These rates have been running between 12 and 15% for the past five years, with a slight increase in excess enrollment each year (Rosengren, 1973, pp. 6-7). Twenty percent of all Swedish parents have children in day care centers *(daghem)* and another 20% leave their children with licensed day care mothers *(familjedaghem)*. The number of places in licensed centers and homes increased about 700% between 1965 and 1970, a huge increase compared with that in the United States during the same period. Places in licensed day care are more available in some parts of the country than others: there are actually unused places in Stockholm, and severe shortages in new towns where many young families live, and in university towns which have a high proportion of married students.

In addition to government approved and subsidized caretakers, it is estimated that 60,000 Swedish children are in private family day nurseries, and there are some 20,000 "home helps," private maids or mother's helpers (Leijon, 1968, pp. 90-91). As in this country, the servant role is a disappearing one, and grandmothers and other relatives are less and less available as child caretakers. Swedish nursery schools *(lekskola)*, like American ones, take children for only about three hours a day. The Swedes acknowledge that at least 40% of the parents of preschoolers have no satisfactory solution to the child care problem, and that the present shortage is expected to continue throughout the 1970s.

Reliable statistics on child caretakers in Israel are harder to obtain. This is partly because child care, like most social services in Israel, has been devised and delivered under emergency conditions, particularly the pressures caused by the waves of immigration, ranging from child survivors of the World War II holocaust to children of the most impoverished Oriental Jewish populations. In one survey, more than half of all Israeli children were diagnosed as "culturally disadvantaged" and in need of some kind of compensatory education or service (interview with Joseph Marcus). Also, until recently, most child care services were provided on a private basis or in institutions set up by the women's voluntary organizations which have initiated so many of the social services and reforms in Israel. Israeli child care and caretakers come from a complex set of organizations and authorities.

Mother and Child Clinics (Tipot Halav)

These clinics are part of the National Health Services and provide prenatal and child health care up to age five. The service includes home visits by nurses. The focus is on inculcating standards of hygiene, good feeding methods, and awareness of children's physical development. The clinics are highly respected and trusted and are used by most Israeli mothers of all social levels. Clinic staff members do not, however, serve as real caretakers of children.

Day Care Homes and Centers

There is no formal system of government approved and subsidized day care for children. Until recently, day care services have been provided almost entirely on a private basis: in small "home nurseries" (where up to a dozen preschoolers are being casually looked after by one or two women) or in centers set up by women's voluntary organizations. A 1969 study by the Demographic Center[2] reported that there were 280 day nurseries in the country taking care of some 9,000 children (less than 10% of the children in this age category). Fifty-two percent of all the nurseries were run by the Working Mothers' Association of the Women Workers' Council of the General Federation of Labor *(Moetzet Hapoalot)*; 22% by the Women's International Zionist Organization (WIZO); 3% by municipalities and local councils, and the rest by a variety of other voluntary organizations. Only about 10% of the centers provided full-day care and meals (Demographic Center, 1971, translated by Laura Starr).

Prekindergartens (Gan Heshut)[3]

These are noncompulsory preschools for 3- and 4-year-olds, subsidized through the state but run through municipalities. About half of the 95,000 children in this age category attend either a municipal or private *gan*. (About 20% are private and attended mainly by children of well-to-do families.) About 32,000 of the 40,000 children attending *ganei* receive subsidies from the Ministry of Education. One important function of the *gan* is to assimilate the children of new Israeli citizens into the society and to narrow the very substantial gaps

[2] A council set up in the Prime Minister's Office in 1968 to coordinate the activities pertaining to family planning and care of preschool children. More will be said about governmental responsibility and activity with respect to children in the next section.

[3] *Gan* is an inclusive word for kindergarten or preschool.

between the various ethnic groups comprising modern Israel. Therefore virtually all the children in immigrant villages, and about 80% of the children in new development towns (populated largely by recent immigrants and members of underprivileged groups), attend a prekindergarten. Most prekindergartens are open five hours daily. There are some current proposals to extend the *gan* day so that children of working mothers could stay until at least 4:00 P.M. (with two hours rest and a light meal in the afternoon); but to date, only about 50 of the 1,500 to 2,000 long-day units have been financed (Harman, 1969).

Kindergarten (Gan Hovah)

These are free and compulsory, and parents have a choice of sending their children to a religious or nonreligious school. Nearly all 5-year-olds attend. Like prekindergartens, kindergartens meet for only a few hours a day. There are efforts to provide "long-day" facilities at this level also. The government has recently begun to support an additional year of compulsory kindergarten for disadvantaged 4-year-olds, with a particular focus upon language skills.

The Demographic Center has tried to determine the professional level of caretakers employed in state-subsidized preschools. Among the 789 day nursery employees in caretaker roles, only 27% are classified as "professional" (that is, have training as *metaplot* or children's nurses). At the *gan* level, where professional training has a pedogogical rather than a health focus, it is estimated that less than 75% of the children are taught by professional teachers *(gan nenet).* Since there is now an increasing emphasis on the educational aspects of day care, the administration of preschool education has been moved from the Ministry of Health to the Ministry of Education. The state offers subsidies to any day care center that can establish that it offers some "teaching" each day. As might be expected, there is a conflict developing between *gan nenet* and *metaplot*. Their training differs in length as well as in substance, with *metaplot* now facing the alternative of getting additional training or losing positions to persons with kindergarten training. However, *metaplot* are members of a very large and powerful nurses' union, which is not likely to give up control of so many positions without a strong fight.

It is true, however, that even in state-subsidized day care settings a large number of caretaker positions are filled by persons with little or no training either in nursing or education. The highest proportion of trained staff is found in the larger cities; the proportion of professionals in development towns is much smaller and declines to about 1% in rural areas (Demographic Center, 1971, translated by Laura Starr; interview with Avima Lombard).

In some of the centers I visited, only the director had had professional training, and most of the staff members were local women whose major caretaking experience had been with their own families. Marcus (1970) describes the "typical" *gan nenet*, as a woman who:

> possesses a smattering of popular psychology and a good deal of the folk culture, may frequently interpret atypical behavior to mother, but for the most part arranges a context for behavior, mediates disputes, supervises safety, and distributes materials and, of course, snacks. The theme of . . . early socialization seems to be a path toward independence with a minimal amount of frustration of immature behavior. Popular notions of psychoanalytic theories are applied in compound with socialist ideology, Jewish theology and folkways, and the various ethnic behaviors included in the immigrants' baggage. Added to all this are a multitude of perceptions of what the ideal Israeli should grow up to become [Chapter 5, p. 22].

In contrast to the day care settings I observed in Sweden, those in Israel had a low ratio of adults to children and a relatively passive role was taken by most caretakers. Except in the kibbutz, caretakers tended to leave children pretty much to their own devices except when they were engaged in formal teaching. My general impression is that caretaking is more of a custodial role in Israel than in any of the other societies I studied. This may be partly explained by the fact that in Israel, social services in general have a more improvisatory quality than in more settled and affluent societies, and developmental care is still a luxury that few can afford.

Some of the most intriguing reports about major innovations in caretaking come from recent visitors to mainland China. There are three levels of preschool care in China today:

1. *Nursery rooms* (for babies from about 2 to 18 months). These facilities are usually located in the mother's workplace, and mothers are given time off, usually twice a day, to breast-feed their babies or just to hold or play with them. Factory nursery rooms are staffed by "aunties" who have no special training but are chosen from among the workers in the factory who are the "most responsible and the most patient" (Sidel, 1972, p. 93). These facilities are widely used. Sidel claims that only about 10% of the mothers of preschoolers are not in the labor market and take full care of their own children.
2. *Nurseries* (for children from about 18 months to 3 years). These are also usually located at the place of employment so parents may be close to their children. A child may be placed in a nursery in his father's as well as his mother's factory. Although reliable figures are not available, it is estimated that about half of all the children in this age category are in nurseries; the other half are cared for by neighbors or grandparents (many of whom live with or near their children). In rural areas, the proportion of children cared for by grandparents is greater.
3. *Kindergartens* (for children from age 3 to school age, about 7½). The majority of Chinese children attend kindergarten (about 80% in the cities, somewhat less in the country). Kindergartens are most likely to be located in the child's neighborhood and are generally run by neighborhood revolutionary committees.

Child care is more informal in the rural communes, and nurseries and kindergartens may be combined. In rural communities, day care is likely to be used sporadically: during the harvest season, for instance, pregnant women and persons with physical handicaps care for little children so that everyone else can work in the fields.

There are several unique features of the caretaker role in contemporary China. Care of infants and young children is characterized by what Sidel terms "multiple mothering." During the course of a typical day, a Chinese child may be cared for by his biological mother (while nursing, before and after work, and on days off), by "aunties" or nursery workers, and by grandparents, when they live in or near his home. Moreover, he is likely to see the same set of caretakers day after day; it is claimed that there is very little turnover of personnel in nursing rooms, nurseries, and kindergartens. There is also a consistency of orientation and very little interpersonal competition among the various persons caring for the young child. Apparently, there is widespread agreement among Chinese caretakers that they wish all children to develop the values of loving and helping each other; of "serving the people" and putting the needs of the society ahead of personal interests; and of identifying with physical labor and those who perform it (Sidel, 1972, p. 82; Committee of Concerned Asian Scholars, 1972, pp. 287-291). There is no move toward professionalism (or credentialism) of caretakers. In fact, the current trend seems to be in the opposite direction. Preschool personnel at all levels "are recruited far more on the basis of personality characteristics than of any kind of formal training, and we had the feeling that the Chinese consider a warm motherly type with common sense the best sort of person to care for small children. This anti-expert bias is, of course, reflective of what is going on in society at large" (Sidel, 1972, p. 126).

While the Chinese seem to have created, within a remarkably brief period of time, an efficient and humane system of child care, it must be remembered that what we know about child care in China is all based upon unsystematic observations made during relatively short visits in settings chosen by the Chinese hosts.

A number of issues have been touched on only peripherally in the previous discussion of the caretaker role and the variety of caretaking patterns in different countries. Questions such as whether children should be cared for in groups or individually and whether institutional care is necessarily harmful are unresolved issues for many societies. (The Chinese have apparently made a clear decision in favor of group caretaking, even for long periods of time.) There seems to be a preference for individualized care in a home setting in the United States, and this preference can be noted even in the pattern of services provided by public and voluntary agencies for neglected, dependent, emotionally disturbed, and other "problem" children. American children receive social services from state and local agencies at a rate of 416 per 10,000 children under

20 years of age. Even among those not living with their own parents, there is a predominance of care in the closest approximation of a home—7% of the children are in foster family homes, while only 2% are in all-group homes and institutions combined (U.S. Department of Health, Education, & Welfare, 1973). This is in contrast to Israel, where programs for children "in distress" tend to concentrate on institutional care "primarily because of the availability of this type of facility as compared to others, and because of the historical respectability associated with group education and ideology-oriented group life" (e. g., the Youth Aliya camps and peer groups within kibbutzim; Jaffe, 1970, p. 345). Since the late 1940s, less than 4% of Israeli children under 18 were reared away from their own homes, and of these children, almost 70% were living in 142 institutions during the 1960s (Ibid., p. 333). Furthermore, according to Jaffe, no significant differences have been found in intellectual or personal development between children in institutions and similar children living in other settings (Jaffe, 1964). While group care can no longer be assumed to be detrimental to children's welfare, we still know too little about the components of good and poor caretakers and caretaking to make a final judgment on any particular form of care.

OTHER SYSTEM ROLES

Government

Until recently there has been little governmental involvement in child care at the national level, and there is still no comprehensive national child care policy: ". . . care of children below school age or during hours not in school was not thought to be a public responsibility except in emergencies" (Fried, Rivlin, Schulze, & Teeters, 1973, p. 161). However, in the last few years there have been substantial increases in federal spending for early childhood programs. In addition to direct program expenditures (such as Head Start and the Work Incentive Program [WIN]), the federal government also provides some indirect subsidies, such as allowing families to increase their income tax deductions for the cost of child care or allowing welfare mothers to deduct such costs from their income computation. What has changed public attitudes and led to this increased public support? According to the Brookings Foundation, there are a number of contributing factors, including women's liberation, the huge increases in welfare rolls, and the influence of child development research showing the importance of early learning experiences upon children's later development.) The result of increasing government involvement in child care is that as a government's investment in child care increases, so does its interest in regulating what it has subsidized. Among the areas in which standards are set by various levels of the government are physical space and facilities, staff ratio, and training requirements. It is often difficult to draw the line between standards that meet real requirements of children's welfare and those that go beyond a society's ability and willingness to invest in its children.

Another result of government involvement in child care is the proliferation of programs and agencies and the almost inevitable competition between them for funds and control. A family seeking welfare services or a group of people attempting to set up a day care center often encounter an enormous amount of red tape. Multiple approvals required for the simplest transactions often raise the costs of child care without enhancing its quality. (For example, because the governmental regulations for Head Start programs and day care centers call for different ways of accounting for food, it is all but impossible for them to share the same building [Day Care Consultation Service].)

The complexity of the governmental role in the child care system is not unique to the United States. In both of the countries I visited during the past year, the parliaments had recently appointed a commission to study preschool problems and to recommend needed programs and legislation; and in both cases this action had brought to the surface long-standing conflicts among the ministries which have responsibility for children. The conflict between the Israeli Ministry of Education and the nurses' union has already been mentioned. Israel has the most complicated governmental arrangements with respect to child care.

In Sweden, conflict between the Ministries of Education, Social Welfare, and Health also exists, but it is less obvious than in Israel. Despite this conflict Sweden has a clearly articulated and comprehensive system of child care services. The most important components of the system are: the "maternity benefit," a lump sum paid to all women following the birth of a child; the children's allowance, now over $200 per child per year; a family housing allowance; and health insurance, which covers hospital care, visits to doctors, and medicine.

Private Industry

Among the institutions which have the most influence over the lives of families in this country are the large corporations and agencies that employ most of us. However, few corporations have actually involved themselves with their employees' child care problems. Probably no more than 5,000 children are currently cared for in centers sponsored by employers, and of the 150 to 200 centers in existence, over half are in hospitals, health care facilities, and other nonprofit institutions (Roby, 1973, Chapter 14; Women's Bureau, 1970, 1971). In fact, industry-sponsored day care was much more extensive in earlier periods of our history: nearly 3,000 day care enters were subsidized under the provisions of the Lanham Act of 1942. It seems likely that arguments about the appropriate care of children follow the trends of the labor market, rather than the reverse. When employers need more women workers they manage to find the means to provide the child care that at other times they claim they cannot afford.

Industry has two reasons for involvement in day care. One is to gain new employees or new kinds of employees; the other is to gain greater retention and low absenteeism among the employees it already has. The pressing need for increasing female labor market participation, for both ideological and economic reasons, is an important factor behind public and private support of day care programs in Israel and China. The United States does not have such an obvious need (one thing that makes the struggle of women's organizations for expanded day care services so difficult now is that their demands are occurring in a time of contracting labor market demands in many crucial areas).

The success of employer child care programs so far is difficult to evaluate, since few have collected data on their results. (Women's Bureau, 1970, 1971, for example, identifies and describes ongoing services without reporting on the response to the services offered.) In recent years, almost as many company-based centers have closed as opened, apparently because commuter mothers find the transportation of young children too arduous. A few employers, including the Ford Foundation, subsidize parents for day care and the parents make their own arrangements (Joan Carroll, personal communication). American Telephone and Telegraph Company is one of the few large corporations which is gathering data on its own day care program, initiated in 1971. The results are not yet published, but preliminary findings indicate that day care centers do cut down on employee tardiness but not necessarily on absenteeism–children in day care centers are more prone to illness than children cared for at home because of the contact with so many other children; and when a child is ill, parents who commute a fairly great distance are likely to extend an absence for several days to care for him (Charles Sherard, personal communication).

In addition to providing or subsidizing day care for its own employees, private industry has also become involved in the selling of child care services. Several companies are attempting to contract with corporations and groups of industries, industrial parks, and government agencies to manage centers for a fee or a percent of operating costs. The most widely publicized and controversial method of operation is the franchise:

> Corporations sell facilities, name, advertising, "training" and program materials to individuals or small groups who operate their own centers. The operators pay an annual fee, usually six percent of the operating costs, to the franchising corporations for continuing use of the name and other central services, such as training, advertising, marketing materials, etc. There are many misgivings about franchises; those educators who think that franchised day care cannot work fear that cutting costs to increase profits means reducing personnel. Certainly personnel is the major cost of day care, and cutting may reduce the quality of service. Studies have shown that day care shows a relatively low profit margin. Two large corporations' in-house studies concluded that "good" day care services could not be sold at a profit. (Day Care Consultation Service, p. 12).

Besides being unable so far to show a very substantial profit, franchisers have yet to show that they can provide care above the custodial level. As the author of a two-year study for the Child Welfare League of America put it, "the kind of child care provided in franchised centers ranged from damaging to fair" (William Pierce, quoted in the *Wall Street Journal*, November 27, 1972; see also Featherstone, 1970). In short, only a very small proportion of the major United States employers have assumed any responsibility for child care, and there is no existing program which is both feasible for the employer and truly responsive to the needs of working parents and their children.

The discussion of government and private industry involvement in child care does not begin to complete our analysis of the child care system. Among other important components or roles which I did not have time to study more than superficially are:

1. *The role of labor unions*. While labor unions have been innovative in providing many kinds of social services to their workers, they seem to have been strangely inactive in the area of day care. Amalgamated Clothing Workers of America is the one union we have located which has attempted to provide quality day care (Joyce Miller, personal communication).
2. *The child advocate*. A new role which has been proposed by observers of the child care system would be a kind of spokesman for children, who would lobby for needed resources and services and would investigate and file suit on behalf of children when it seems that their legal rights are jeopardized. A recent class action filed in a New York court against all of the public and private child welfare agencies of the city and their chief administrators argued that the entire system of child welfare services is unconstitutional, since the city funds and relies upon systems that are permeated by religious and racial discrimination, that lack adequate services for the children most in need of care, and that place such children in detention homes and other institutions in violation of their right not to be subjected to cruel and unusual punishment (Shirley Wilder *et al.* versus Jule Sugarman *et al.*). Research and legal action is also being planned by Marian Wright Edelman, creator of the Children's Defense Fund, to investigate the more than 1.5 million school-age children who are not enrolled in public or private schools.
3. *The role of mass media*. In both Israel and Sweden, I met with producers of educational television programs who are committed to a role for television in the lives of children which is quite different from the mindless, mechanical babysitter TV has become for many American children. In both countries, TV is available only a few hours a day (so Israeli and Swedish children cannot yet spend more hours in front of a television set than they do in school), and the educational channel is often the only one. Besides producing a series of programs aired during the hours most day care centers and nurseries are open, both countries have developed some sophisticated substantive courses for use in elementary, secondary, and college classrooms (the foreign language programs being among the most impressive). Finally, both countries have examined the

possibility of importing the American "Sesame Street" programs, and have rejected the idea (Israel even broadcast some "Sesame Street" programs translated into Hebrew, but they were not very successful); they decided that the values and life-styles presented in the program were contrary to the ones they wished to inculcate in their own children (interviews with Frederic Fleisher and other members of the TRU committee; interview with Jaacov Lorberbaum).

Society and Its Child Care System

It should be clear from much in the preceding sections that the society in which a child is raised affects the kind of care he will receive. During the past year, I have given some thought to what characteristics of societies as total systems have the most important effects upon children and the child care system.

Each of the countries I studied has serious unresolved problems concerning the care of young children. Only China seems not to have a critical shortage of caretakers; and this may not last when the present generation of grandmothers passes on, a phenomenon which has occurred in other societies. However the forms in which the problems manifest themselves are distinct for each society. Only Israel faces masses of immigrants from diverse backgrounds, a phenomenon which requires a strong focus upon programs for assimilation. Perhaps because of the constant crisis atmosphere in which Israelis live they have been the most inventive about social programs for children (to list just a few: the kibbutz children's home, Youth Aliya and children's villages, boarding schools for culturally disadvantaged gifted students, home intervention projects using mothers and neighborhood aides to encourage cognitive skills in preschool children, *Korath Gag*, a temporary foster-placement program to remove children from immigrant camps during especially severe winters, and vacations for mothers of large families). Indeed there is an improvisatory quality about children's programs in Israel that is rather refreshing, as is the evident concern for every human life displayed by the society as a whole. The problem, of course, is in coordinating the proliferation of both public and private programs which have sprung up. One analysis concludes rather gloomily that "it is rather difficult, at present, to envisage the situation in which the particular interests of various ministries, departments, and organizations will cease to circumvent coordination and integration" (Roby, 1973, p. 428).

Unlike Israel, Sweden has the advantage of having only one language, no national minorities, relatively small status differences between society members, and the absence of war and other major national emergencies. Major concerns are how to revise and extend a system of social benefits so as to wipe out remaining pockets of need (including the unmet need for day care places and service to mistreated children) and how to achieve even higher levels of equality. Sweden has probably gone as far as any nation in the world in envisioning settings for human beings that cut across age and class boundaries and which nurture the cooperativeness and nonagression so highly valued by Swedes (e.g., the brother–sister *daghems* which contain children of relatively broad age range and allow children from the same family to attend together, and experiments with neighborhood co-ops for all ages, as opposed to physically separated day care centers).

In comparison with Israel, Sweden, and nearly all socialist states in which women work outside the home as a matter of course, the United States has not managed to break free from guilt and ambivalence about the working mother or about any kind of child care arrangements outside the home, except for very poor children. We have consequently been slow to develop the kinds of social inventions which would make the relationships between children and adults and between men and women less stressful. Perhaps the most disturbing thing about the child care system in this country is how impoverished the interpersonal lives of many American children really are. Children not only need environments that meet minimum standards of health and safety; they are also highly social beings who need the attention of interested adults and the company (under appropriate adult supervision) of friends. A child development specialist asked to identify the greatest hazard facing young children today in our city centers and suburbs replied "loneliness" (Roby, 1973, p. 13).

CONCLUSIONS

The general conclusion that can be drawn about the child care system, in this country and elsewhere, is that it is not providing enough of the kinds of care children need most. Roby argues that child care in America is a nonsystem. I think a more accurate conceptualization is that it is a system which is out of balance, in which there is a substantial gap between the needs of children and the ability or the willingness of the system to provide these needs.

A second conclusion is that children are best served in systems in which responsibility is relatively diffused. The environment of many American children, with its isolation of the mother and child, is hardly conducive to intellectual or social growth. The burden of being solely responsible for raising children is more than many parents can bear (and probably explains the rejection of parenthood among growing numbers of young people).

In this country especially, there seem to be discontinuities between our values and our behavior with respect to children. Several logical possibilities exist concerning the relationship between values and behavior: (a) that we actually value children less than we used to, and therefore our neglect of them is consistent; (b) that we value children as much as ever (though perhaps for different reasons) but that our institutional arrangements do not allow us to care for them in a way consistent with our values; (c) that we value children but we now value other things more (especially self-development), and this interferes with our behaving responsibly toward children. Which, if any, of the above models most clearly fits the American situation is unknown from currently available data.

One's choice of strategy for reform of the child care system depends upon a variety of factors, including personal bias and political realities as well as objective evaluation of how to maximize children's development. The one kind of strategy that seems doomed to failure is one based upon large numbers of women returning to the home and full-time motherhood. This still leaves a great number of different strategic approaches, of which the relative merits and feasibility are largely untested. Some of the alternative strategies suggested in current debates on child care are: greater public investment; greater involvement by corporations, agencies, and labor unions as employers; new kinds of family, neighborhood, and community arrangements which involve greater sharing of the pleasures and perils of childrearing; getting more adults involved in part-time relationships with children (including adults not related by blood); pushing for greater specialization and professionalization of the caretaker role—or the reverse, encouraging the identification of people with an affinity for working with children and providing them with the minimum necessary training; and planning a comprehensive set of centers and services for children.

REFERENCES

Aries, P. *Centuries of childhood*. New York: Knopf, 1962.

Benson, L. *Fatherhood: A sociological perspective*. New York: Random House, 1968.

Berelson, B. The value of children: A taxonomical essay. In *Population Council Annual Report*. New York: The Population Council, 1972. Pp. 19-27.

Bernard, J. *The future of marriage*. New York: World Publishing Company, 1972.

Bettelheim, B. *The children of the dream*. New York: Macmillan, 1969.

Bowlby, J. *Maternal care and mental health*. Geneva: The World Health Organization, 1952.

California Commission on the Status of Women, Transcript of the Public Hearings on Day Care, held jointly by the Advisory Commission on the Status of Women with Senate and Assembly Social Welfare Committee of the California Legislature, San Francisco, October, 1968.

Campbell, A. A. In *The family in transition*. A Round Table Conference Sponsored by the John E. Fogarty International Center for Advanced Study in the Health Sciences, National Institutes of Health, Nov. 3-6, 1969. Fogarty International Proceedings No. 3. Washington D.C.: U.S. Government Printing Office, 1969.

Chapman, J. E., & Lazar, J. B. *A review of the present status and future needs in day care research*. Washington, D.C.: Office of Child Development, 1971.

Child Welfare League of America. *Standards for day care service*. New York: Child Welfare League of America, 1969.

Committee of Concerned Asian Scholars. *China! Inside the People's Republic*. New York: Bantam Books, 1972.

Cottman, G. Baby dolls. *Los Angeles Times West Magazine*, November 21, 1971, pp. 7-16.

Day Care Consultation Service. *Day care and industry in New York City: A report on the problems and alternatives*. New York: Bank Street College of Education, Day Care Consultation Service, n. d.

Day Care Council of New York. *Children at risk: The growing problem of child abuse*. New York: Day Care Council of New York, 1972.

Demographic Center. *Survey of day nurseries*. Jerusalem: Demographic Center, Prime Minister's Office, 1971 (in Hebrew).

de Shalit, N. Children in war. In A. Jarus et al. (Eds.), *Children and families in Israel*, New York: Gordon and Breach, 1970. Pp. 151-182.

Duncan, O. D. Schuman, H., & Duncan, B. *Social change in a metropolitan community*. New York: Russell Sage Foundation, 1973.

Featherstone, J. Kentucky fried children. *The New Republic*, September 12, 1970, pp. 12-16.

Fried, E. R., Rivlin, A. M., Schultze, C. L., & Teeters, N. H. *Setting national priorities: The 1974 budget*. Washington, D.C.: The Brookings Institution, 1973.

Gerson, M. Women in the kibbutz. *American Journal of Orthopsychiatry*, 1971, *41*, 566-573.

Grotberg, E. H. (Ed.). *Day care: Resources for decisions*. U. S. Office of Economic Opportunity, Office of Planning, Research and Evaluation, 1972.

Handlin, O., & Handlin, M. *Facing life: Youth and the family in American history*. Boston: Little Brown, 1971.

Hannerz, U. *Soulside: Inquiries into ghetto culture and community*. New York: Columbia University Press, 1969.

Harman, Z. *Services for the young child*. Jerusalem: Demographic Center, Prime Minister's Office, 1969. Mimeographed report.

Hawes, J. *Children in urban society: Juvenile delinquency in nineteenth century America*. New York: Oxford University Press, 1971.

Hoffman, L. W. Effects on children: summary and discussion. In F. I. Nye & L. W. Hoffman (Eds.), *The employed mother in America*, Chicago: Rand McNally, 1963. Pp. 190-212.

Hoffman, L. W., & Hoffman, M. L. The value of children to parents. In J. T. Fawcett (Ed.), *Psychological perspectives on population*. New York: Basic Books, 1973. Pp. 19-76.

Hunt, D. *Parents and children in history*. New York: Basic Books, 1970.

Jacoby, S. Who raises Russia's children? *Saturday Review*, August 21, 1971, pp. 41-43, 53.

Jaffe, E. D. Child welfare in Israel: An overview of institution care, foster home care and adoption. In A. Jarus, T. Marcus, J. Oren, and C. Rapaport (Eds.), *Children and families in Israel*. New York: Gordon and Breach, 1970. Pp. 331-350.

Kahn, E. J., Jr. Who, what, where, how much, how many? *New Yorker*, October 15, 1973, pp. 137-157.

Komarovsky, M. Cultural contradictions and sex roles: The masculine case. *American Journal of Sociology*, 1973, *78*, 873-884.

Komarovsky, M. *Unemployed man and his family*. New York: Octagon, 1971.

Larrabee, E. Childhood in twentieth-century America. In E. Ginsberg (Ed.), *The nation's children*, Vol. 3. New York: Columbia University Press, 1960. Pp. 199-216.

Laslett, P. *Household and family in past time*. Cambridge: Cambridge University Press, 1972.

Leijon, A. G. *Swedish women-Swedish men*. Stockholm: Swedish Institute for Cultural Relations, 1968.

Liebow, E. *Tally's corner*. Boston: Little Brown, 1966.

Linner, B. *Sex and society in Sweden*. New York: Pantheon Books, 1967.

Lombard, A. D. *Home instruction program for preschool youngsters*. NCJW Center for Research in Education of the Disadvantaged, School of Education, Hebrew University of Jerusalem, 1971. (Mimeographed report)

Low, S., & Spindler, P. G. *Child care arrangements of working mothers in the United States* (Children's Bureau Publication No. 461-1968). Washington, D.C.: U.S. Department of Health, Education, and Welfare, 1968.

Marcus, J. Early child care in Israel. Unpublished manuscript. Henrietta Szold Institute, Jerusalem, 1970.

Mead, M., & Wolfenstein, M. (Eds.). *Childhood in contemporary cultures*. Chicago: University of Chicago Press, 1955.

Munro, D. J. Egalitarian ideal and educational fact in communist China. In J. M. Lindbeck (Ed.), *China: Management of a revolutionary society*. Seattle: University of Washington Press, 1971. Pp. 256-301.

Nelson, R. R., & Krashinsky, M. *Public control and the economic organization of day care for young children*. Mimeographed paper, Yale University, Institution for Social and Policy Studies, 1972.

Orleans, L. A. China: Population in the People's Republic. *Population Bulletin*, 1971, *27*, 5-37.

Otto, H. Man-woman relationships in the future. *The Futurist*, 1973, *7*, 55-61.

Polatnick, M. Why men don't rear children. *Berkeley Journal of Sociology*, 1973, *18*, 45-86.

Printz, P. The Chen family still has class. *The New York Times Magazine*, October 14, 1973, pp. 43-70.

Robinson, J. P., & Converse, P. E. Social change reflected in the use of time. In A. Campbell & P. E. Converse (Eds.), *The human meaning of social change*, New York: Russell Sage Foundation, 1972. Pp. 17-86.

Roby, P. (Ed.). *Child care–Who cares? Foreign and domestic infant and early childhood development policies*. New York: Basic Books, 1973.

Rosengren, B. *Pre-school in Sweden: Facts, trends, and future*. Stockholm: The Swedish Institute, 1973.

Rossi, A. Transition to parenthood. *Journal of Marriage and the Family*, 1968, *30*, 26-39.

Schultze, C. L., Fried, E. R., Rivlin, A. M., & Teeters, N. H. *Setting national priorities: The 1973 budget*. Washington, D.C.: The Brookings Institution, 1972.

Senn, M. J. E., & Hartford, C. (Eds.). *The firstborn: Experiences of eight American families*. Cambridge, Massachusetts: Harvard University Press, 1968.

Sidel, R. *Women and child care in China*. New York: Hill & Wang, 1972.

Sorel, G. *Reflections on violence*. London: Collier-Macmillan, 1950.

Spiro, M. E. *Children of the kibbutz*. New York: Schocken Books, 1965.

Statistical Abstract of Israel, 1970, *22*, p. 284.

Talmon, Y. *Family and community in the kibbutz*. Cambridge, Massachusetts: Harvard University Press, 1972.

Talmon, Y. Sex-role differentiation in an equalitarian society. In T. G. Lasswell, J. Burma, & S. Aronson (Eds.), *Life in Society*, Chicago: Scott, Foresman, 1965. Pp. 145-155.

U.S. Department of Health, Education, and Welfare. *Children served by public welfare agencies and voluntary child welfare agencies and institutions*. (DHEW Publication No. (SRS) 73-03258). Washington, D.C.: Department of Health, Education and Welfare, National Center for Social Statistics, 1973.

Waldman, E., & Gover, K. R. Children of women in the labor force. *Monthly Labor Review*, July 1971, pp. 19-25.

White House Conference on Children. *Profiles of children*. Washington, D.C.: U.S. Government Printing Office, 1970.

Wolfenstein, M. Fun morality. An analysis of recent American child-training literature. *Journal of Social Issues*, 1951, 7, 15-25.

Women's Bureau. *Child care services provided by hospitals*. Washington, D.C.: U.S. Government Printing Office, 1970.

Women's Bureau. *Day care services: Industry's involvement*. Washington, D.C.: U.S. Government Printing Office, 1971.

Women's Bureau. *Day care facts* (pamphlet 16 [revised]). Women's Bureau, Employment Standards Administration, U. S. Department of Labor, 1973.

Zablocki, B. *The joyful community*. Baltimore: Penguin Books, 1971.

Zalba, S. R. Battered children. *Trans-action*, 1971, *8*, 58-61.

5

Sex Role and Pupil Role in Early Childhood Education

Patrick C. Lee
Gita Kedar Voivodas

Teachers College, Columbia University

Society's increasing concern with sexism has persuaded educators to examine the school's potential for fostering sexist values in children. The issues which have attracted the greatest scrutiny have been the sexist content of children's books (e.g., Saario, Jacklin, & Tittle, 1973), sex typing of school-related activities and objects (e.g., Kagan, 1964b; Paley, 1973), and sterotyped sex-role expectations of teachers (e.g., Feshbach, 1969). These kinds of stereotypy, however, are not peculiar to schools, but are endemic to most institutions in American society.

Our position is that the school is neither more nor less sexist than other American institutions. Its unique contribution to sex-role socialization is more through its implicit indoctrination of children to "pupil role" than through explicit support of the larger society's sex-role expectations. It is the special nature of pupil role and its resulting interaction with sex role which has important and differential implications for boys and girls and which should be of major concern to educators.[1]

Accordingly, this paper has three objectives: to discuss the origins of pupil role and its relationship to sex role in early childhood settings (from nursery

[1]This interaction has been analyzed elsewhere (e.g., Brophy & Good, 1974; Lee, 1973; Lee & Gropper, 1974). However, these previous treatments differ from the present one in three important respects. First, none has focused specifically on the interaction between pupil role and sex role in early childhood settings. Second, with the exception of Lee (1973), none has attempted to analyze the etiology and specific nature of pupil role as an institutional phenomenon. Third, none has described and documented a viable and valid alternative to pupil role.

school through second grade); to indicate the problems this interaction presents for both boys and girls; and to offer recommendations for teacher training and school reform.

PUPIL ROLE

During the early years, young children assume a variety of roles as a way of adjusting to the complexities of human society and its institutions. In the family, the child usually plays multiple roles; for example, son or daughter, little brother, older sister, etc. Upon entering school, he is faced with a new set of roles that are peculiar to the school as an institution. For the first time in his life he is expected to be a formal learner and a *pupil*. As a learner the child masters the school's official curriculum; his pupil role, however, defines the accommodations he must make to the school as a social institution. The ideal pupil is often viewed as a conforming, dependent, docile, and manageable child. Most practicing educators assume that adoption of this behavioral profile is prerequisite to effective learning, a view probably derived from the nature of teaching as a profession and of schooling as an institution.

In comparison with other professionals, such as physicians and lawyers, teachers receive only brief academic preparation for their jobs. Moreover, the period of student teaching is probably too short and comes too late in training, when one considers the responsibilities they are expected to assume once they take their first real teaching assignments. Katz (1972b) has referred to the first year of teaching as the "survival stage" of teacher development, and Fuller (1969) has found that beginning teachers have anxieties about their own adequacy as teachers which often lead to rigidity and an overinsistence upon maintaining classroom control. With increasing maturity, some teachers shift focus from their own performance as teachers to children's performance as learners; but, many teachers continue to place a high premium on effective classroom management and prefer those students who are easy to control. This preoccupation with control is found in nursery school teachers as well as those in early elementary classrooms.

Schools and child care centers are probably the most crowded institutions in American urban culture, as whole neighborhoods of children are gathered into selected buildings for three to eight hours a day (see Jackson, 1968, p. 8). These great numbers of only partially socialized youngsters create serious problems of crowd control. Given these realities of schooling, pupil role may be viewed as a necessary alternative to chaos in the hallways, the cafeterias, and the bathrooms, as well as in the classrooms.

Most states have statutes requiring universal, compulsory schooling starting with kindergarten. This means that public schools do not select their clientele, nor do the students voluntarily choose to go to school. From the perspective of institutional analysis, then, one can appreciate why the school would place such emphasis on controlling the behavior of its involuntary clientele and why it invokes pupil role as the proper role for students.

From kindergarten on, most schools have an age-graded system. This means that teachers have to move their students through a carefully scheduled sequence of curricula so that they are prepared for the next grade. As a result, there is great pressure on students to move through the school year in an orderly and predictable fashion. Those who have approximated ideal pupil-role status are the ones most likely to be on schedule, exactly where the teacher wants them to be. With the recent introduction of academic instruction in many preschool settings, there is often the same concern with "curriculum" appearing in nursery school classrooms. In preschools serving lower socioeconomic populations some "pre-academic" programs explicitly require the child's accommodation to pupil role. For certain periods of the day, he is expected to sit in place, receive direct instruction, and answer questions just as if he were in first or second grade (e.g., Engelmann, Osborne, & Engelmann, 1972). In schools serving more economically privileged populations, admission to prestigious private elementary schools is often based upon an evaluation of the child's performance in nursery school. Such evaluations usually rely heavily upon the child's "potential" for assuming acceptable pupil-role status.

Some readers might argue that the early childhood settings described above are not representative of the typical setting for young children, least of all of nursery schools. Little research has been conducted on this question, but the few studies which have been done indicate that teachers begin socializing children to pupil role as early as nursery school. Jackson and Wolfson (1968), for example, found that the average nursery school child receives almost three constraints per hour from his teacher. In a school consisting of 97 children, six teachers, and ten assistant teachers, they counted approximately 3,500 constraints every morning: 25% of these were imposed by the teachers. The observations took place in a university laboratory school generally regarded as an outstanding example of good nursery school practice. In another study, LaBelle and Rust (1973) found even more instances of control in their sample of 20 nursery school teachers. These teachers averaged 35 control episodes during a 45-minute observational period. Forty-nine percent of these controlling responses were for the specific purpose of socializing children to the rules of the classroom, while another 32% constituted assertions of "personal control" by the teacher. LaBelle and Rust commented that a number of these personal assertions were closely related to institutional objectives, thus indicating further pressure on the children to adopt pupil role, to be conforming and manageable. Ironically, only 19% of the controls were designed to introduce children to the cultural values of the larger society. It would seem, then, that pupil role is a reality of schooling which begins in nursery school and usually becomes an accepted part of the child's experience by first and second grade.

SEX ROLE

Just as pupil role is a creation of schools and teachers, sex role is a creation of the larger culture. Sex role consists of a set of cultural prescriptions which are delivered to the child by the significant figures in his or her life. Parents, peers, and television characters use a variety of techniques (including modeling, reinforcement, expectations, and direct teaching) to draw the child's attention to the essential parameters of his or her "appropriate" sex role. As the child incorporates early lessons in sex-role identity, he increasingly views sex role as a central component of self-concept and begins to more actively select and assimilate characteristics which are congruent with his emerging sex-role identity. There is no need to review the complexities of sex-role acquisition here, as they have been adequately presented elsewhere (e.g., Maccoby, 1966). A few selected points, however, should be considered:

1. Both adults and peers socialize children to their culturally assigned sex-role identity. Socialization by adults begins during the first year of life (e.g., Goldberg & Lewis, 1969), while the influence of peers is apparent among three-year-olds (Fagot & Patterson, 1969).
2. Most boys and girls are aware of their gender by their third birthday (Gesell, Halverson, Thompson, Ilg, Costner, Ames, & Amatruda, 1940, p. 228); and, whether aware of it or not, behave in predictably different ways by three years of age (Fagot & Patterson, 1969).
3. Although there are broad areas of similarity, both boys and girls tend to adopt society's differentially prescribed sex roles (see Lee & Gropper, 1974). The male sex role generally incorporates characteristics such as dominance, aggressiveness, physical assertiveness, and large muscle mobility, as well as distinct preferences for certain objects, games, and activities. The traditional female sex role, on the other hand, emphasizes dependence, passivity, neatness, politeness, affiliative skills, and small motor dexterity, as well as toys and activities which allow for expression of these characteristics (see Kagan, 1964a; Sutton-Smith & Savasta, 1972; Ross & Ross, 1972).

THE INTERACTION OF SEX ROLE AND PUPIL ROLE

An examination of the characteristics of sex role and pupil role indicates that there is an uncanny correspondence between pupil role and the female sex role, while the exact opposite holds for the relationship between pupil role and the male sex role. One would expect, then, that boys would have a more difficult time adjusting to school than girls. The available evidence seems to bear this out, even at the early childhood levels. One nationwide study, for example, found that girls have much higher promotion rates from first to second grade than boys. Of 402 schools surveyed, 73.2% reported higher rates for girls, 23.6% reported no difference, and only 3.2% had higher rates for boys (AASA, 1958). Another study, conducted in Maryland, found that girls are referred to extra-classroom specialists much less frequently than boys are, *especially at first grade* where the referral ratio is three boys to every girl (Bentzen, 1966). A recent survey of the Boston school system discovered that boys constituted 62% of children in classes for the mentally retarded, and that they probably accounted for approximately 70% of the false positives assigned to these classes. The same survey found that, in the five to seven year age range, 33% more boys than girls are "excluded" from school (Task Force, 1970, pp. 38-40, 82).

Moreover, first-grade boys receive more criticism from teachers than do first-grade girls, while the two sexes receive about the same amount of praise (Brophy & Good, 1970). At the preschool level, however, Biber, Miller, and Dyer (1972) found that girls received more positive reinforcement than boys did. Another preschool study observed that boys were significantly more disruptive than girls and that boys received three times as many "loud reprimands" from their teachers as did girls (Serbin, O'Leary, Kent & Tonick, 1973). McNeil (1964) and Davis and Slobodian (1967) found that first-grade children were apparently aware of these differences in treatment, since they perceived boys as receiving more negative comments from teachers than girls received. Finally, Gregersen and Travers (1968) asked first and second graders to draw pictures of their teachers. As might be expected, two out of three boys produced drawings expressing negative feelings toward their teachers, while the opposite ratio held for girls.

One might attribute these differences in school adjustment to the relative social and physiological immaturity of boys as contrasted with girls. For example, Bentzen (1966) estimates that at the time of entry into first grade, girls are approximately one year ahead of boys in general maturity. Yet boys and girls are officially expected to meet approximately the same standards of performance. This marked difference in maturity doubtlessly accounts for some portion of the total variance between boys and girls in initial school adjustment; but we are still left with the striking incongruity between sex role and pupil role for boys and the equally marked congruity between the roles for young girls. Moreover, sex-role differences between boys and girls are not a function of maturity, but of cultural indoctrination. Boys, at whatever level of maturity, seem to have difficulty in coordinating the conflicting demands of sex role and pupil role. This conflict leads to demonstrable stress, starting at the earliest school levels.

The foregoing might seem to imply that schooling is a benign experience for young girls. On the contrary, the close match between sex and pupil roles for the typical young girl carries its own problems which, on balance, may be more pernicious than the problems experienced by boys. There are three studies which shed light on the young girl's status in school, one concerned with teacher expectations, and two with teacher behaviors.

Levitin and Chananie (1972) found that first-and second-grade teachers perceived boys as being "typically" more aggressive than girls, and girls as being more dependent, revealing traditional sex-role expectations. Moreover, the same teachers significantly *approved* of achievement and dependent behaviors over aggressive behaviors, regardless of sex of child, indicating their pupil-role expectations. The teachers *liked* dependent girls more than aggressive girls, but did not like dependent boys more than aggressive boys. Thus all three judgments converged for girls, while diverging for boys.

Two other studies indicate that these expectations are reflected in the teacher's behavior with children, even at the preschool level. Fagot and Patterson (1969) empirically identified a repertoire of "sex-role behaviors" among 36 nursery school children. They then observed four nursery school teachers and found that 97 and 86% of the sex-role behaviors reinforced in girls and boys, respectively, were female-typed. The effect of this consistent reinforcement schedule was that boys adopted cross-sex-typed behaviors almost twice as frequently as did girls, although for both sexes the proportion of cross-sex-typed behavior was small (13.5 and 7.6%, respectively). Serbin *et al.* (1973) essentially corroborated and extended these results by finding that nursery school teachers were highly reinforcing of various dependent behaviors in both boys and girls. One interesting difference was that teachers attended more to physically proximal girls than to girls in distant parts of the classroom whereas boys received the same amount of attention regardless of their distance from the teacher. To the degree that physical distance is an index of independence, this latter finding would seem to indicate that teachers foster greater dependency in girls than in boys. Moreover, boys were found to be about three times as "disruptive" as girls and received about nine times as many teacher reprimands as girls for their disruptiveness. If one were to view disruptive behaviors as assertions of autonomy, then boys were obviously receiving more teacher attention (i.e., reinforcement) for autonomy than girls were. Most teachers, however, probably do not realize that their reprimands often reinforce precisely those behaviors they would prefer to eliminate.

These studies indicate that nursery school teachers both expect and reinforce appropriate pupil-role behaviors in children, irrespective of sex, although their reinforcement procedures appear to be more successful with girls than with boys. Teachers apparently have different sex-role expectations for boys and girls, and are, in fact, faced with real differences in the sex-typed behavior of boys and girls. The typical teacher's expectations for pupil role interact with her[2] expectations about sex role so that she is defensively sensitized to marked discrepancies between the two and tranquilized by interrole correspondence.

[2]All 59 teachers used as subjects in these three studies were female. Whether or not the preponderance of females among early childhood teachers is a significant factor in the

Thus, the relatively poor fit between pupil role and sex role for boys leads to ongoing stress and conflict in the educational setting. Girls, on the other hand, are victimized by the close fit between pupil role and their traditional sex role. They are, in a sense, locked into cumulatively reinforcing cycles of conformity, docility, and dependence and many eventually come to accept receptivity as the proper stance for learning. While schooling may be a more benign experience for girls than for boys over the short run, boys usually resist full indoctrination to receptive modes of learning. The long-term implications of the typical girl's relatively easy accommodation to pupil role are probably counterindicative of her ever becoming a fully active learner.

LEARNING AS AN ACTIVE PROCESS

The above analysis argues that pupil role subsumes all other roles associated with school and that, due to its demands for conforming and manageable behavior, it predisposes children more toward receptive than active modes of learning. This critique of pupil role is based on the assumption that there is some special value to "active learning" and that educators have a clear idea of what it is. Our suspicion is that most advocates of active learning have simply asserted rather than demonstrated its superiority and that, at least during the last decade, it has been defined more as a reference point for polemics and contention than as a denotable way of acquiring information about the world. Accordingly, if our case against pupil role is to have anything more than intuitive value, we must first specify what active learning is and, second, cite evidence and theory which would indicate its superiority to receptive learning.

In attempting to define what is meant by "active learning" it is helpful to review the ideas of three noted theorists in the development and education of children. Over 70 years ago, in his famous essay, "The Child and the Curriculum," Dewey (1956) reminded us that "subject-matter never can be got into the child from without. Learning is active. It involves reaching out of the mind. It involves organic assimilation starting from within [p. 9]." Thirty years ago, Montessori (1967) wrote about the interaction of learning and activity in young children:

> When mental development is under discussion, there are many who say, "How does movement come into it? We are talking about the mind." And when we think of intellectual activity, we always imagine people sitting still, motionless. But mental development must be connected with movement and be dependent on it. It is vital that educational theory and practice should become informed by this idea [pp. 141-142].

---

sex-role ecology of the school is a matter of conjecture (Lee, 1973). However, since 98% of teachers at grades three and below are female, these samples would seem to be representative of the sex distribution in the population of early childhood teachers (NEA Research Division, 1971-72, 1972).

Montessori believed that bodily movement was somehow "connected" with mental development and Dewey wrote in terms of a "reaching. . . mind," but neither had a fully articulated theory which adequately described in what sense the mind was active. More recently, Piaget has fashioned an epistemological system which postulates that the human intellect operates on reality in a manner analagous to sensory-motor manipulation. In young children, mental operations are mapped upon perceptual-motor manipulations of objects, which, in turn, are external manifestations of the very same mental actions they serve to develop (Piaget & Inhelder, 1971). This does not mean that perceptual-motor manipulations are necessary to each and every mental operation. It simply means that, in the long run, the child's covert mental activity proceeds best when he has the option of physically manipulating the world in ways which are spontaneously his own. Dewey, Montessori, and Piaget, then, would seem to agree that the young child's learning should be a mobile, proactive engagement of reality and that enforced receptivity would interfere with effective and meaningful learning.

There have been a number of studies on the relationship between perceptual-motor activity and young children's performance on simple tasks. Goodnow (1969), for example, found that kindergartners were able to suggest more unusual uses for objects when they were allowed to handle and look at them than when they were restricted to looking only. The ability to generate nonstandard uses is generally regarded as an index of "creative" or divergent thinking. Other studies have indicated the contribution of manipulation to *convergent* modes of thinking. For example, Wolff and his colleagues have found that children learn paired-associates better when they actively manipulate the objects to be paired than when they are confined to observing manipulation by another person (e.g., a peer or a teacher). These results would indicate that active engagement of materials is associated with better performance on both divergent and convergent tasks than is simple reception of information. That is, experimental treatments which encourage subjects to approximate pupil role are less effective than those which allow for more active modes of thinking (Wolff & Levin, 1972; Wolff, Levin, & Longobardi, 1974).

Active learning can thus be defined as learning which is mediated by active thinking in the Piagetian sense. In young children mental activity is usually (but not always) accompanied by some form of physical activity since these actions serve as mutual guidance and marking systems. Accordingly, if one observes a group of young children and finds that they are not actively, spontaneously, and physically manipulating their environment, one can probably infer that they are not thinking actively. Such children are probably more disposed to receptive than to active modes of learning.

It would seem that the kind of active learning proposed here corresponds fairly well with the degree of mobility and object manipulation found in most preschool settings, that it is somewhat less evident in kindergarten, and that it is generally considered counterindicative of effective learning by most first- and second-grade teachers. Thus, the typical child, as he moves through the early childhood grades, probably begins as a relatively active learner, gradually adjusts his learning style to the demands of pupil role, and ends as a less active and less efficient learner than he was at the outset. The irony of this socialization to pupil role is that it is inconsistent with clear evidence of the superiority of active modes of learning for both convergent and divergent outcomes. Unfortunately, practitioners often view "activity" of any kind as preliminary to chaos, despite the conclusions of respected theorists and researchers to the contrary. Teachers are apparently unwilling to risk the benefits of active learning because of its presumed association with lessened classroom control.

RECOMMENDATIONS FOR EDUCATIONAL POLICY

Teachers' professional behavior is a function of their training, their working conditions, and their individual sensibilities. The last would seem to be beyond policy recommendations, but we do have recommendations regarding teacher training and working conditions as they relate to the issues discussed in this paper.

Teacher Training

There is a basic body of knowledge which ought to be included at both the preservice and in-service levels as a systematic and integral part of teacher training. First, teacher trainees should be given general anthropological information about the school as an institution. To be fully effective, any professional, whether a tax accountant or a teacher, must know the folkways of the system within which he works. It is not enough that a tax accountant, for example, be able to compute deductions and fill in tax forms; to be truly professional, he must understand the tax code and know how to manipulate the subtle realities of taxation to work for, rather than against, his client. Similarly, a professional teacher must know more than methods, materials, and content; she must know the code of the school so she can use it to the benefit of her clients. General treatments of the school as an institution can be found in Jackson (1968), Silberman (1971), and Sarason (1971). There has been very little anthropological work on the early childhood setting per se, but one might want to begin with Shure (1963) and Jackson and Wolfson (1968).

In particular, teacher trainees should receive systematic instruction about the interaction of pupil role and sex role, and how these interactions lead to detrimental consequences for girls and boys. Trainees should also be exposed to pedagogical theory and research which compare active and receptive modes of learning, and should be encouraged to relate to children as learners rather than pupils.

Finally, teacher trainees should familiarize themselves with the principles of behavioral analysis and techniques of behavior change in order to avoid the common pitfall of fostering precisely those behaviors they wish to discourage. On this last point, we are aware that there are potential dangers in the misapplication of behavioral techniques, and we are not recommending that teachers indiscriminately use systematic reinforcement with any and all children (see Katz, 1972a). But there are also potential risks in allowing people to become teachers of young children when they are unaware of both the reasons for much of what they do in the classroom and the possible consequences. Teachers should know about the folkways of the school, about the realities of sex role and pupil role, and about the contingencies of human behavior; and colleges of education should assume responsibility for imparting this basic knowledge.

Beyond the content of teacher training, there is the matter of training format. It would seem imperative that the formal presentation of knowledge just recommended be accompanied by group discussions and workshops. Such seminars could be a vehicle for trainees' analysis of their own roles as actual or potential teachers and of their place in the overall workings of the school as an institution.

One item for analysis would be the teacher's dual role of custodian and educator. In her custodial role she views the child as a pupil, that is, a consumer of school-based experience. But when the teacher educates she engages the child as a learner, as a producer of educational experience. A second item for analysis would be the teacher's *apparent* dominance in the classroom, a myth which dissolves rather quickly under careful scrutiny. Teachers, for example, are usually tacticians who implement the strategies of curriculum experts. Moreover, their posture in the classroom is essentially reactive rather than proactive. Their behavior is often influenced by the behavior of children and this is particularly true where there is one adult (the teacher) who is responding to 20 or 25 children (see Yarrow, Waxler, & Scott, 1971). A final and related agenda item would require that teachers analyze their own modeling value for children. It is enlightening to observe children "playing teacher"—and also embarrassing. Apparently, teachers' most obvious behaviors are managerial and disciplinary in nature. Thus, it would be advisable for teachers to reconstruct themselves as models of active learning. This would put them in more active control of their own classroom experience, enhance their appeal to children, and attach value and prestige to active modes of learning. Unless teachers are helped to develop a pedagogical strategy which is firmly grounded in an awareness of institutional folkways and the contingencies of human behavior, they will continue to expend primary energies in the management of minor crises, rather than in the creation of educational experiences.

School Reform

Sweeping proposals for school reform are usually futile because they threaten the basic structure of the institution and fail to recognize that much of what goes on in school is unintended. Thus, the most profound criticism of the school usually evokes the institution's most obtuse response. For this reason, our recommendations are modest and specific.

The school should attempt to provide teachers with at least the rudiments of a professional support system. This means, first, that teachers should have access to expert supervisory input. Such support would be especially important to new teachers who, feeling constrained to establish their own professional adequacy, are particularly prone to impose inflexible versions of pupil role on their students. The purpose of supervisory support would be to move inexperienced teachers through the "survival stage" as expeditiously as possible. Some innovative school systems have teacher resource centers and a cadre of roving supervisory personnel. It would be desirable to have all schools provide the same support to their teachers. Second, some attempt should be made to reduce the isolation of teachers through the provision of time and space for group discussion of common institutional and professional problems (see Sarason, 1971, pp. 105-108). These discussions would probably be facilitated by representatives of resource centers or by educational directors who could keep the sessions goal directed and task oriented as well as provide constructive feedback. The point of these two recommendations is to help teachers achieve conscious and purposeful control over their classroom behavior and to promote continuity between training and professional practice. Such continuity can be achieved only if the school supports the teacher's efforts to translate her training into application.

The key to school reform lies in finding permeable points in the structure of the institution. One such point is the consciousness of the teacher. We can safely assume that most teachers would want to open, rather than close, experiential options to their children, if only they knew how. Therefore, we have placed our greatest emphasis on getting teachers to know what they are doing and why they do it. This is the essence of professionalism and may well be the best hope for eradicating those aspects of pupil role which are most detrimental to young children.

SUMMARY

Schools for young children do not play a disproportionate role in socializing them to sexist expectations or stereotypic values. Most other childhood institutions are at least as responsible as schools for such socialization. What makes schools unique is that they constitute the young child's first contact with formal, group-based learning. In order to manage large numbers of involuntary, partially socialized children, each with his own set of individual differences, schools have invented a cultural vehicle, which we have defined as pupil role. Examination of the few studies available indicates that pupil role is in effect at the earliest levels of schooling, including nursery school.

Pupil role places first priority on conformity and receptivity as the proper stance for school-based learning. As such, it ignores theory and research which holds that learning is facilitated by activity and inhibited by passivity. Pupil role also corresponds very poorly with the male sex role, thus making for ongoing stress and conflict between young boys and their schools. Ironically enough, young girls are victimized by pupil role for precisely the opposite reason. The close correspondence between pupil role and the traditional female sex role seduces most girls into becoming well-behaved students and receptive learners. The short-to-medium-range implications of these role interactions are probably more damaging for boys. Girls, however, probably suffer more over the long run due to the relatively dysfunctional modes of learning they adopt. It would seem that both sexes would benefit from considerable loosening of the constraints imposed by pupil role.

REFERENCES

American Association of School Administrators and Research Division of the NEA. Pupil promotion policies and rates of promotion. *Educational Research Service Circular*, No. 5, 1958, Washington. D. C.

Bentzen, F. Sex ratios in learning and behavior disorders. *National Elementary Principal*, 1966, *46* (2), 13-17.

Biber, H., Miller, L., & Dyer, J. Feminization in preschool. *Developmental Psychology*, 1972, *7*, 86.

Brophy, J. E., & Good, T. L. Teachers' communication of differential expectations for children's classroom performance: Some behavioral data. *Journal of Educational Psychology*, 1970, *61*, 365-374.

Brophy, J. E., & Good, T. L. *Teacher-student relationships: Causes and consequences*. New York: Holt, Rinehart, & Winston, 1974.

Davis, O. L., & Slobodian, J. Teacher behavior toward boys and girls during first-grade reading instruction. *American Educational Research Journal*, 1967, *4*, 261-269.

Dewey, J. *The child and the curriculum and the school and society*. Chicago: University Of Chicago Press, 1956.

Engelmann, S., Osborne, J., & Engelmann, T. *Distar language program*. Chicago: Science Research Associates, 1972.

Fagot, B. I., & Patterson, G. R. An in vivo analysis of reinforcing contingencies for sex role behaviors in the preschool child. *Developmental Psychology*, 1969, *1*, 563-568.

Feshbach, N. D. Student teacher preferences for elementary school pupils varying in personality characteristics. *Journal of Educational Psychology*, 1969, *60*, 126-132.

Fuller, F. F. Concerns of teachers: A developmental conceptualization. *American Educational Research Journal*, 1969, *6*, 207-226.

Gesell, A., Halverson, H. M., Thompson, H., Ilg, F. L., Costner, B. M., Ames, L. B., & Amatruda, C. S. *The first five years of life: A guide to the study of the preschool child.* New York: Harper, 1940.

Goldberg, S., & Lewis, M. Play behavior in the year old infant: Early sex differences. *Child Development*, 1969, *40*, 21-31.

Goodnow, J. J. Effects of active handling, illustrated by uses for objects. *Child Development*, 1969, *40*, 201-212.

Gregersen, G. F., & Travers, R. M. A study of the child's concept of the teacher. *The Journal of Educational Research*, 1968, *61*, 324-327.

Jackson, P. W. *Life in classrooms*. New York: Holt, Rinehart, & Winston, 1968.

Jackson, P. W., & Wolfson, B. J. Varieties of constraint in a nursery school. *Young Children*, 1968, *23*, 358-367.

Kagan, J. Acquisition and significance of sex typing and sex role identity. In M. L. Hoffman & L. W. Hoffman (Eds.), *Review of child development research*, Vol. 1. New York: Russell Sage Foundation, 1964. (a)

Kagan, J. The child's sex role classification of school objects. *Child Development*, 1964, *35*, 1051-1056. (b)

Katz, L. G. Condition with caution. *Young Children*, 1972, *27*, 277-280. (a)

Katz, L. G. Developmental stages of preschool teachers. *The Elementary School Journal*, 1972, *73*, 50-54. (b)

La Belle, T. J., & Rust, V. D. Control mechanisms and their justifications in preschool classrooms. *Small Group Behavior*, 1973, *4*, 35-46.

Lee, P. C. Male and female teachers in elementary schools: An ecological analysis. *Teachers College Record*, 1973, *75*, 79-98.

Lee, P. C., & Gropper, N. B. Sex-role culture and educational practice. *Harvard Educational Review*, 1974, *44*, 369-410.

Levitin, T. E., & Chananie, J. D. Responses of female primary school teachers to sex-typed behaviors in male and female children. *Child Development*, 1972, *43*, 1309-1316.

Maccoby, E. E. (Ed.). *The development of sex differences*. Stanford, California: Stanford University Press, 1966.

McNeil, J. D. Programmed instruction versus usual classroom procedures in teaching boys to read. *American Educational Research Journal*, 1964, *1*, 113-119.

Montessori, M. *The absorbent mind*. New York: Holt, Rinehart, & Winston, 1967.

NEA Research Division (or Research Division of NEA). *Estimates of school statistics, 1971-72*, (1971-R13, NEA). Washington, D. C. pp. 13-14.

NEA Research Division. New profile of the American public school teacher. *Today's Education*, 1972, *61* (5), 14-17.

Paley, V. Is the doll corner a sexist institution? *School Review*, 1973, *81*, 569-576.

Piaget, J., & Inhelder, B. *Mental imagery and the child*. New York: Basic Books, 1971.

Ross, D. M., & Ross, S. A. Resistance by preschool boys to sex-inappropriate behavior. *Journal of Educational Psychology*, 1972, *63*, 342-346.

Saario, T. N., Jacklin, C. N., & Tittle, C. K. Sex role stereotyping in the public schools. *Harvard Educational Review*, 1973, *43*, 386-416.

Sarason, S. B. *The culture of the school and the problem of change.* Boston: Allyn & Bacon, 1971.

Serbin, L. A., O'Leary, K. D., Kent, R. N., & Tonick, I. J. A comparison of teacher response to the preacademic and problem behavior of boys and girls. *Child Development*, 1973, *44*, 796-804.

Shure, M. B. Psychological ecology of a nursery school. *Child Development*, 1963, *34*, 979-992.

Silberman, M. L. (Ed.). *The experience of schooling*. New York: Holt, Rinehart & Winston, 1971.

Sutton-Smith, B., & Savasta, M. Sex differences in play and power. Paper presented at the annual meeting of the Eastern Psychological Association, Boston, Massachusetts, April, 1972.

Task Force on Children out of School. *The way we go to school: The exclusion of children in Boston*. Boston: Beacon Press, 1970.

Wolff, P., & Levin, J. R. The role of overt activity in children's imagery production. *Child Development*, 1972, *43*, 537-548.

Wolff, P., Levin, J. R., & Longobardi, E. T. Activity and children's learning. *Child Development*, 1974, *45*, 221-223.

Yarrow, M. R., Waxler, C. Z., & Scott, P. M. Child effects on adult behavior. *Developmental Psychology*, 1971, *5*, 300-311.

6

Relations between Piagetian and Psychometric Assessments of Intelligence[1]

Rheta DeVries

University of Illinois at Chicago Circle

Lawrence Kohlberg

Harvard University

Since the mid 1960s, many researchers have been evaluating federally funded early education programs by studying changes in children's IQ. A strong impetus to this approach was the book *Intelligence and Experience*, published in 1961, in which J. M. Hunt suggested that large increases in children's IQs could be achieved through early stimulation and education. Hunt presented Piaget's interactional stage theory as a central justification for his conclusion that intelligence is not genetically fixed and may be modified by experience.

We questioned the use of Piaget's theory as a valid basis for new hopes or new approaches to raising IQ because the psychometric conception of intelligence is basically different from Piaget's. Let us first examine these two conceptions.

The psychometric conception of intelligence is characterized by two basic related assumptions: the Binet assumption and the Spearman assumption. The assumption reflected in Binet's operational definition of intelligence was that it was represented by school success. Thus, he chose test items which simultaneously discriminated older children from younger and discriminated children whom teachers thought able from those they thought not able. Binet's intent was to avoid achievement items which he believed contaminated by motivation and other nonintellectual components. Rather, Binet's strategy called for avoiding achievement items in a test which would predict achievement. This strategy led Binet to define intelligence in terms of individual differences on a wide variety of items which have no theoretical significance in themselves (that

[1]An earlier draft of this paper was presented in March, 1969, at a conference on "The Natural Curriculum of the Child," held in Urbana, Illinois. We thank Dr. Dorothe Weinberg and Dr. Constance Kamii for their helpful suggestions.

is, one cannot conclude anything about a child's general intelligence from his response to a single item).

The Spearman assumption was that the term "intelligence" represented a general hereditary capacity (*g*) which would be reflected by a significant level of positive correlation on all tests of intelligence. Spearman's strategy was thus to maximize the role of *g* by using novel tasks and randomized sampling which presumably reduce the effects of training and experience.While Spearman recognized the role of *s* (specific ability in a task), he deliberately attempted to minimize the effect of *s* in his measurements of intelligence. Both the Binet and Spearman assumptions led to assessment based on the number of right answers the child gives, relative to other children of the same chronological age.

In contrast with these psychometric assumptions about intelligence, Piaget views intelligence in terms of an individual's place in a universal and invariant sequence of development toward formal operational reasoning. He came to this view as a result of research aimed at the epistemological issue of how knowledge develops. For this research, Piaget and his collaborators in Geneva devised tasks with which to study how children view and reason about such aspects of reality as space, time, substance, dreams, etc. Thus, these tasks have theoretical significance, and each in itself reveals something important about the individual's general development of his intelligence. (In fact, Piaget deliberately avoided school-type subject matter in his tasks because he found children responded with a lot of verbalism which he termed "school varnish," rather than with convictions.) In further contrast with psychometric methods, moreover, assessment with Piagetian tasks is not limited to consideration of right versus wrong answers, but includes assessment of kinds of wrong answers as well. Piaget and his co-workers have found that some "wrong" answers are more advanced developmentally than some right ones.

On the issue of heredity, Piaget says the following:

> First, obviously genetic factors play a role in the development of intelligence. But they can do no more than open certain possibilities. They cannot do anything about actualizing these possibilities. That is, there are no innate structures in the human mind which simply come into being; . . . all our mental structures must be constructed. So genetic factors or maturational aspects are not adequate for explaining what really takes place at any given stage [Evans, 1973, pp. 31-32].

Piaget places innateness, the hereditary program, as only one of four factors in intellectual development. He (Piaget, 1972) also cites an active interaction among (1) the physical environment, (2) social transmission, and (3) equilibration, in addition to heredity. Moreover, Piaget views intelligence as integrated with personality and socioemotional development. He points out (Piaget, 1965)[2]

> . . . the important and essential problem for pedagogy, of the methods of estimating a student's intellectual value and his particular personal aptitudes. The term "intel-

[2]References to Piaget's publications are dated according to their first appearance in French. Quotations, however, are from English translations, listed in the References.

lectual value" is to be taken here in the very broadest sense, since it is obvious that thorough work habits, an inventive disposition, etc., are as much the result of character, emotional balance, and social behavior as they are of intelligence, imagination, and memory: it is not difficult, for example, to find individuals in scientific circles who possess everything needed to achieve brilliant success except self-discipline, application, ability to make choices, etc. What then are the methods that will enable us to judge and, even more important, to predict the effective work of an individual subject, and especially of a child or adolescent [pp. 106-107]?

Further, the Genevan perspective on intelligence includes a recognition of individual differences in rate of development. For example, Inhelder (1943) studied children (and some adults) classified as retardates on the basis of IQ and found that Genevan tasks could differentiate between children who eventually became formal operational (but whose rate of development was slow) and true retardates who never progressed past the concrete operational stage.

Given the opposition of Piaget's conception of intelligence to the psychometric conception, it seems implausible that IQ tests would reflect changes in intellectual development on Piagetian tasks.[3] What intrigued us was the possibility that Piagetian measures might be psychometrized to provide a more useful assessment of psychoeducational efforts than the IQ test. Indeed, Laurendeau and Pinard (1962) have also made such a suggestion. The intent of the study reported here is to explore this possibility.

Although Piaget has never recommended that his tasks be used as measures of individual differences, it is clear in the following quotations that he expects his tasks to define basic thought structure better than psychometric tests:

It is indisputable that these tests of mental age have on the whole lived up to what was expected of them: a rapid and convenient estimation of an individual's general level. But it is no less obvious that they simply measure a 'yield,' without reaching constructive operations themselves. As Pieron rightly pointed out, intelligence conceived in these terms is essentially a value-judgment applied to complex behavior . . . Inhelder was able to distinguish moronism from imbecility by the presence of concrete groupings (of which the imbecile is not capable) and slight backwardness by an inability to reason formally. This is one of the first applications of a method which could be developed further for determining level of intelligence in general [Piaget, 1947, pp. 153-155].

. . . Is intelligence measured only on the basis of some performance, or are we really getting at the competence, the internal structure? I am afraid that in studies of this sort (Jenson, 1969) people have always measured performance, and it is quite obvious that performance will vary according to the social environment. For my part, I have no faith in measures that are based on intelligence quotients or on any other performance measure [Evans, 1973, pp. 31-32].

However, if the development of a Piagetian scale is possible and/or desirable, it must first be demonstrated that it would meet the minimal condition of measuring something distinguishable from the psychometric tests now in existence.

[3]The theoretical background of the study reported here will be discussed at greater length in *Early education: A cognitive-developmental view*, by L. Kohlberg (Aldine, in press).

Thus, we set out in this research to study the empirical relationships between Piagetian and psychometric conceptions of intelligence. Basically, the issue addressed in the study reported here is: Do Piagetian tasks simply measure in a different way what is measured by the general factor (*g*) found on psychometric tests? Or, do they measure something distinguishable?

METHOD

Subjects. Subjects were 67 middle-class white kindergarten children enrolled in the University of Chicago Laboratory School and first-grade children enrolled in a suburban public school. The rationale for this selection was that the sample would represent a range of psychometric ability from average to above average, and that it would represent the presumed age of transition to concrete operations.

Procedure. Psychometric tests or subtests were selected to represent the distinguishable mental abilities often reported by those following Thurstone and Guilford. In Table 1 the factors reported at age 6 are indicated (Thurstone, 1938; Guilford, 1954; Meyers, Orpet, Atwell, & Dingman, 1962; McCartin, 1963), and the marker tests we included in our battery. In Table 2 the Piaget-type tasks included are listed. All tasks were individually administered. (See Appendix A for a summary of procedures used in the Piaget-type tasks.)

Analysis. Each subject's performance on the psychometric tests was assessed by means of mental age, using published norms for each test. Performance on Piaget-type tasks was assessed by means of Guttman scales constructed for each task (see Appendix A for scaling and scoring details). Product-moment correlations among all tasks were obtained, and factor analyses were performed (unrotated and varimax rotations).

RESULTS

The product-moment correlations among tasks are shown in Table 3. Since the correlations among Piagetian tasks were high enough to warrant a factor-analytic search for consistency, this analysis was then undertaken. In Table 4 unrotated factor loadings and loadings resulting from an orthogonal varimax rotation are shown. Four factors are listed, although the fourth factor is extremely weak, and therefore questionable.[4] Hence, we will discuss only the first three factors.

[4]The first general mental age factor accounts for 35% of the variance; the second, 12%; the third, 9%; the fourth, 6%; with several more hovering around 5% with equivalences around one.

TABLE 1
Tests Representing Primary Mental Abilities[a]
at Mental Age 6

I. Linguistic
- V. Vocabulary and comprehension of verbal meaning
  1. Quick Test—a picture vocabulary test (Ammons & Ammons, 1962; McCartin, 1963)
  2. W.I.S.C. Information Subtest (Wechsler, 1963; McCartin, 1963)
- W. Verbal fluency
  3. Monroe classification test (Monroe, 1935)
     "Tell me as many things to eat (toys, etc.) as you can (in 30 sec)" (McCartin, 1963; Meyers *et al.*)
- M. Immediate memory (P)
  4. Digit Span, Stanford Binet Form L-M (Terman & Merrill, 1960)

II. Reasoning
- R. Verbal reasoning
  5. W.I.S.C. Comprehension (McCartin, 1963)
  6. W.I.S.C. Similarities (McCartin, 1963)
- R. Spatial reasoning
  7. Raven's Matrices, colored board from (Raven, 1956; Meyers *et al.*)

III. Psychomotor
- M. Hand-eye psychomotor
  8. Line Drawing (Thurstone & Thurstone, 1954)
     "Draw lines from the top dot to the bottom dot as quickly as you can—timed 60 sec"
- P. Perceptual speed
  9. Pacific Perceptual Speed (Meyers *et al.*, 1962)
     "Mark the one geometric figure that looks like that one" – 60 sec. Meyers *et al.*
  10. Total mental age (sum of tests 1–9 based on converting raw scores on each task to mental age equivalents)

[a] Abilities defined by studies of Thurstone (1938), Meyers, Dingman, Atwell, and Orpet (1962), and McCartin (1963).

The first rotated factor is defined by all the psychometric tests, with loadings ranging from .59 to .97. The Piaget-type tasks divided into two factors. The first Piagetian factor (including object sorting, class inclusion, objective responsibility, and causality of dreams and magic) is a classification and causal reasoning factor. The second Piagetian factor is a conservation factor with an additional high loading on the sex identity task.

The unrotated results indicate a first factor of general intelligence including both psychometric and Piagetian tasks, but more heavily loaded on the psychometric tasks. The second and third factors are common only to Piaget-type tasks.

DISCUSSION

The results of this study indicate that Piaget-type developmental stage tasks measure something in common with each other that is distinguishable from *g*. Studies done subsequently (DeVries, 1974; Hathaway, 1973; Stephens, 1972; Stephens, McLaughlin, Miller, & Glass, 1972) support this conclusion. In the present study, it is particularly significant that when primary mental abilities are included in a factor analysis with Piagetian tasks, primary-mental-abilities tests define a single factor. Thus, it seems that Piagetian tasks are even more distinctive than the usual psychometric factors are from one another.

This basic finding contradicts Hunt's theoretical marriage of psychometric and Piagetian conceptions of intelligence, and calls into question his expectation that early stimulation and education will necessarily bring increases in children's *psychometric* intelligence. In fact, most of the research in recent years on the effects of preschool programs has indicated that changes on IQ scores do not persist beyond the second or third grade (see White, Day, Freeman, Hantman, & Messenger, 1972, for review and summary of these studies).

TABLE 2
Piaget-Type Tasks

IV.	Conservation tasks	
	11.	Length conservation–movement
	12.	Area conservation–ring segment illusion
	13.	Liquid conservation
	14.	Number conservation
V.	Generic identity tasks	
	15.	Sex
	16.	Age
VI.	Classification	
	17.	Object-sorting tasks
	18.	Class inclusion
VII.	Causal thinking	
	19.	Dreams
	20	Magic
VIII.	Moral judgment	
	21	Objective versus subjective responsibility
	22.	Sanctions versus rules orientation

The psychoeducational issue concerns the meaning and use of Piaget-type tasks for assessing individual differences. We should note first that our results suggest the Piagetian tasks will not be better tests of psychometric intelligence than are psychometric tests themselves. The fact that the Piagetian tasks do not well define *g* indicates that they will not cover the correlational ground that a good test of *g* does. Piagetian tasks would not be expected to match psychometric tests with regard to their success in long-range prediction of IQ and school success. However, by using items linked with school achievement, Binet opened a Pandora's box in the culture's conception of cognitive growth or cognitive education. Essentially the IQ tests introduced a relativistic criterion of intellectual competence. Intellectual competence is not defined by a basic set of operations or achievements, but by position on the normal curve. The rudderless nature of educational aims which results from this conception of intelligence is well expressed by Edward Zigler's facetious statement that the official aim of compensatory education in the United States is to bring 100% of the population above the 50th percentile on IQ and achievement tests!

Despite the predictive success of psychometric tests, McClelland (1973) recently challenged the validity of IQ tests as measures of intelligence. His review of the literature led him to argue convincingly that the high correlations between IQ scores and various measures of occupational success or life adjustment are likely due to social class rather than to intelligence.

It should be noted, too, that the kinds of achievement tests used to validate IQ tests have also been under attack recently. It might seem that school achievement test items are more significant than psychometric items because achievement tests are intended to assess whether children have learned what teachers have tried to teach them. However, Kohlberg and Mayer (1973) reviewed the literature and found that school achievement only predicts further school achievement and fails to predict anything else of value (such as occupational success).

Thus, if the value of the kinds of school achievement used to validate the IQ is questioned, then the validity of the IQ itself must be questioned. The crumbling assumptions that an IQ score represents intelligence and that school achievement prepares children for later success lead to a demand for alternatives in testing theory and practice. Kohlberg and Mayer (1973) suggest that Piagetian measures provide a more rational basis for evaluation of educational intervention than psychometric intelligence tests. This alternative suggestion is congruent with McClelland's (1973) less specific advocacy of tests with scores which "change as the person grows in experience, wisdom, and ability to perform effectively on various tasks that life presents to him [p. 8]." Therefore, the Piagetian alternative to psychometric methods seems worth examining.

Piagetian tasks are significant because they represent natural and culturally universal general sequential organizations of the child's world. They are important because they reflect the child's construction of his world. Because the

TABLE 3
Product-Moment Correlation Matrix

	Quick test 1	Information 2	Monroe class 3	Digit span 4	Comprehension 5	Similarities 6	Raven matrices 7
I. Linguistic							
1. Quick test		.82	.39	.43	.59	.75	.61
2. Information	.70		.42	.32	.33	.59	.58
3. Monroe classification	.56	.57		.20	.18	.28	.41
4. Digit span	.36	.45	.39		.25	.33	.24
II. Reasoning							
5. Comprehension	.48	.46	.44	.45	.40	.43	.27
6. Similarities	.51	.57	.51	.47	.37		.46
7. Matrices	.62	.60	.54	.41		.52	
III. Psychomotor							
8. Line drawing	.63	.59	.62	.57	.36	.50	.50
9. Perceptual speed	.70	.72	.66	.50	.42	.63	.64
10. Mental age	.80	.81	.72	.71	.66	.77	.74
IV. Classical conservation							
11. Length	−.07	−.09	−.12	−.11	−.09	−.17	−.02
12. Area segment	.16	.25	.16	−.22	.21	.28	.11
13. Liquid	.20	.30	.12	.05	.10	.39	.36
14. Number	.14	.19	.25	.11	.10	.34	.24
V. Generic identity							
15. Sex	.16	.12	.18	.27	.23	.28	.20
16. Age	.47	.35	.31	.18	.06	.27	.40
VI. Classification							
17. Object sorting	.31	.21	.18	.29	.07	.30	.27
18. Class inclusion	.22	.22	.28	.12	.07	.29	.25
VII. Subjective causality							
19. Dream	.31	.24	.22	.22	.25	.40	.32
20. Magic	.18	.01	.20	.14	.18	.20	.19
VIII. Moral realism							
21. Objective responsibility	.39	.32	.33	.33	.34	.44	.47
22. Sanctions	.12	.08	.23	−.00	.12	.08	.18

Piagetian notion of intelligence is relative to an individual's place in a universal sequence of development rather than being relative to the performance of other individuals, it may provide a much more serviceable guide to education. A study by Kuhn, Langer, Kohlberg, and Haan (in press) indicates that at least on the pendulum and correlation tasks, only about 60% of adults are able to consistently use formal operational reasoning, and that many adults with high IQ are in this group. If formal operational reasoning is considered a desirable educational goal, then Piaget's theory and research may provide helpful guides to curriculum development and educational evaluation.

TABLE 3 (*continued*)
Product-Moment Correlation Matrix

ing	Perc. speed 9	Mental age 10	Length 11	Area ring 12	Liquid 13	Number 14	Sex 15	Age 16	Obj sort 17	Class inc. 18	Dream 19	Magic 20	Obj. res. 21	Sanc-tions 22
0	.66		−.27	−.06	.44	.37	−.07		.45	.32	.33	.05	.42	.13
5	.82		−.32	.05	.37	.16	−.04		.46	.24	.47	.07	.27	.05
7	.49		−.19	.22	.17	.23	−.03		.06	.11	.16	.28	.30	.22
7	.21		−.21	−.03	.04	.15	.21		.27	.11	.26	.06	.23	.07
3	.32		−.30	.01	.26	.18	.07		.11	.05	.01	.27	.36	.28
37	.53		−.48	.07	.39	.37	.05		.14	.27	.26	−.08	.53	.34
3	.51		−.03	−.01	.33	.32	.15		.17	.02	.23	.05	.27	.09
	.63		.03	−.05	.17	.07	−.02		.40	.19	.34	.07	.40	.04
73			−.27	.09	.23	.34	−.20		.33	.37	.14	.02	.30	.00
78	.84													
04	−.17	−.13		.11	.06	−.03	.29		.15	−.08	−.26	.01	−.47	−.17
06	.18	.26	−.02		.30	.09	.25		−.12	−.14	−.22	.18	.05	.19
14	.31	.30	.16	.36		.15	.18		−.01	.16	.20	.01	.16	.12
09	.25	.24	−.08	.07	.18		.06		.17	.11	.32	.05	.27	.36
08	.12	.26	.21	.65	.45	.16			.04	−.17	.03	.24	.09	−.03
39	.46	.40	−.09	−.16	.22	.07	−.11							
26	.25	.32	.08	−.08	.18	.11	.16	.59		.10	.13	.04	.02	−.02
27	.31	.28	−.06	−.13	.26	.18	.06	.46	.68		.07	.02	.18	.14
17	.22	.36	.02	−.04	.19	.40	.19	.29	.44	.31		.09	.16	.05
07	.13	.19	.11	.22	.20	.27	.30	.30	.48	.39	.33		.23	.18
31	.29	.48	−.11	.17	.29	.49	.34	.42	.51	.40	.52	.55		.14
06	−.03	.10	−.06	.09	.11	.40	.19	−.10	.17	.23	.31	.23	.43	

Whether it is possible or even desirable to develop a Piagetian scale of intelligence is debatable. Perhaps it is not possible to develop *any* single meaningful scale of intelligence. As researchers continue to ponder the problem of psycho-educational evaluation, however, we would like to point out Piaget's emphasis on the importance of knowing what it is we are trying to measure before we attempt to measure it. The following are illustrative of his comments in this regard:

> Psychology has too often chased the shadow instead of the fox by searching for applications, and more particularly for measurements, before understanding the

TABLE 4
Factor Loadings: Product-Moment Correlations[a]

	Unrotated				Varimax rotation			
	F_1	F_2	F_3	F_4	F_5	F_6	F_7	F_8
I. Linguistic								
1. Quick test	*77*	−26	−08	07	*79*	17	04	−0[illegible]
2. Information	*77*	−33	04	−04	*83*	00	08	−1[illegible]
3. Monroe	*72*	−23	07	−08	*74*	09	−01	−1[illegible]
4. Digit span	*63*	−22	07	03	*65*	04	13	−08
II. Reasoning								
5. Comprehension	*60*	−16	17	−21	*59*	−11	14	−2[illegible]
6. Similarities	*77*	−05	09	−05	*69*	13	20	−28
7. Matrices	*75*	−10	−04	02	*70*	20	11	−18
III. Psychomotor								
8. Line drawing	*71*	*−41*	−16	16	*82*	17	−04	12
9. Perceptual speed	*81*	−35	−08	06	*88*	13	02	−03
10. Mental age	*95*	−29	02	00	*97*	11	13	−16
IV. Classical conservation								
11. Length	−10	20	19	*49*	−20	24	*40*	26
12. Area ring	30	09	*79*	10	20	−26	*79*	−12
13. Liquid quantity	*41*	26	38	32	21	23	*61*	−08
14. Number	39	*42*	−03	*−46*	13	11	01	*−72*
V. Generic identity								
15. Sex	37	36	*66*	24	12	07	*85*	−19
16. Age	39	31	20	*−42*	17	−06	18	*−63*
VI. Classification								
17. Object sorting	*47*	*42*	*−46*	*43*	20	*86*	04	−08
18. Class inclusion	*44*	36	*−51*	30	21	*78*	−08	−13
VII. Subjective causality								
19. Dream concept	*51*	*45*	−20	−17	21	*42*	01	*−56*
20. Magical causality	37	*58*	−06	26	03	*60*	33	−28
VIII. Moral realism								
21. Objective responsibility	*66*	*51*	−09	−12	32	*46*	18	*−62*
22. Sanctions	27	*52*	−03	*−43*	−03	15	03	*−71*

[a] Loadings over .40 (generating significant correlations) *italicized.*

formative mechanisms and the significance of the factors measured [Piaget, 1965, 109].

In working out his intelligence tests, Binet had the excellent idea of applying them to the most diverse functions, convinced that intelligence is everywhere and constitutes a sort of summation of all cognitive activities. But when afterwards he was asked what intelligence was, he replied with ready wit: "It is what my tests measure," a very wise reaction but a little disturbing when one thinks of the theoretical knowledge acquired by the instrument of measurement thus constructed. A physicist, on the contrary, does not measure a form of energy until a far more thorough theoretical study has been made of what is to be measured and of the instrument of measurement itself.

. . . it is important to diagnose not so much what the subject can do when undergoing the test, as what he would be capable of doing in many other situations. Intelligence was therefore "measured" long before it was known what it consists of, and we are only just beginning to have some inkling of the complexity of its nature and functioning [Piaget, 1970, p. 59].

In summary, the findings of this study contribute to a growing body of literature which indicates the need to reassess the widespread use of psychometric measure such as IQ for educational purposes. As Piaget put it:

in particular, his (Binet's) practical achievement in devising intelligence tests has led to innumberable research projects involving the measurement of mental development and individual aptitudes. And though the tests have not produced all the results expected of them, the problems they raised are of far greater interest than could have been foreseen at the time they came into use: either we shall one day find good tests, or else intelligence tests will go into history as an example of a fruitful error [1970, p. 150].

The research described here was aimed at contributing to a broadened perspective on intelligence testing that will generate better methods of educational evaluation.

APPENDIX A: DESCRIPTION OF PIAGET TASKS[5]

11. Length Conservation. Two cylindrical sticks of bubble gum 4 in. and 4¼ in. long, differing in color, ends closest to child aligned.

1. "See, one stick is bigger than the other. Now I put them like this (extending shorter stick ¾ in.). Now I want you to choose, to point to the bigger one because you can have the bigger one to eat."
2. Same but retracting shorter stick.
3. Measurement trial, nonaligned arrangement, "Pick the bigger. Show me how you can tell it is bigger, how you can make sure."

[5] A Guttman scale was constructed for scoring each task, using Green's (1956) summary statistics. The coefficients of reproductibility and Index of Consistency reported were calculated according to Green's formulas.

Scale score

1. Discriminates length correctly.
2. Measures spontaneously or to prove.
3. Consistently conserves length.
4. Verbalizes conservation principle.

reproducibility = .99, index of consistency = .80

12. Conservation of Length–Ring Segment. Green (3.69 in.) and white (3.5 in.) cookies in ring segment portions for Jastrow illusion (in which bottom segment appears longer).

1. "See, one cookie is bigger than the other (objectively bigger green cookie at bottom). Now I put them like this. Pick the bigger cookie; you can have it to eat."
2. Random arrangement–see which is bigger; repeat as above.
3. Rapid position reversal and questioning.

Scale score (Similar to magic causality)

1. Unquestioning acceptance of change of size.
2. Surprise, amusement over change but accepts as completely real. Thinks it is magic.
3. Reserved belief in change.
4. Uncertainty, suspicion about change.
5. Suspicion, seeks for a trick by E.
6. Definite disbelief. Tries to prove it does not change. Sharply discriminates appearance and reality but views change in appearance as somewhat magical.
7. Categorical disbelief. Categorical disbelief in magic. Views it as an illusion.

13. Liquid Conservation. "Point to the glass of coke which has more to drink because you can have the one with more to drink."

1. The greater quantity in one of two 10 ml beakers is poured into a 100 ml beaker (that is, a much wider one).
2. The lesser quantity poured into a tall thin graduate.
3. The liquids returned to original glasses and repoured.

Scale score

1. Has some expectation of constancy.
2. At least conserves after demonstration.
3. Consistently conserves.
4. Gives categorical reason for conservation.

reproducibility = .99, index of consistency = .96

14. Conservation of Number

1. "One plate has more candy than the other plate. You can have this plate (with 5 M&Ms in short vertical line) or you can have this plate (4 M&Ms in a longer line). Take the plate with more to eat. Which do you want?"
2. Repeat with new plates, left–right position reversed.

Scale score

1. Takes the plate with most candy. Associates the meaning of most with counting or number.
2. Counts correctly.
3. Chooses correct plate on second trial.
4. Chooses correct plate, all trials.
5. Verbalizes principle of quantitative comparison.

15. Sex Identity. Three girl paper dolls, four boys, one snow-suited ambiguous figure. "Let's say these dolls are real people. I'm a lady, a girl, so I'll put this girl here next to me. Put all the girls here and the boys here."

1. "Now, here is a girl, Heidi. Let's say it's a real girl and put it with the other girls here. It's got girl clothes on. Now let's take off the girl clothes and put on boy clothes. Now what is it, where does it go?"
2. "Now we cut Heidi's pony tail hair off."
3. "Now we put on boy clothes" (in addition to hair cut).
4. Return to girl's clothes.
   "Can that really happen? Can a girl be a boy if she wants to?"

Scale score

1. Shows some resistance to gender change.
2. Says a girl cannot really be a boy if she wants to.
3. Denies has changed gender after one of changes.
4. Denies gender change because of clothes.
5. Denies gender change with both hair and clothes.
6. Verbalizes principles.
7. Consistently denies possibility of gender change.

reproducibility = .94, index of consistency = .93

16. Age Identity. Interviewer dons fireman's hat and nurse's hat. Has child do the same. Asks "Am I (you) a real fireman (nurse) now?"

Scale score

1. Child says he cannot be the real adult identity, even if he wears hat, that is, even though he says he changes to fireman; holds he is not a real fireman when pushed.

2. Child says E cannot be opposite-sex occupational role.
3. Maintains this even if E wears hat.
4. Child says he is not opposite-sex adult identity wearing the hat.
5. Says he is not the same-sex adult identity though wearing the hat.
6. Says even though he grows up, may not be (able to be) the fireman (nurse).

reproducibility = .97, index of consistency = .76

17. Object Sorting. "Put the ones together that go together. Put them in order" for a set of dolls including three infants, boys, girls, fathers, mothers, dogs. Two of each set are cloth (Flagg), one is plastic jointed (Renwall). Testing limits on sorting by similarity.

0. All groupings are associative ("the boy and the girl because they play together").
1. On request, can make groupings on the basis of *similarity* (but most groupings are associational).
2. Most groupings are *not associational.*
3. Spontaneously *includes all 21 objects* in one group or another.
4. Spontaneously *includes all members of a class* in the relevant class group in more than 50% of the spontaneous groupings.
5. *Complementarity.* When asked, constructs a system of two complementary classes including all objects. Examples of complementary classes are males and females, children and adults.
6. *Categorical set.* More than 50% of weighted groupings are true categorical concepts.
7. *Hierarchy.* Understands the quantitative inclusion of a subclass in a higher-order class without probings (that is, scores 3 on inclusion task).
8. *Shifts* spontaneously from one system of classification to another. When asked to make just two groups, makes a different set of complementary classes than those used spontaneously. Examples are those in which groupings were initially by sex, and are now by age or vice versa.

reproducibility = .98, index of consistency = .85

18. Class Inclusion. Here are some pieces of candy. "Some are chocolate (four brown M&Ms); one is a mint (one white M&M). Are these chocolates pieces of candy? Is this mint a piece of candy? They are all pieces of candy. Now I want you to pick some candy, pick the most you can. Pick either all the chocolates or all the candy."

1. Initial choice.

2. Practice in seeing all are candy after removal.
3. Choice again.

Scale score

1. Understands that if all chocolates removed, there is still some candy left.
2. Concludes there is more candy than chocolates at end of interview.
3. Chooses the candy set at first choice.
4. Verbalizes the principle.

reproducibility = .90, index of consistency = .94

19. Dream Concept. See Laurendeau and Pinard (1962) for interview adapted from Piaget (1926).

1. Dream object is not real.
2. Action or object of dream is not really there.
3. Dream is not visible to others.
4. Dreams do not originate in the external physical world.
5. Thinks dreams may take place inside the body or head.
6. Some dreams take place inside.
7. Dreams are not material things.
8. Dreams are caused in a subjective or psychological fashion by the child himself.

reproducibility = .97, index of consistency = .83

20. Magical Causality. A magician's change bag to effect an apparent transformation of a small toy cat into a toy bird. The experimenter waved his hand in a circular motion over the bag as he said, "Abracadabra Allakazam" and surrepitiously turned the handle which moved the inner lining over the cat and uncovered the bird. An interview explored the child's beliefs about the nature and cause of the event. At the end of the interview, the handle was locked in a fixed position and the child was asked to see if he could change the cat into the bird; any imitation of the experimenter's magical words as well as any gestures were noted. Subjects were classified in one of the following descriptive levels.

1. *Premagical level.* Matter of fact unquestioning acceptance of transformation without surprise and without concept of magic. Does not think a transformation occurred, for example, "The cat went away. It's a bird." Accordingly, is not sure that it "really turned into a bird" on probe, but not because of suspicion. Does not seem to have a concept of magic, does not know whether it was magic, who can do magic. May think he can make the change by holding the bag, saying "Abracadabra" (transitional to Level 2).

2. *Active magical belief.* Active surprise and amazement, thinks really transformed, it is real magic, E is a magician, and wants it repeated, done to other things, wants to be transformed himself, spontaneously introduces notion that it is magic.
3. *Reserved belief.* Says it is real magic on probe, really changed, is same, but is not surprised or excited. Some reservations about changing, still a cat, only hair changed, etc.
4. *Uncertainty.* Some suspicion and uncertainty. Says changed to a bird but does not know how, whether it really changed, if it is the same. Not sure that it is real magic. Believes or does not know whether there is magic.
5. *Desire to find a physicalistic explanation.* Some belief that it might be magic but tends not to believe and searches for a trick. Has some concept of a substitution. Active effort to find out how it is done.
6. *Definite disbelief.* Aware must be a substitution, some trick to it. Says there may be a hole in the side, etc. But has to prove to himself concretely that it is not magic. There tends to be some residual belief in magic in some remote context.
7. *Categorical disbelief.* Categorically sure it is a trick even without working out a concrete explanation, and does not believe in magic in other contexts.

21. Objective Responsibility (with Pictures). The two stories are given below:

Story 1–The Fight (Equal Consequences). Jimmy sees a boy who is teasing a little girl and hurting her. Jimmy tells the boy to stop teasing the girl. Jimmy and the boy get into a fight. Jimmy gets beaten up.

Billy sees a boy playing with some blocks. He goes and kicks the blocks over. Billy and the other boy get into a fight. Billy gets beaten up.

Story 2–The Cups (Unequal Consequences). Tommy's mother is setting the table in the dining room. Tommy thinks that he will help her by pushing the cart into the dining room from the kitchen. Tommy pushed the cart too fast. The cart falls over. The cups fall on the kitchen floor and all of them break.

Larry's mother told him not to take any cookies. But Larry wants some. He climbs up to take some cookies. A cup falls on the floor and breaks.

1. Was Jimmy a good or bad boy?
2. Why?
3. Was Billy a good or bad boy?
4. Why?

5. Which boy was worse? (Jimmy or Billy)?
6. Why?

Scale: objective responsibility

1. Does not call Billy worse than Jimmy or calls Billy good.
2. Calls Billy worse than Jimmy (Story 1) and calls Billy bad.
3. Calls Jimmy good and Billy bad.
4. Calls Larry worse than Tommy and Larry bad.
5. Calls Tommy good and Larry bad.

22. Internality

The boy wants to play.
But the mother has to leave the house to shop.
She tells the boy to watch the baby until his big sister gets home.
The mother leaves.
The boy watches the baby.
The mother comes home in time to see the boy watching the baby.
She gives the boy a spanking.

The teacher has to leave the room.
The children are allowed to play.
After she has gone, the children start to play in the sand box.
They try to build a sand castle.
A little boy comes over and kicks the sand castle to pieces.
The teacher comes back in time to see the boy kick the castle.
She kisses him.

(a) "What do you think of that?"
(b) "Was the boy (girl) good (bad)?"
(c) "Why was the boy (girl) good (bad)?"
(d) "Why was the boy (girl) kissed (spanked?)"
(e) "How does the child feel?"

Internality scale

0. Sanction-oriented. An obedient child who is punished is called bad; a disobedient child who is rewarded is called good.
1. Vacillating. The subject vacillates between a sanction and an obedience orientation.
2. Amoral. The subject does not switch to a sanction orientation when the inconsistent ending is added. The obedient child is called good and the disobedient child bad, in spite of the sanction. But the subject gives no moral reason for his choice.
3. Distorting. The subject is obedience-oriented, gives a moral reason for his choice, but distorts either the deed or the sanction to make them congruent with one another.
4. Norm-oriented. The subject's choice is based on a stated norm; he does not distort either the sanction or the deed.

REFERENCES

Ammons, R. D., & Ammons, C. H. *The quick test.* Missoula, Montana: Psychological Test Specialists, 1962.

DeVries, R. Relationships among Piagetian, IQ, and achievement assessments. *Child Development*, 1974, *45*, 746-756.

Evans, R. I. *Jean Piaget: The man and his ideas.* New York: Dutton, 1973.

Green, B. F. Method of scalogram analysis using summary statistics, *Psychometrika*, 1956, *21* (1), 79-88.

Guilford, J. P., *et al.* A factor analysis study of human interests. *Psychological Monographs*, 1954, *68*, No. 4.

Hathaway, W. E., Jr. The degree and nature of the relations between traditional psychometric and Piagetian developmental measures of mental development. Paper presented at annual meeting of the American Educational Research Association, March, 1973.

Hunt, J. M. *Intelligence and experience.* New York: Ronald Press, 1961.

Inhelder, B. *The diagnosis of reasoning in the mentally retarded.* New York: John Day, 1968. (First published in French in 1943 by Delachaux and Niestle, Neuchatel.)

Kohlberg, L., & Mayer, R. Development as the aim of education. *Harvard Educational Review*, 1973, *42* (4), 449-496.

Kuhn, D., Langer, J., Kohlberg, L., and Haan, N. The development of formal operations in logical and moral judgment. *Genetic Psychology Monographs* (in press).

Laurendeau, M., & Pinard, A. *Causal thinking in the child.* New York: International Universities Press, 1962.

McCartin, R. Primary mental abilities at age 6. Paper presented at the Society for Research in Child Development, 1963.

McClelland, D. C. Testing for competence rather than for "intelligence." *American Psychologist*, 1973, *28* (1), 1-14.

Meyers, C. E., Dingman, H. F., Attwell, A. A., & Orpert, R. E. Primary abilities at mental age six. *Monograph of the Society for Research in Child Development.* Serial 82, *27* (1), 1962.

Monroe, M. *Reading aptitude tests.* Boston: Houghton Mifflin, 1935.

Piaget, J. *The child's conception of the world.* Totowa, New Jersey: Littlefield, Adams, 1960. (Originally published in French in *1926.*)

Piaget, J. *Psychology of intelligence.* Totowa, New Jersey: Littlefield, Adams, 1966. (First published in French in 1947.)

Piaget, J. *Science of education and the psychology of the child.* New York: Viking Press, 1971. (First published in French as Education et instruction. *Encyclopedie Francaise.* Vol. XV. Paris: Librairie Larousse, 1935, and *Education et instruction depuis 1935.* Paris: Librairie Larousse, 1965.)

Piaget, J. Problems of equilibration. In C. F. Nodine, J. M. Gallagher, & R. D. Humphreys (Eds.), *Piaget and Inhelder on equilibration.* Philadelphia: The Piaget Society, 1972.

Piaget, J. *Main trends in psychology.* New York: Harper & Row, 1973. (First published as Chapter 3 in *Main trends of research in the social and human sciences*, Part 1, Mouton/Unesco, 1970.)

Raven, J. C. *Raven progressive matrices.* New York: The Psychological Corporation, 1956.

Stephens, W. B. The development of reasoning, moral judgment, and moral conduct in retardates and normals: Phase II. Mimeographed report, 1972.

Stephens, W. B., McLaughlin, J. A., Miller, C. K., & Glass, G. V. Factorial structure of selected psycho-educational measures and Piagetian reasoning assessments. *Developmental Psychology*, 1972, *6*, 343-348.

Terman, L. M., & Merrill, M. *Stanford-Binet intelligence scale*. Boston: Houghton Mifflin, 1960.

Thurstone, L. L., Primary mental abilities. *Psychometric Monographs*, 1938, No. 1.

Thurstone, T. G., & Thurstone, L. L. *SRA primary mental abilities for ages 5 to 7*. Chicago: Bureau of Child Study of the Chicago Public Schools, 1954.

Wechsler, D. *Wechsler intelligence scale for children*. New York: The Psychological Corporation, 1963.

White, S. H., Day, M. C., Freeman, P. K., Hantman, S. A., & Messenger, K. P. *Federal programs for young children: Review and recommendations*. Washington, D.C.: U.S. Government Printing Office, 1972.

7

Federal Involvement in Early Education (1933-1973): The Need for Historical Perspectives

Ruby Takanishi

University of California, Los Angeles

The history of early childhood education has not been considered an especially significant aspect of the professional training of America's teachers of young children. Theoretical findings and research influences in developmental psychology have dominated the field, especially in the last two decades.[1] In the past few years, however, there has been a resurgence of interest in the history of childhood and of the family[2] as well as in analyses of the use of early education as a means of broad social reform (Lazerson, 1970). The compensatory early education programs of the 1960s are compared to the child-saving, Americanizing efforts of the kindergarten movement and philanthropic groups at the turn of the century.

During this recent period, the major documents on day care have discussed the role of the federal government in programs of early education.[3] There have

[1]See the contents of the National Society for the Study of Education Yearbooks (1928, 1947, 1972) related to early education.

[2]A new journal has emerged from current interest in the history of childhood, *The History of Childhood Quarterly*.

[3]Since the research and writing of this paper were completed, Sheldon White and his associates have published a four-volume series on federal programs for children. One chapter presents an historical discussion of the development of public programs (see White, Day, Freeman, Hartman, & Messenger, 1973, pp. 15-79). This paper comes to similar conclusions regarding recurring themes in federal programs. However, a substantial part of this paper is directed toward an agenda for historical inquiry into areas which are not covered in the White and associates chapter. Discussions of the federal role are included in Fein and Clarke-Stewart (1973), Roby (1973), and Steinfels (1973).

been large-scale federal programs aimed at the education and care of young children. Such programs as the Economic Opportunity Act of 1964, which in turn fostered the Head Start Program, the 1967 Amendment to the Social Security Act under Title IVA and IVB, the Demonstration Cities and Metropolitan Development Act of 1966, and the Manpower Development Training Act, all are grist for continued historical research and perspective into the role of federal government in early childhood programs.

Many influential groups labeled these federal efforts a failure. The fallout from these groups' attacks has resulted in disenchantment among segments of the population that are concerned with federal intervention in the lives of young children. It can be safely stated that, for the most part, the opposition groups are made up of the same people who favor restricted federal involvement in social welfare strategies (Emergency Committee, 1971) and of those, like social science researchers, who favor allocation of federal resources to adolescents versus young children. There are, however, equally influential and diverse political forces that urge continued and expanded federal involvement in child development programs. These groups include feminist movements, child development researchers, professionals in early education, labor unions, policy planners who see programs as a means of welfare reform, and private industry which is either focused on providing care for children as a work benefit or providing care for profit.

During the period 1967-74, there were at least four national commissions working on policy for young children.[4] Historical perspective can serve several functions for policy planning. Examination of the goals which were associated with each federal entry into early education can provide a means of appraising current and future directions as well as assumptions and motivations which led to federal intervention. For example, what has been the nature of the federal role regarding the goals of early education; and, have those goals changed over time? Which individuals and groups supported or opposed the federal presence? What political and legislative strategies were enlisted among the forces of support and of opposition? What issues and value positions were evoked in the disputes? What were the anticipated consequences of federal involvement?

Most importantly, what was the impact of federal involvement on the development of early education institutions and on practical and public perceptions of early education? *The nature of historical inquiry is well-suited for research into the long-term social and cultural consequences of federal involvement in the lives of children.* Central to these questions is the potential role of historical research in demythologizing assumptions and beliefs regarding the federal role.

[4]These committees were: The Presidential Task Force of 1967; Gorham Committee of 1967; Joint Commission on the Mental Health of Children (1969); and National Research Council Advisory Committee on Child Development (1972). An analysis of these reports and their impact on policy is yet to be undertaken.

The main purpose of this paper is heuristic—to identify and raise pertinent questions which will stimulate further intensive historical inquiry into the federal role in early childhood programs. Recurring themes which emerge from past federal programs in early education will be described. The focus, however, will be on identifying areas for historical research which examine the nature of the federal role.

A Definitional Aside

Before proceeding further, the term "early childhood education" needs to be defined. Historically, within American society, the distinction between the nursery school (or preschool) and the day care center was defined as follows: the nursery school was to provide an educational program for children of the middle and upper classes; the day care centers, run by social welfare agencies, were to provide all day "custodial" care for children who fitted within identified categories of "problems."

Actually, there is no hard and fast distinction. First, day care centers do provide educational programs, and preschools sometimes function as baby-sitting centers. Second, early education—whether in preschool or day care—is inseparable from early socialization. Contrary to the view of certain noted writers (Bereiter, 1972), children have the potential to learn values and acceptable modes of behavior in custodial units as well as in those which consciously provide an educational program. Third, day care is increasingly characterized as part of a total educational program in current federal legislation and in the official standards of the welfare agencies.[5]

Hence, in this discussion, early education will refer to both preschool and day care programs which have been sponsored by the federal government.

Federal Involvement in Early Education (1933-1973): Recurring Themes

During the twentieth century, the federal government was involved in at least three national programs of early education: The Works Progress Administration (WPA) Nursery Schools (1933-1943); the Lanham Act Child Care Centers (1943-1946); and the Head Start Programs (1965-present). In examining these three programs, several identical themes reappear.

Federal involvement in early childhood education has been temporary in nature and responsive primarily to social, political, and economic crises. "As a demonstration of the public usefulness of nursery schools," the WPA nursery school ruling stated, "we will assist the community in establishing and conducting this project. But the WPA aid cannot be promised beyond the fiscal year,

[5] *Child Welfare League Standards*, 1969.

and such aid will end entirely when large-scale unemployment ends [Final Report, 1943, p. 60]."

The Lanham Act Centers were created to deal with a war-caused problem—the care of children whose parents were employed in war-related industrial production. Funds were distributed only to communities where war-related federal activity created a strain on existing community facilities. Funds for child care were clearly to be terminated at the end of the war. In effect, the temporary nature of the funding was stressed by its most ardent advocates and contributed to its political acceptance.

The Head Start program originated out of the Economic Opportunity Act of 1964. In Section 205a of the Act which provided the funding for Head Start, the early education of the low-income child was not even mentioned. Head Start was initially conceived as a program which was to be integrally a part of the Office of Economic Opportunity's community action strategy to reduce poverty. However, many leaders in developmental psychology and early education became involved in creating a child development program.[6]

The professional advocates who stood behind the War on Poverty argued that disadvantaged children needed a head start which would allow them to enter school on an equal basis with middle-class children. These children of the poor needed cognitive enrichment and acquisition of school-appropriate behaviors. The possibilities appeared unlimited—school failure common to minority students would be considerably reduced or even eliminated. They would achieve in school, stay in school longer, have better jobs and incomes, and thus improve their social and economic status in the society. Early education was seen as the primary antidote for social inequities; the vicious cycle of poverty in America would come to an end (Hunt, 1964).

During the poverty war era, construction and rehabilitation funds for day care centers were embedded in legislation to improve the physical and social environment of people who lived in slum areas of American cities. The legislation included the Housing and Urban Development Act of 1965 which provided for the construction of day care centers in low-rent public housing projects and the Demonstration Cities and Metropolitan Development Act of 1966.

It must be pointed out that, in connection with its responsiveness to social and economic crises, *federal aid has been targeted toward a narrow range of children*—those presumed to suffer disadvantages which families themselves cannot ameliorate and/or which pose a potential threat to public safety. In other words, aid was not intended for the education and care of *all* children. Possibly as a consequence of this situation, the fact that present-day legislation

[6]Bettye Caldwell (1972) recalls this period of optimism: "So excited were many of us by the possibilities of Head Start that we did not go on record to protest that a six-week summer program could not hope to do all that it was being requested to do—develop a positive self-concept, produce new levels of language competence, discover and correct an accumulation of five years' work of medical and nutritional problems, and convince parents that education was the solution to all their problems. Plus many other miracles [p. 57]."

is perceived as nontargeted may be the reason it so often becomes the rallying point for those who oppose federal involvement. An example of this attitude may be found in the Comprehensive Child Development Bill of 1971 which was intended to include children from a wider range of income levels than previous federal programs. In the conservative press, the Bill was characterized as follows: "(It) is more than an antipoverty measure. It is blatantly a social experimental scheme to change the nature of American society by undermining the basic unit of that society: the family [Report, 1971, p. 902]."

Clearly, this targeting of federal aid is related to the *theme of early childhood education as a means of social reform* (Lazerson, 1970). Compare, for example, the announcement of Harry Hopkins, Administrator for the WPA in 1933, with the recent view expressed by the Kerner Commission in 1968. Speaking of preschool age children of unemployed parents, Hopkins (1933) stated: "The education and health programs of the nursery school can aid as nothing else in combating the physical and mental handicaps being imposed upon these young children [p. 155]." And the recent Kerner Commission's recommendations for national action: "Early childhood education is at the very heart to reconstruct the environment which incapacitates disadvantaged children educationally, even before they enter the school system [National Advisory Commission, 1968, p. 446]."

Federal legislation in the 1960s in early education reflects the themes of narrow targeting of programs and of early education as social reform. In Title I of the Elementary and Secondary Education Act (ESEA) of 1965, preschool programs were provided to meet special needs of "educationally deprived" children. Under Title III of ESEA (1965), supplementary centers and services for preschool children were authorized.

Marvin Lazerson has presented the argument that early education has been used as a substitute for broader social reform (Lazerson, 1970). However, the origins of this reform strategy in American history remain unclear. But that this theme is persistent is indicated by the Kerner Commission's cited recommendation, made in the face of evidence suggesting Head Start programs were not accomplishing their compensatory objectives.

The association of federal programs with children of the poor and the fact the programs were intended to serve economic and production needs may have seriously hampered future federal efforts to deal with a broader range of American children. This viewpoint was integrally related to the *longstanding federal policy that the family was critically important as an agent of early socialization.*

As far back as 1909, in a declaration of the First White House Conference on the Care of Dependent Children, the position of the federal government vis-a-vis the family stated that, "Home life is the highest and finest production of civilization. . .Children of parents of worthy character, suffering from temporary misfortune, and children of reasonably efficient and deserving mothers who are without the support of the normal breadwinner, should as a rule be kept with their own parents, such aid being given as may be necessary to maintain suitable homes for the rearing of children [quoted by Lundberg, 1928, p. 1]."

Even during the war period when woman power was so critically needed in defense-related industries, the policy announcement of the War Manpower Commission on the Employment of Women on August 12, 1942, read: "The first responsibility of women with young children, in war as in peace, is to give suitable care in their own homes to their children. In order that established family life may not be unnecessarily disruptive, special efforts to secure in industry women with young children should be deferred until full use has been made of all other sources of labor supply [U.S. Department of Labor, 1942]."[7]

A dominant theme in Congress has been the fear of the federal government becoming a child rearer; proposed federal legislation today still reflects the primacy of the family, specifically the mother in the care of her children. In the Comprehensive Head Start, Child Development, and Family Services Act of 1972, the bill begins: "The Congress finds that child development programs must build upon the role of the family as the primary and the most fundamental influence on the development of children, and must be provided only to children whose parents or legal guardians request them [U.S. Congress, 1972, p. 1]." However, a curious double standard has developed in federal policy in relation to low-income families in recent federal legislation; child care has been provided to poor families contingent on the employment or training of the mother. Title VA of the Economic Opportunity Act (1964) authorized funds for the care of children whose parents or guardians were enrolled in the Work Experience and Training Program. Similarly, under the Social Security Act Amendments of 1967 (Title IVA), child care services must be provided for children who are affected by their mother's participation in the Work Incentive Program (WIN).

Federal programs of early education all have common themes:

1. Federal programs for young children have been created in response to immediate social, political, and economic crises. Related to this mode of crisis intervention, programs are planned to be temporary in nature.
2. Federal programs are targeted toward special groups of children, specifically those designated in distress.
3. Federal programs of early education have been used as a means of broad social reform.
4. Federal policy has been intensely concerned with the primacy of the nuclear family as an agent of early chilhood socialization.

These themes are related to the general one which has characterized federal involvement: programs are temporary in conception and will be phased out by

[7]Contrary to their past practices, many industries hired married women under the assumption that when the emergency was over, they could be discharged more easily than single women.

improvements in economic and social conditions for poor and/or distressed families.

There appears to be an insufficiently analytic stance regarding the federal presence in the literature and research done in this area. Their major emphases were directed primarily toward descriptions of programs, their official goals, the implementation of the programs, and their outcomes as seen from the perspective of individuals who were closely involved in the day-to-day functioning of the programs. In Table 1 this *descriptive versus analytic distinction* is illustrated.

In addition to the need to shift from the descriptive to the analytic level of inquiry, there are important facets of the federal role which remain obscure for the researcher. The goals and political resources of the groups who supported or opposed the programs are unclear in reports and in the literature. The individuals who administered the programs, those who implemented them, and these individuals' relationships with professional and other groups in the community

TABLE 1

Descriptive Versus Analytic Historical Inquiry Into the Federal Role—Early Education as an Example

Descriptive statement	Analytic question
Federal programs are responsive to crisis; programs are temporary	What have been the effects of this mode of federal involvement on future programs? What does it tell us about how the child and family are perceived? Did the programs have their intended effects? Why was early education part of a crisis intervention program?
Programs are targeted toward special groups	How has the targeted nature of programs influenced its acceptability and adoption in the public and private institutions of child care and education? Have these special target groups benefited in the long term from federal entry?
Federal programs are means of achieving social reform	Why have early childhood education programs been viewed as a means of large-scale social reform?
Federal policy reflects intense concern over the role of the family	What has *been* the impact of federal programs on the family as a socializing agency? Have they strengthened or weakened the role of the family in the child's life?

are missing even from the descriptive accounts. Nowhere have the dynamics and impact of federal early education program creation and the issues involved received serious consideration so that needed new historical perspectives can be gained.

The further discussion of historical inquiry into aspects of the federal role in early education is intended to stimulate additional historical and public policy research in this area. As such, this paper may be viewed as an agenda for research into the federal role in the lives of young children.

AN AGENDA FOR HISTORICAL RESEARCH

Selected Aspects of the Federal Role in Early Education

The Dynamics of Federal Program Creation

Perhaps the most intriguing aspect of this current but sketchy research–thus far –is the discovery that past programs were not created by legislative action of the Congress, but that the programs originated out of staff and administrative decisions in the federal bureaucracies.

For example, in 1933, the WPA nursery schools were started when the Federal Emergency Relief Administration (FERA) administrator authorized the expenditure of work-relief funds for nursery schools serving children from low-income and unemployed families. These schools met the needs of the time by creating jobs for teachers, nurses, nutritionists, cooks, and janitors. The nursery schools were placed under the jurisdiction of the public school system, but in 1943, when federal funding ended, few were adopted by the public school system.

The Lanham Child Care Centers followed a different pattern. The centers received funds under Title II of the 1941 Community Facilities Act (Lanham Act) which read: "Title II: Defense Public Works. As used in this title, the term 'public works' means any facility necessary for carrying on community life substantially expanded by the national defense program . . . [U.S. Statutes, 1942, pp. 361-363]." The Act became a major source of funding for child care centers in a decision made in 1943 by the House Committee on Building and Grounds from where the Act originated.

On February 17, 1943, President Roosevelt transmitted to Congress a supplemental estimate of appropriations to enable the Office of Defense, Health, and Welfare Services (functions subsequently referred to the Federal Security Agency) to provide "payments to the states for expenditure in accordance with state plans for the care and protection of children of employed mothers [U.S. Senate, 1943, p. 2]." This resulted in a bill (S.1130) providing the legislative authorization for the necessary funding.

It was the first time in the country's history that there would be hearings and congressional debate over a bill whose stated intent was to provide for the group care and protection of children. It is noteworthy that at the time when the hearings were taking place, child care was being funded by the Lanham Act in the amount of $9,000,000.[8] These funds were being administered by the Federal Works Agency (FWA) and were direct grants to local sites.

Thus the central issue was not whether to fund child care centers, but whether federal activity in child care "should be covered by definitive legislation of Congress prescribing the scope and basis of federal participation in the field [U.S. Senate, 1943, p. 1]." A related issue was whether the two existing federal agencies that had traditionally been involved with children–the Office of Education and the Children's Bureau–would administer the programs through established state agencies, thus recognizing the states' rights in matters related to the education and care of children.

On June 8, 1943, Mrs. Florence S. Kerr, Assistant to the Administrator of the Federal Works Agency distributing Lanham funds, testified before the Committee on Education and Labor regarding S.1130: "First, funds are allotted solely as a war emergency measure in order to facilitate the employment of women needed in the war industries. *We are not subsidizing an expanded educational program nor a federal welfare program* . . . [U.S. Congress, 1943, p. 34]."

S.1130 would have vested administrative responsibility in the Office of Education and the Children's Bureau which would have then developed with the states education and welfare services for children. Thus the bill would have superseded the FWA, but more importantly it would have had the clear directive of providing *nonemergency* education and welfare services which were negated by the Lanham funding pattern.

S.1130 was passed by the Senate on June 30, 1943, but it remained in the House Education Committee where it slipped into obscurity. The hearings before the Congressional committees and the debates on the floor of both Houses, however, provide a context for examing the controversies surrounding the limits of the federal role which continue to the present.

Federal control of education has a long history of being the bogeyman issue for those fearful of the erosion of family influence with respect to the early education of young children (see, for example, Hales, 1954). The debates and fate of S.1130 in the House indicated a majority of influential legislators preferred the existing emergency measures, even though massive financing of child care centers with little federal control over local operations resulted in wide variations in program quality and community acceptance, to the alternative possibility of creating permanent federal agencies and federal-state channels

[8]Testimony of Mrs. Florence S. Kerr, Assistant to the Administrator of the Federal Works Agency (U.S. Congress, 1943, pp. 33-45).

of regulations and funding. The ad hoc Lanham Act continued to finance child care during the war, and funds were terminated on February 28, 1946. In only one state (California) did the centers continue functioning by means of state funding.

Close examination of current child care legislation points to the fact that the history of S.1130 is not an isolated case. The Child Development Bill of 1971, for example, was amended to Office of Economic Opportunity (OEO) legislation. This tactic of attaching the bill as an amendment to extend the life of OEO consequently precluded the possibility of extensive debate and examination of the bill on its own merit.

The questions now arise: What does the nature of the legislative strategy and debate tell us about how the young child is perceived and valued in the society? What do the dynamics of program creation reveal regarding the nature of the federal commitment to early childhood programs? The strategy by which bills are introduced, the opposition and support which they receive, and the resulting legislation and programs which finally emerge during a given period should be an important agenda item for future inquiry.

The Impact of Federal Involvement

It appears that every federal entry into early education occurred under the assumption that it would provide an impetus and create models for future efforts in the field. During each period of federal involvement, optimistic writers extolled the virtues of the nursery schools and child care centers and their essential contributions to American society (Davis, 1934; Langdon, 1935; Langdon & Robinson, 1940). Table 2 presents the intended outcomes of the three national programs. Although the emphases differ in the narrative account, the outcomes show remarkable similarity even in the language used by the reporters.

Educational evaluation and formal evidence dominated the assessment of the compensatory programs of the 1960s focusing on their cognitive, and to a lesser extent, on their affective outcomes in children. There is a paucity of existing studies on the impact of federal entry into early education along with a number of other equally important dimensions. Following is a detailed account of the thrust of federal programs in four major areas.

1. The impact of federal programs in the development of early education institutions in America. The use of census and survey data on enrollment of children under six gives us a quantitative fix on the impact of federal programs on the development of early education institutions and the kinds of children they served. The data were gathered by the U. S. Office of Education in 1930, 1936, and 1942. Due to the difficulties encountered in the collection and compilation of the survey data, only hypotheses regarding the impact of federal entry on the numbers and kinds of schools can be made.

TABLE 2
Three Federal Programs of Early Education

oals	WPA Nursery Schools	Lanham Centers	Head Start
cial and economic	To provide work for individuals on relief during Depression	To provide child care for mothers employed in war industries during World War II	To provide programs to deal with conflict over race and poverty in context of urban unrest[a] and minority militancy
hild	"Health services, nutrition, good physical, social and mental development [p. 54]."[b]	"Direct contribution to child life and the prevention of physical and emotional wreckage [pp. 45-47]."[c]	"Improving the child's physical health and abilities; helping the emotional and social development of the child . . . [p. 1]."[d]
rents	Parent education programs	Parent education and enabling mothers to work	"Strengthening the family's ability to relate positively to the child and his problems [p. 1].[d]
ublic schools	Increased opportunities for public schools to realize the value of nursery schools for adoption into the public system	"Opportunity for public school to incorporate preschools into its system [p. 47]."[c]	To prepare children for the public school experience

[a] See Lazerson (1970, p.84).
[b] Salley (1943).
[c] Baruch (1945).
[a] Office of Economics Opportunity (1964).

TABLE 3
Dates for the Establishment of
Nursery Schools in Operation in 1942[a]

Years	Nursery school	
	Number	Percent
1880-1900	13	1.6
1901-1910	9	1.1
1911-1920	37	4.5
1921-1930	215	26.2
1931-1940	481	58.6
1941-1942	66	8.0

[a]Adapted from Table 11 in Davis (1947, p. 42).

Table 3 shows the dates for the establishment of nursery schools in operation in 1942. Between the years 1921 and 1930, 26.2% of all nursery schools were organized. This was also the greatest period of growth of "college laboratory nursery schools," 42% of which were organized during the period. The next ten-year period, 1931-1940, brought the greatest expansion with 58.6% of the nursery schools opening during the decade. This was the time in which the WPA nursery schools were organized. Taking the period 1930-1942 and comparing the numbers of nursery schools by group type allows us to speculate on the kind of children who were served (see Table 4).

In 1930, the distribution among the types of nursery schools was somewhat even. Tuition schools declined during the Depression period, but constituted one-fourth of the preschool centers in 1942, or 64% of all the nonfederal programs. Thus it appears that while the WPA schools served a large number of low-income children during the period 1933-1942, public school nurseries which were expected to be a consequence of federal funding experienced the least growth during the period. Meanwhile, middle-class tuition nursery schools increased steadily, a trend which continued after World War II (Prescott, Milich, & Jones, 1972, p. 8).

There are no data on the crucial postwar period and into the middle 1960s when the federal government reentered the early education realm on a national scale. There is reason to believe that the federal government stopped collection of preprimary enrollment data during this period, presumably because of its noninvolvement. One wonders whether H. H. Anderson's statement as far back as 1934, "Nursery education is now available only for the very rich and the very poor [p. 11]," holds true also for the 1960s when large-scale federal programs were aimed at poverty groups.

TABLE 4

Comparisons of Numbers of Nursery Schools
by Group Type, for the Period 1930-1946[a]

Group Type	1930		1936		1942		1944	1945[b]	1946[b]
	Number	Percent	Number	Percent	Number	Percent			
Tuition	73	36.0	144	8.0	622	26.0	—	—	—
College	74	36.4	77	4.0	122	5.0	—	—	—
Philanthropic	43	21.2	53	3.0	156	6.0	—	—	—
Special	—	—	—	—	35	1.0	—	—	—
Public School	13	6.4	11	1.0	30	1.0	—	—	—
Federal Programs	0	0.0	1,500	84.0	1,500	61.0	3,100	2,800	1,497[c]

[a]Adapted from Table 7 in Davis (1947, p. 38). See also Davis (1946, p. 56).
[b]Numbers for first five group types for years 1944, 1945, 1946 are not available.
[c]Numbers on the last day of the program, February 28, 1946.

Based on the October 1965 survey, Samuel Schloss reported: "Project Head Start, the federal preschool program for needy children, which was carried out so successfully in the summer of 1965 apparently has little effect on the size of nursery and kindergarten enrollments when the regular school year began in the fall [p. 6]." The critical point which appears consistently in later reports of the National Center for Educational Statistics is that attendance at each age level greatly favored children who came from "middle-class and above" family backgrounds than children from "poverty" backgrounds.

Based on the October 1967 survey, there was a continued upward trend in preschool enrollment based on the period 1964-1967. Diane Gentler (1968) of the Center reported: "Increase in percentage of children enrolled at each year of age was larger for children in the two lower income groups (under $3,000, $3,000-$4,999) than for families with $5,000 or more. However, it did not close the gaps between enrollment rates of 3-5-year-olds in the lowest income categories with those of upper income ($7,500-$9,999, $10,000, and above) [p. 3]."

Again, a paucity of data precludes answering the question of who benefits in the long term from early education programs, especially under conditions when federal funding tends to dwindle after the peak of a crisis. While the Head Start programs did temporarily benefit low-income families, financial support for the programs dropped in succeeding years. In 1970, five years after the debut of Head Start, the National Center survey indicated that at each age level, private schools served a significantly larger proportion of preschool children than did publicly financed ones (National Center, 1970).

In their survey of day care and preschool services, Ronald Parker and Jane Knitzer (1972) conclude: "A two-pronged pattern reflecting economic and racial stratification has evolved . . . . White (affluent) children are more likely to be enrolled in preschool programs, and minority group children are more likely to be enrolled in day care programs. Federal involvement . . . is directed primarily at serving children of the poor. In actual numbers, only a small percentage of this group is reached [pp. 18-19]."

2. *Impact on the development of the professional organizations.* Early education has two points of reference with respect to its American origins. First, around the turn of the century, Margaret and Rachael McMillan, who had worked in nursery school settings with slum children in London, were involved in establishing kindergarten projects in the large American cities (Dowley, 1971). Through the kindergartners, the early care and education of children had its roots in the philanthropic, child-saving orientation of the settlement houses. The second point of origin is to be found in the laboratory schools which were associated with institutions of higher education and which served middle- to upper-class children.

There are few data on the role of these two interest groups in the early care and education of young children. It is known that each developed into a separate professional group with an established territory of care for children. During World War II, both groups worked in the same settings and in the same community groups which centered about child protection. At the end of the war, they again developed separate agendas and went separate ways (Close, 1945).

Recently proposed federal legislation merges early education with the care and protection of children (Searcy & Ouellet, 1971). However, legislative language and child welfare standards do not necessarily ensure such a merger will take place in the delivery of services. Historical inquiry into the work of the settlement houses and the laboratory schools is needed to focus on the social welfare and early education professional ranks, their past relationships with and perceptions of each other, and the conditions under which cooperation did occur. A fascinating narrative is still to be written about the individuals involved—most of whom were women—and their influence on the development, both in numbers and in character of the professional organizations.

Two related questions are: (1) How did professional organizations evolve? and (2) Did their philosophy affect their orientation toward governmental involvement in early education, and the political strategies they used? Margaret Rosenheim has distinquished between two themes of child legislation in the United States. The first is the "deviancy control" approach or the reform of individuals, and the second is called "structural reform" or direct manipulation of public institutions (Rosenheim, 1973). Like most distinctions, neither of these exists in pure form, but both are potentially useful as a framework for examining strategies in early education and their implications for the state of the field at present.

From its beginnings, the National Association of Nursery Education (NANE) (now National Association for the Education of Young Children) had a legislative specialist to keep the membership informed regarding the status of legislation affecting early education. In 1946, after the termination of federal funds, NANE joined other groups to form the National Committee for Group Care of Children. The work of the committee reveals the nature of their strategy: "(The committee) did not promote any particular bill or pattern of governmental aid nor did it attempt to outline or establish an all-inclusive program for children. The committee felt it would be most effective if it published a series of bulletins which would serve as a clearinghouse of concrete suggestions for methods of mobilizing community forces on the state and local levels to meet the needs of children [p. 3]." NANE shied away from the rough and tumble of political activity, lobbying, and the creation of organized pressure groups. As a result, even moderate activity in support of public early education did not materialize.

The question of the role which the various organizations played in the formulation of federal programs and legislation also needs more scrutiny. The impression is that early educators entered the scene *after* the programs had been authorized. Thus they often worked under regulations/program requirements which they had no part in formulating. The consequences of noninvolvement in policy development are clear in the area of personnel training both in the WPA and Headstart periods. At the 1933 NANE annual conference in Toronto, the organization protested, but "acceded" to a federal request to provide technical assistance to the WPA nursery schools (White, 1935). The protest was based on the grounds that NANE had not been consulted in the development of the program and that there was a paucity of trained teachers to work in the nursery schools. Likewise, at the beginning of Head Start in the summer of 1965, there was no group of early education specialists who were prepared to deal with the target population of "disadvantaged" children.

The National Association for the Education of Young Children has currently adopted a "Children's Cause" strategy which encourages active lobbying and coalitions with other organizations for the promotion of its goals. The evolution of and the factors which led to the adoption of this activist strategy within the organization also need further exploration.

3. Impact on public attitudes regarding early education. Another question is: How did the previously described federal role and policies influence public attitudes regarding early education? In 1945, Professor J. Norton, Teachers College, noted that past federal policies in the establishment of nursery schools may have produced consequences that would hinder their expansion: ". . . The emphasis has been and is on the production by adults and employment of adults rather than the education of children . . . (nursery schools) are established for noneducational purposes and financed by funds obtained outside the educational budget . . . (they) tend to grow up as separate agencies rather than as part of the continuous, free, public education system to which the United States has been long committed [p. 215]."[9]

Although this is an area for much more intensive inquiry, my research suggests that there was disparity of opinions held by various groups. The differing viewpoints of people in different positions is a vehicle for understanding the miltiplicity of motivations and assumptions with which the programs were viewed.

The impact of the federal programs on parents' expectations and desires for early education is not clear. The Lanham funds were extended for a year because of a deluge of parent protests across the country.[10] However, as previously

[9]In the intervening years in which faith in the public schools has faltered, the question is now posed: Should early education be part of an educational system that has failed children?

[10]A survey taken a month after the final termination of the Lanham funds indicated that the number of centers and children were not adversely affected. However, such figures are not adequate evidence for long-term effects. Further inquiry of a census sort is needed to look at the fate of these centers.

noted, it was only in one state (California) where the Lanham centers continued to be financed on a year-to-year basis for 13 years until they became a permanent part of the State Department of Education. This achievement is partially attributable to a strong and organized parent group (Prescott, Milich, & Jones, 1972).

A number of surveys taken during 1945 indicated that mothers in Los Angeles and Detroit (60%) planned to continue working and needed the services of child care institutions.[11] At that time, the *Nation's Schools*, a journal for school administrators, conducted a poll on the future of child care services. Of the 480 school administrators selected at random to answer the following question: "Who should assume responsibility for administering a program for children of working mothers?" 38% opted for schools, 36% for welfare, 25% for industry, and 1% for parents.[12] To the question, "Who should pay for the program of child day care?" the responsibility for the financing of the program is revealing. The burden was placed squarely upon parents (34%) and the federal government (22.5%), and to a lesser extent on industry (9%) (see footnote 12). The results of this survey are also consistent with the state governors' reply to FWA administrator Phillip Fleming's 1946 inquiry regarding state funding of day care in 1945. All the governors replied that they saw the Lanham programs as purely a wartime undertaking and hence solely the responsibility of the federal government.

A related question is why the impetus for child care faltered after federal funds were terminated. The answer is important because the federal effort in early education has never been a long-term commitment, but was more intended to provide models which then presumably were to be adopted at the private, state, and local levels. But it is a complex question. There are great problems involved in federal withdrawal, the most prominent being that of financing. The examination of these problems sheds light on problems still faced today by proponents of early education, especially in the public domain.

What is beginning to emerge is a sense of the social, political, and economic conditions which led to and sustained federal disengagement from early education for approximately 20 years. Following World War II, women continued to work in large numbers. Private companies which had provided models of excellent child care, such as the Kaiser Industries, withdrew their support from the programs partially because it was not economically advantageous to them to continue. For the school people, the shifting population caused by the war resulted in overcrowded school facilities. Many child care facilities built during the war period under the Lanham Act were projected to become elementary school buildings once the war would be over.

In August 1949, George Stoddard, president of the University of Illinois, stated to the World Organization of Early Childhood Education: "Resistance

[11]See "Children of working mothers still need day care." *The Child*, 1946, *11*, p. 563.

[12]See "What about war nurseries?" *Nation's Schools*, 1943, p. 17.

to nursery schools, like war, begins in the minds of men; presently in the mental habits of the male administrative animal [p. 12]." The "blocking" attitudes found by Stoddard ran as follows:

Blocking No. 1: I got along without nursery school and kindergarten. Why can't the children of today?

Blocking No. 2: The worst home is better for the child than the best institution.

Blocking No. 3: What can a child of three, four, five learn?

These are some of the arguments presented by those who find clear evidence that early childhood is not the "prime time" for learning to take place (Rowhrer, 1971). The style of opposition after 1960 depends heavily on the citation of "research evidence," and obscures the implicit value positions which are taken by the questioners.

Blocking No. 4: Aren't mothers better off if they stay at home and take care of their children instead of visiting nursery schools or attending parent education meetings?

This theme goes back a long way in history. Namely, mothers who do not want to care for their children on a full-time basis are said to be shirking their primary responsibility as women. To which Stoddard's (1949) reply was: "There is no joy in the sense of captivity [p. 14]."

Blocking No. 5: Educational services for young children will cost too much. We can't afford them.

There is no doubt that early childhood education is expensive. And with a crunch on school budgets throughout our history and no enduring commitment to put funds where rhetoric reigns, this issue promises to be with us for some time without an easy resolution.

The political context of early education at the end of the war also needs further examination. In many cities, community groups were organized (New York Times, 1946), supported by professional groups such as the Educational Policies Commission, the Research Division of the NEA, the National Society for the Study of Education, the American Association of School Administrators, as well as labor and parent groups (Goodykoontz, Davis, & Gabbard, 1947, pp. 44-49). Why they did not have a greater impact is an intriguing consideration in relation to the problem of effecting change in educational policy and practice.

One strategy adopted by early educators favored general grants-in-aid to the states which would then be pressured to provide for nursery schools versus the aid from the federal government aimed specifically at nursery education. The issue of specific versus general aid goes back a long way in the relations between federal-state education. More exploration is needed to obtain the full implications of the adoption of this strategy by the early education groups. Another line of analysis—already indicated in this paper—is the need for examination of the structures at the state and local levels created by the pattern of federal funding. Goodykoontz suggests two reasons why the emergency-relief nursery schools did not change the conditions for acceptance of such schools in the public school system (Goodykoontz *et al.*, 1947, p. 50). First, the funding required local sponsoring committees to be set up which evolved as separate policy-making bodies from the public school system. Second, the efforts to maximize employment during emergencies created large staffs at the nursery level and thus militated against eventual adoption.

On the other hand, Goodykoontz argues, the nursery schools established as part of extended public school services had a greater probability of being adopted as part of school units. She cites the cases of the cities of Cleveland, Detroit, Milwaukee, and the states of California, New York, and Massachusetts. It is important to note that these were also situations in which there existed active parental or professional groups, or both.

Finally, it is possible that federal support of child care may have actually hindered the continuation of the programs once the funding sources were withdrawn. The targeting of federal funds on specific groups may have contributed to the lack of a broad-based constituency for child care. New York City, for example, was not designated a defense area, and hence did not qualify for Lanham funds. Cornelia Goldsmith (1972), a noted early educator and child advocate, observed, "New York City, forced by circumstances to work out its own day care destiny without federal assistance, (found that) day care had gained sufficient strength, know-how and community support to survive at the end of the war [p. 16]."

4. Impact on the development of the private sector. This particular line of inquiry is important in order to assess the long-range effects of federal programs which were intended to be short range and targeted toward "needy" children in terms of the question (Berke & Kirst, 1972): "Who benefits?" Private nursery schools flourished after the war. However, it is likely that these programs did not serve needy children, but rather became resources for middle- and upper-income families. This inquiry is also important in light of the potentially large "day care industry" and poverty-education complex.

What historical precedents do we have for child care provided by industry and supported by government? During World War II, a large program of early education was provided by the Kaiser Shipbuilding Corporation for children of mothers who were working in the Portland shipyards. The Kaiser Child Service Centers were mainly financed by the Kaiser Company. However, the buildings were financed by a grant from the U. S. Maritime Commission. Many of the key participants, the administrators and teachers, have settled since into careers within the early education field. The position taken by Kaiser was that an industry which needs the labor of women must shoulder responsibility for the children of these women. The centers were located within easy access to the shipyards, were open 24 hours a day, and flexible for the schedules of individual parents and children. The emphasis was on "meeting needs" (Kaiser Centers). They provided meals, take-home dinners for families, mending services, shopping services, and drop-in centers to enable mothers to devote attention to their children after work.

The Kaiser Centers were seen as models for postwar nursery schools: "If this demonstration has been successful so that all levels of education learn that the job is to meet needs, this lesson may outrank the nursery school's good care of children as a wartime contribution [p. 4]." It would be beneficial to all early childhood professionals to have access to a careful study of the Kaiser Child Service Centers since it closely examines the role of industry versus the federal government in the provision of early child care.

Finally, the impact of federal policies on the emergence of franchise day care programs needs careful examination. The expansion of such programs has been aided by federal funds to care for children of welfare mothers (e. g., Title IVA and IVB of the Social Security Act, 1967). The issue of control of day care programs is related to both the mode of financing and the quality and nature of the services provided.

Themes Shared with Other Federal Educational Programs

The ongoing research on the federal presence in early education suggests common themes with other inquiries into the federal role in American education. First, the policies and programs appear responsive to social, economic, and political crises outside the field of education itself. It would be perfectly safe to conclude that no federal bill on early child care and education has yet been passed without an economic rationale or as a rider on another nonchild-related bill.

Second, the federal role in early education can be characterized by a piecemeal approach reflecting a lack of comprehensive social policy and the formation of temporary policy in times of crisis. This particular feature makes any research in this area frustrating and elusive. Examing the federal presence is particularly complex when viewed in relation to other countries which have centralized planning, coordination, and delivery of services for children (Robinson & Robinson, 1972). In the United States, there are at least three different levels of government, as well as private agencies with overlapping spheres of influence, all engaged in the care and education of young children. Within the federal level there are bureaus and agencies which are involved in a series of uncoordinated programs which may or may not have relationships to agencies at the state level.[13] Furthermore, different agencies of the federal government

[13]Lazar (1970) describes over 200 federal programs for young children.

may have different goals for childhood programs which may be opposing (Steinfels, 1973, p. 190). In addition, the manner in which programs were developed and implemented cannot be subjected to the traditional means of examining legislative records. As we have seen, national programs of child care and education were funded by bills in which no specific mention of children was made.

The history of programs, as remembered by the decision-making administrators in federal agencies, is a valuable untapped information source. Many of these administrators are still active within the professional organizations and concerned with childhood legislation. Their reflections and recollections comprise valuable data for historical research.

Finally, federal programs related to the early childhood years raise age-old questions regarding the role of the family vis-a-vis the state in the care and education of young children. Although the importance of the family in relation to the state has shifted slightly during the twentieth century, the prominence of the family has remained strong.[14] The origins of the ideology of the family in American social and cultural history is an important area for inquiry.

The nation's most faithful advocate of children, Senator Walter Mondale (D-Minnesota) has conducted hearings on the impact of federal policies on the welfare of American families (U.S. Congress, 1973). The thrust was to determine the extent to which government policies strengthen or weaken the family and what changes need to occur in areas of work, mobility, taxes, welfare, and housing (U.S. Congress, 1973, p. 2). For example, welfare-reform plans which coerce low-income mothers to work in exchange for custodial day care may have the potentiality of undermining parental influence, particularly if the programs are not controlled by parents.

A theme that projects into the 1970s may well be, what was the impact of federal preschool programs on the families whose children participated? The assessment of "family impact" is an important aspect of understanding the state versus the family approach. Has the family indeed been "undermined," as the opponents of the programs have claimed? The extent to which parent involvement was actually implemented and affected the lives of both parents and children remains unclear. A history of parent roles in the federal programs remains to be written.

Another persisting theme has been the fear that federal funding would result in governmental child rearing which allegedly homogenizes political and social values of children. J. J. Kilpatrick (1971), echoing earlier opposition, called the Child Development Bill of 1971, "the boldest and most far-reaching scheme advanced for the Sovietization of American youth [p. 851]."

The record of past federal programs does not support this view. If anything, community or site control was preeminent. In a National Advisory Council of

[14]For an analysis of the family as portrayed at the White House Conferences on Children, see Rochelle Beck (1973).

Education of Disadvantaged Children report (1967), it was noted that, "for the most part . . . projects are piecemeal, fragmented efforts at remediation or vaguely directed 'enrichment.' It is extremely rare to find strategically planned comprehensive programs for change [p. 10]." It was unlikely, given the past nature of federal involvement in early education, that the government could dictate guidelines or even programs. Local communities and individuals ruled the day.

CONCLUSION

At several points in this paper, I suggested that the historical perspective might provide a critical context for policy formation in the future. In order to provide this context, historical research into the federal role in early education must shift from the descriptive to the analytic level of inquiry. Conceptual frameworks that link levels of analysis are needed. Some potential frameworks include Matthew Miles' (1964) analyses of educational innovations which illustrate linkages among the nature of specific innovations; their introduction, installment, and eventual fate; and the individuals and groups involved at different stages.

Another fruitful approach might be that of social policy paradigms which are described by Martin Rein (1973) as "a curious admixture of psychological assumptions, scientific concepts, value commitments, social aspirations, personal interests, and administrative constraints [p. 6]." My examination of the federal role in early education illustrated each of the above components. I have not touched upon the development and change of federal policy models in early education, nor upon the development and implementation of the individuals and groups who were involved, and the social context in which their activity took place. It is in these areas of federal policy patterns that social historians must begin to work.

The task ahead for a "new history" of the federal presence in early education lies not so much in answering the questions which are raised but in the identification of alternative frameworks which organize the questions in relation to each other. Within these frameworks there must be room for the impact of different ideologies, strongly held assumptions about childhood, the family, and the role the government should play in the lives of young children. In the final analysis, the federal role in early childhood programs can be defined as a political issue. As such, it will reflect the complex political factors which operate in policy and program development.

ACKNOWLEDGMENTS

I would like to acknowledge the research assistance and personal support of Louis L. Knowles in the preparation of this paper. Edith M. Dowley, Director of Bing Nursery School, Stanford University, provided me with documents and personal contacts related to the period under study. Norma D. Feshbach, Sol Cohen, Marvin Lazerson, David Tyack, and Edith Dowley provided critical reviews of drafts of this paper. Responsibility for the final version of this paper, however, is solely that of the author. Sipora Gruskin provided editorial services.

REFERENCES

Anderson, H. H. Emergency nursery school. *Childhood Education*, *11*, 1934.

Baruch, D. When the need for wartime services for children is past—What of the future? *Journal of Consulting Psychology*, 1945, *9*.

Beck, R. The White House Conferences on Children: An historical perspective. *Harvard Educational Review*, *43*, 1973, 653-668.

Bereiter, C. E. Schools without education. *Harvard Educational Review*, *42*, 1972, 390-413.

Berke, J. S., & Kirst, M. *Federal aid to education: Who benefits? Who governs*? Lexington, Mass.: Lexington Books, 1972.

Close, K. After Lanham Funds—What? *Survey Midmonthly*, *81*, 1945, 131-135.

Caldwell, B. Consolidating our gains in early childhood. *Educational Horizons*, 1972, *50*, 57.

Davis, M. D. Children of working mothers still need day care. *The Child*, 1946, *32*.

Davis, M. D. Emergency nursery schools. *Childhood Education*, 1934, *10*, 200.

Davis, M. D. Schools for children under six. *Office of Education Bulletin*, 1947, No. 5. Washington, D.C.: U.S. Government Printing Office, 1947.

Dowley, E. M. Perspectives on early childhood education. In R. Anderson & H. Shane (Eds.), *As the twig is bent: Readings in early childhood education*. Boston: Houghton, Mifflin, 1971.

Emergency Committee for Children Gaining Steam. *Human Events*, October 3, 1971, p. 845.

Fein, G., & Clarke-Stewart, A. *Day care in context*. New York: Wiley, 1973.

Final report on the WPA Program, 1935-1943. Washington, D.C.: U.S. Government Printing Office, 1943.

Gentler, D. B. *Preprimary enrollment of children under six*. Washington, D.C.: National Center for Educational Statistics, 1968.

Goldsmith, C. *Better day care for the young child*. Washington D.C.: National Association for the Education of Young Children, 1972.

Goodykoontz, B., Davis, M. D., & Gabbard, H. F. Recent history and present status of education for youth children. *Early childhood education* (Fourty-sixth Yearbook of the National Society for the Study of Education, Part II). Chicago: University of Chicago Press, 1947. Pp. 44-49.

Hales, D. *Federal control of public education*. New York: Bureau of Publications, Teachers College, Columbia, 1954.

Hopkins, H. L. Announcement of emergency nursery schools, *Childhood Education*, 1933, *10*, 155.

Hunt, J. McVicker The psychological basis for using preschool enrichment as an antidote for cultural deprivation. *Merrill-Palmer Quarterly*, 1964, *10*, 220-240.

Kaiser Child Service Centers Pamphlets for Teachers, No. 2. *Meeting needs: The war nursery approach*. Undated.

Kilpatrick, T. *Human events*, October 30, 1971.

Langdon, G. Facts about emergency nursery schools. *Childhood Education*, 1935, *11*, 258.

Langdon, G., & Robinson, I. J. Nursery schools plus. *School Life*, 1940, *26*, 48-51.

Lazar, I. *Federal programs for young children*. Washington, D.C.: Appalachian Regional Commission, 1970.

Lazerson, M. Social reform and early childhood education: Some historical perspectives. *Urban Education, 5*, 1970, 83-102.

Lundberg, E. O. Public aid to mothers with dependent children. *Children's Bureau Publications*, No. 162, 1928.

Miles, M. (Ed.) *Innovation in education*. New York: Teachers College Press, Columbia, 1964.

NANE Bulletin, 1946, mimeoed.

National Advisory Commission on Civil Disorders. New York: Bantam Books, 1968.

National Advisory Council on the Education of Disadvantaged Children, House Report No. 188, 90th Congress, 1st Session. *Elementary and Secondary Amendments of 1967.* Report of the Committee on Education and Labor, House of Representatives together with separate and individual views to accompany HR 7819.

National Center for Educational Statistics. *Preprimary enrollment of children under six* (October 1970). Washington, D.C.: U.S. Department of Health, Education, and Welfare, 1971.

National Society for the Study of Education Yearbook, 1928. *Preschool and parent education*. Bloomington, Illinois: Public School Publishing Company, 1928.

National Society for the Study of Education Yearbook, 1947. *Early childhood education.* Chicago: University of Chicago Press, 1947.

National Society for the Study of Education Yearbook, 1972. *Early childhood education*. Chicago: University of Chicago Press, 1972.

New York Times, October 25, 1946, p. 30.

Norton, J. K. The place of nursery schools in public education. *Childhood Education*, 1945, *21*, 215.

Office of Economic Opportunity Panel of Authorities on Child Development (Robert Cooke, Chairman, 1964).

Parker, R., & Knitzer, J. *Day care and preschool services: Trends and issues*. Atlanta: Avatar Press, 1972.

Prescott, E., Milich, C., & Jones, E. *The politics of day care*, Vol. 1. Washington, D.C.: National Association for the Education of Young Children, 1972.

Rein, M. Values, knowledge, and social policy. In S. White, M. L. Day, P. K. Freeman, S. A. Hartman, & F. D. Messenger (Eds.), *Federal programs for young children: Review and recommendations,* Vol. III. Washington, D.C.: U.S. Government Printing Office, 1973. Appendix IIID.

Report on Proposed "Child Development" Program. Radical federal plan. *Human Events*, October 13, 1971, p. 902.

Robinson, N. J., & Robinson, H. D. A cross-cultural view of early education. *In Early childhood education* (Seventy-first Yearbook of the National Society for the Study of Education, Part II). Chicago: University of Chicago Press, 1972. Pp. 291-316.

Roby, P. (Ed.) *Day care: Who cares?* New York: Basic Books, 1973.

Rosenheim, M. K. The child and the law. In B. Caldwell & H. Riciutti (Eds.), *Review of child development research*, Vol. III. Chicago: University of Chicago Press, 1973. Pp. 515-520.

Rowhrer, W. D., Jr. Prime time for education: Early childhood or adolescence? *Harvard Education Review*, 1971, *41*, 416-341.

Salley, R. *Some factors affecting the supply and demand for preschool teachers in New York City* (Bureau of Publications: Contributions to Education, No. 870). New York: Teachers College, Columbia, 1943.

Schloss, Samuel. *Nursery-kindergarten enrollment of children under six* (October 1965). Washington, D.C.: National Center for Educational Statistics, 1966.

Searcy, E., & Ouellet, R. *The history and current status of federal legislation pertaining to day care programs*. Washington, D.C.: Socail Research Group, George Washington University, 1971.

Steinfels, M. O'B. *Who's minding the children*? New York: Simon & Schuster, 1973.

Stoddard, G. D. The tasks which await us. *World Organization of Early Childhood Education.* Report on the 2nd World Conference held at UNESCO House, Paris, August 24-26, 1949, p. 12.

U.S. Congress, Senate, Committee on Education and Labor. *Hearing on wartime care and protection of children of employed mothers.* 78th Congress, 1st Session, June 8, 1943.

U.S. Congress, Senate, Subcommittee on Children and Youth of the Committee on Labor and Public Welfare. *Hearings, American families: Trends and pressures, 1973.* 93rd Congress, 1st Session, 1973.

U.S. Congress, Senate, Subcommittee on Employment, Manpower, and Poverty of the Committee on Labor and Public Welfare. *Comprehensive Head Start, child development, and family services Act of 1972* Bill text and section-by-section analysis. 92nd Congress, 2nd Session, 1972, p. 1.

U.S. Department of Labor, Children's Bureau. *Defense of children series* (No. 2). 1942.

U.S. Senate Reports, Report No. 363, 78th Congress, 1st Session, 1943, p. 2.

U.S. Statutes, Vol. 55, Chapter 260, pp. 361-363. 1942.

White, S., Day, M. L., Freeman, P. K., Hartman, S. A., & Messenger, F. D. *Federal programs for young children.* Vol. I: *Goals and standards of public programs for children.* Washington: U.S. Government Printing Office, 1973.

White, E. N. History of the program and role played by the National Advisory Committee for Emergency Nursery Schools. *Proceedings of the Sixth Conference of the National Association for Nursery Education*. St. Louis: October 31-November 2, 1935, p. 79.

8

Parents as Teachers: A Rationale for Involving Parents in the Education of Their Young Handicapped Children

Edith Levitt
Shirley Cohen

City University of New York

Formal professional efforts to involve parents as educators of their young children are a recent development. They have been stimulated in part by a belated realization on the part of educators that parents play an important role in the intellectual development of their young children. While the present trend toward home-based instruction has been most visible in the case of the disadvantaged, educators working with handicapped children have begun to develop similar programs.

Barsch (1968) has commented that no parent is ever prepared to be the parent of a handicapped child. Yet all parents shape their young children's behavior, select and mediate their experiences, and, in effect, serve as their child's first teacher. The role of teacher in relation to a handicapped child is frequently difficult and baffling even for the skilled professional. It must seem overwhelming to untrained parents who often have to cope with this role unassisted.

There are poignant accounts by parents (Anderson, 1963; Kastein & Trace, 1966) which reflect the bewilderment and hopelessness they have felt in trying to deal with their handicapped children. At the same time, these same parents have obviously shown an extraordinary determination and ingenuity in nurturing their children's development. Apparently these parents had special resources that enabled them to assume the parent-teacher role and produce favorable results. Their accomplishments suggest that if the average parent of a handicapped child received systematic professional support, she (or he) might more nearly approximate these accomplishments.

There has been a long-standing tradition of professional home visits to parents of the handicapped, particularly the blind and the physically handicapped. However, these visits have been geared more to the teaching of self-help skills or to physical therapy than to the stimulation of intellectual development. This latter focus has been reserved for professional educators. Even in those cases where "home instruction" was offered, parents were excluded from the instructional process. This attitude—that intellectual development is the purview of educators only—has not only prevented educators from offering badly needed help to parents in their parent-as-teacher role, but has hindered educators from perceiving that such a role exists. Meanwhile, parents have had to fulfill this role as best they could, while often being criticized by educators for not having fulfilled their responsibilities.

Today, the field of special education has finally begun to assume professional responsibility at a sophisticated level for helping parents function as teachers of their children. However, home-based instruction for the handicapped is still an almost uncharted area badly in need of exploration.

HOME-BASED PROGRAMS FOR THE DISADVANTAGED

During the past decade, the field of early childhood education has been caught up in a period of experimentation and expansion. Two factors have helped to shape its direction. The first was a demand by disadvantaged parents and by society at large that their children be given a better foundation for academic achievement. The second was the argument by Hunt (1961) and others that appropriate early stimulation was critical for normal intellectual growth and that the lack of such stimulation contributed to the learning problems of disadvantaged children. Thus, it was natural for innovative childhood educators to undertake programs to help counteract early environmental deprivation in the disadvantaged. The large-scale Head Start Program (Westinghouse Report, 1969) was launched specifically for that purpose, as were programs directed by Bereiter and Engelmann (1966), Caldwell and Richmond (1968), and Klaus and Gray (1968).

While these programs utilized diverse approaches, all of them aimed at arresting the cumulative deficit characteristic of disadvantaged children. Thus, the finding that they produced only temporary benefits was a disappointment. It became evident that early childhood educators would have to try new directions before they could hope for a permanent effect on the intellectual development of the disadvantaged. It was in this atmosphere of search for alternative approaches that home-based programs for disadvantaged mothers and their young children began to proliferate. Klaus and Gray (1968) had pioneered the first of these programs. Within a short period, similar programs were undertaken by Karnes (1968), Gordon (1969), and Weikart (1967). The most ambitious efforts at home-based programs for the disadvantaged to date are designed as supplements to Head Start. They are the Parent and Child Centers for children under three, and the Home Start Centers for those between the ages of three and six.

The trend toward home-based instruction for disadvantaged was more specifically stimulated by an important insight that has recently emerged from the child development literature. This centers on the unique contribution of parents to the early intellectual development of their children. A recognition of this contribution has impelled educators to search for new ways to support the mother in her role as "first teacher" of her child. Their expectation is that facilitation of this role will create a useful additional channel for counteracting the learning problems of the disadvantaged.

Parent education in the form of group meetings and parent-teacher conferences has been a long-standing tradition in the preschool field. However, it has always been viewed as secondary to the main concern of preschool education—the classroom program. The current emphasis on the instructional role of the mother has added a new dimension and new importance to parent education. In the case of programs that are exclusively home-based, this recognition of the instructional role of the mother has become a central professional focus. It is also being accorded prime status in bicurricular programs, that is, those based both in home and school. The new emphasis on parent education is reflected in an address by Zigler (1972) at the inception of Home Start. He commented that the program that "impacts the child the most" was one that involves parents in direct interaction with their own child.

This argument for involving parents in their children's education has been presented most prominently in relation to the disadvantaged. However, it applies even more forcibly to the handicapped. Whereas disadvantaged children generally develop normally for the first year or so and slow down thereafter (Meier, Segner, & Brueter, 1970), children with constitutional handicaps are confronted by adverse developmental factors from their earliest days. Thus, participation of their mothers in efforts to stimulate intellectual development takes on added urgency. There are two reasons for expecting parents to respond positively to the concept of home-based instruction. The first is their special investment in the handicapped child and his problems. The second is the opportunity to try a new approach to a personal problem which engenders a feeling of bafflement and helplessness.

HOME-BASED PROGRAMS FOR THE HANDICAPPED

According to Calvert (1971), three-quarters of the project proposals considered under the Federal Handicapped Children's Early Assistance Act in 1969 were disapproved for reasons related to inadequate planning for parent participation in the proposed programs. Calvert's statement points up the growing emphasis by educational leaders on active participation of parents in programs for young handicapped children. This emphasis, along with the influence of the burgeoning home-based programs for the disadvantaged, probably portends a growth in home-based programs for the handicapped in coming years.

Sporadic examples for such programs are currently visible. Programs for the blind have a long tradition of home visiting which dates back to early in the century. This tradition of home visiting is still apparent in current service-oriented programs for the blind. At least one program (Fraiberg, Smith, & Adelson, 1969), has focused on specific guidance of mothers' interactions with their blind infants. While there is a history of home-visiting programs for cerebral palsied children, these programs have generally been medically oriented. More recently, home-visiting programs for the cerebral palsied have also provided assistance with day-to-day management (Weider & Hicks, 1970), along with counseling services for parents. Additional programs conducted by United Cerebral Palsy Associations have used the nursery school cooperative model in which mothers assist in the classroom and attend parent education classes (Headley & Leler, 1961). The long-standing focus on residential treatment for the deaf has tended to curtail home guidance for parents of the deaf. This lack is currently being remedied by programs at centers such as the John Tracy Clinic in Los Angeles, the Bill Wilkerson Speech and Hearing Center in Nashville (Horton, 1968), and the Robbins Speech and Hearing Center in Boston (Luterman, 1967). The John Tracy Clinic has also developed correspondence courses for parents of preschool deaf children (Tracy & Thielman, 1972), and deaf-blind children (Thielman & Meyer, 1973). A scattering of home-based programs for retarded children are reported in the literature, the most comprehensive being that conducted by Weikart (1967) with mildly retarded subjects with disadvantaged backgrounds. The Portage Project (Yavner, 1972) involved home training of young multiply handicapped children, mostly retardates, with mothers carrying out educational prescriptions defined for a week at a time by Home Trainers. Only one formal home-based program for emotionally disturbed children was identified through the literature, that of the League School in Brooklyn (Doernberg, Rosen, & Walker, 1968). Susser (1974) described a program for young brain injured children in which parents were used as both teaching assistants in the classroom and as home teachers.

ABERRANT DEVELOPMENT

In developing the present rationale for home-based instruction of the handicapped, a major consideration has been the early adverse factors that produce cognitive dysfunction in these children.

The seriously handicapped child, like all children, is subject to general developmental laws. However, he also seems to be subject to special subprinciples within these laws—subprinciples which pertain to an aberrant developmental course. These subprinciples center around specific adverse factors, both intrinsic and extrinsic, that appear in almost all seriously handicapped children. They are exemplified by a cumulative intellectual deficit, and by impairment in affective aspects of the mother–child relationship. These adverse factors are seen as operating in a mutually reinforcing manner to produce a negative impact on the child's overall development. The sections which follow provide expansion and documentation of the thesis that early adverse factors reinforce each other in producing cumulative dysfunction in handicapped children. A better understanding of these factors should pinpoint ways of compensating for their effects.

Intrinsic Factors

Intrinsic factors which are seen as having an adverse effect on cognitive function in the handicapped are cumulative deficit, "critical period" problems, and sensory deprivation. They have received a great deal of attention in the literature, notably from those concerned with disadvantaged children. They are viewed here as central determinants of cognitive dysfunction in the handicapped child. Other intrinsic factors which play a distinctive role in the aberrant developmental course of handicapped children involve temperament and motivation.

Cumulative deficit. Hebb (1949) has discussed the initially diffuse character of the infant's sensory input and has described the way in which it takes on cortical organization. He has defined this process as "primary learning" and has stated that it forms a basis for all subsequent learning. Hunt (1961) has elaborated on Hebb's theory, suggesting that primary learning includes early information-processing strategies. Organismic factors in the handicapped child would hamper this initial priming, or tuning up, of the cognitive apparatus. Thus, the process of cumulative deficit would be activated from the child's earliest days.

Fowler (1971) has pointed out another aspect of the cumulative deficit problem that has special application to the handicapped. "Failure to early establish a high-level cognitive baseline for learning is thus to generate alternative, poor modes of functioning. These alternative modes become preferred, but poorly adaptive systems, leaving the child to meet each new encounter with the same old, less effective means [p. 255]." The "poorly adaptive systems" noted by Fowler are most frequently encountered among the handicapped. In sufficiently severe cases, as in the profoundly retarded, these can lead to a virtually total arrest in cognitive growth.

Problems relating to the "critical period" hypothesis. A child who is subject to cumulative deficit would also suffer from a related set of problems. As the lag in cognitive functioning increases relative to the normal developmental timetable, the child becomes increasingly vulnerable to problems associated with the "critical period" hypothesis. According to Caldwell (1962), these arise from the fact that there is an optimal developmental period for the emergence of various skills in the young child. If these are not mastered within normal time limits, they will be bypassed, or else will appear in an attenuated form. In terms of the handicapped child, his developmental lag, if sufficiently severe, would lead to "critical period" problems. These, in turn, would hinder the acquisition of more advanced skills, and so would contribute further to the process of cumulative deficit.

Sensory deprivation. An important consequence of impairment in early sensory learning of the handicapped child would be a vulnerability to sensory deprivation. As noted by Meier *et al.* (1970), sensory deprivation can stem both from extrinsic factors, as in the case of the disadvantaged, or from intrinsic factors, as in the brain-injured. Intrinsic factors could be expected to produce analogous sensory deprivation in other types of handicap.

DiLeo (1967) has described the newborn normal infant as being "in constant exchange" with the environment and thus seeking out his own stimulation. However, the handicapped child may be hampered in this goal because of inadequate sensory processing mechanisms. Deprivation in sensory stimulation could be expected to produce an apathetic reaction to environmental stimuli similar to that seen in institutionalized children (Provence & Lipton, 1962). The early sensory deprivation experienced by handicapped children may help to explain the motivation problems often manifested by them.

The developmental factors just reviewed point up the urgency of early remedial planning for handicapped children. These factors also pose special hazards for the affective relationship between parent and child. Thus, the cumultive deficit factor, manifested in poor progress on the part of the child, would produce a reaction of disappointment and anxiety in the parent. Again, repeated failure in efforts to evoke a response to play materials in the child would give the parent a feeling of helplessness and discouragement.

Temperament. Longitudinal studies (Escalona, 1968; Thomas, Chess, & Birch, 1968) indicate that infants start out with distinctive temperamental characteristics and that these help to shape adult responses toward them. According to Thomas, Chess, and Birch, the "easy" child is one who shows a positive response to new stimuli, adapts readily to change, exhibits a preponderance of positive moods, and has reactions that are mild to moderate in intensity. Such a child differs markedly from the "difficult" child who responds to new stimuli with negative moods, and has reactions of high intensity. A major finding by these authors was that the temperamentally difficult child was more likely to be diagnosed at a later date as suffering from a behavior disorder.

Kahn's (1969) description of psychological characteristics in the brain-damaged fits into the general picture of the difficult child. According to Kahn, such a child exhibits lability of mood, reduced tolerance to frustration, problems in impulse control, a tendency toward disorganized or regressed behavior, and a pervasive reaction of anxiety.

The autistic child also fits readily into the picture of a temperamentally difficult child. Kanner (1957) describes such a child as seriously lacking in response to interpersonal contact, and generally to objects as well. He is highly resistant to change, and his moods are predominantly passive or apathetic, interspersed in some cases with sudden spells of irritability, or outbursts of temper.

Sensorily impaired children present temperamental difficulties of a different kind. As a result of the exclusion of the visual world, the blind infant is described (Burlingham, 1961) as initially passive and withdrawn. However, after interpersonal contact was established, such children typically develop an overdependent response to the adult. Ewing and Ewing (1964) have referred to the deaf child as "exceedingly vulnerable to a sense of insecurity." They also cite research findings which show that the deaf child has twice as many tantrums as the hearing child.

Intensification of the temperamental difficulties of handicapped children can be expected on several counts. First, such children are subject to specific organismic problems and discomforts which accompany severe handicaps. Secondly, they tend to be impaired in the ability to have satisfying exchanges with the social and/or physical environment. Finally, the problems of responding to and handling these difficult children create adverse reactions in their mothers, which have a negative effect, in turn, on their children.

Motivation. Clinical experience suggests that seriously handicapped children have limited intrinsic motivation. This contrasts with the high level of intrinsic motivation manifested by the well-functioning normal child and the self-activated learning which accompanies it. Several aspects of the child development literature help to explain the motivational problems characteristic of the handicapped child. First, the sense of competence (White, 1959) which spurs the normal child to further activity might be impaired in the handicapped child because of faulty or erratic performance. Secondly, as Hunt (1961) has suggested, an important incentive for interaction with the environment stems from incongruity between "what is known and what is perceived." Since many handicapped children would be less capable of grasping this incongruity, they would also be less motivated to interact with the environment and learn from it.

Another factor which has potential importance for motivation in the handicapped should be noted here—the mother's role as mediator of experiences for the young child. This role may be disrupted when the child is handicapped. This postulate and its ramifications are considered in more detail in a later section.

Extrinsic Factors

This section focuses on factors which are not inherent in the child's impairment, but rather which involve an environmental reaction to this impairment. These factors include: maternal mourning, the affective interaction between mother and child, and the mediational role of the mother.

Maternal mourning. Meadow and Meadow (1971) have discussed some of the factors underlying the assumption of the parental role when a child is handicapped. They state that transition to the role of parenthood requires "socialization," that is, learning ways of behaving and seeing oneself in a given role. However, parents undergo a different sort of socialization process when they are confronted with the task of becoming the parent of a handicapped child. It is then experienced not simply as a transition to parenthood but as "an unwanted and distasteful status." The power of this feeling is suggested by Burlingham's (1961) comment that the mother of a blind infant may wish for its death.

Solnit and Stark (1961) have interpreted the reaction of mothers to newborn defective babies as one of mourning. Touching on the mother's image of the expected child and her psychological preparation for its arrival, they contrasted these with the sudden loss of that baby, and the sudden appearance instead of a "feared, threatening, anger-evoking child." Absorption of this trauma is inevitably a slow process characterized by disappointment and a feeling of helplessness. Thus, at least in cases where the defect is apparent or known to the mother, the very fact of childbirth lays the groundwork for a negative response to the mothering role. While dynamics would vary somewhat in cases in which awareness of defect occurs at a later time, a similar mourning reaction could be anticipated at that point.

Affective interaction between mother and child. It was previously noted that constitutional deficits in the child may impair the affective interchange between mother and child. This reaction in the mother would intensify such response patterns as withdrawal, dependency, or hostility. Yarrow (1968) has stated that the most distinctive aspect of the human environment for the young infant is the affective interaction with the caretaker. This must be even truer for the handicapped child, with his special need for acceptance and support. Hence, hindrance of this interchange would have a proportionally more serious effect. Yarrow has described this interchange as including "protecting, buffering, gratifying, and responsive" functions on the part of the mother. However, the fulfillment of these functions would be difficult even under favorable circumstances because the responses of the handicapped child tend to be delayed, erratic, or generally "off kilter." The undependable communication system between the handicapped infant and his mother contrasts with the efficient signaling system which is developed between the normal infant and his mother.

Obviously, the mother's temperament and personal needs also enter into the affective interchange with her child, whether he is normal or handicapped. As Caldwell and Hersher (undated paper) have noted, the "affiliative" mother will feel frustrated by an aloof baby, while the aloof mother has special problems with the overdependent child. Such reactions would be intensified under the special pressures engendered by a handicapped child.

Mothers who have a very stressful reaction to the child's handicap, or mothers with unfavorable temperamental and emotional characteristics, will clearly have a negative influence on the child's overall development. However, by the same token, potential developmental problems in the handicapped child can be alleviated when maternal responses have an appropriately supportive quality. In the study by Thomas *et al.* (1968), three children were identified as suffering from brain damage. The variation in their subsequent development led the authors to conclude that the nature of behavioral response in such children is not a direct manifestation of brain damage. Rather it is the result of the interaction of a child with a damaged nervous system and the interpersonal environment.

While the main focus of the present discussion has been on the troublesome problems encountered by mothers of the handicapped, it should be noted that mothers are also able to assimilate these problems to a considerable extent, and often successfully assume the traditional nurturing role in relation to their child. Furthermore, in working through these problems, mothers are apt to invest a special feeling of involvement and concern for their handicapped child. These positive maternal attitudes should constitute a favorable base for mothers who take on the "parent-teacher" role.

The mother's mediational role. The role of the mother as mediator of experience for her child has recently been receiving increased attention. Miller (1970) has discussed such mediational functions as ordering the physical and spatial environment for the child, directing his attention to relevant dimensions of objects, and providing a general response model for him to imitate.

In a similar vein, Fuerstein (1970) has described the mediating adult as interposing herself between the child and external sources of stimulation, and as "framing, selecting, focusing, and feeding back" environmental experiences so that they create appropriate learning sets. In his view, such mediation is a prerequisite to autonomous nonmediated learning by the child. In touching on negative factors which might hinder mediated learning, Fuerstein referred to socioeconomic class and to various problems inherent in the parent or the child.

Fuerstein's view that intrinsic factors in a child can hamper the mediational role of the adult is particularly relevant to the handicapped child. The adverse factors previously cited, be they developmental, temperamental, or motivational, all hinder the mother in her efforts to mediate experience and learning for the child. She brings to this role two added problems: a history of complex affective interchange with the child; and the investment of the mediational role with overtones related directly to the child's handicap. These overtones may range from a feeling of futility in attempting to teach the child anything to an expectation of having a "magical" affect on his development. As a consequence of these factors, learning frequently becomes an emotionally charged area for the handicapped child and his mother.

Mothers of normal young children generally present experiences to their children in a pleasurable context, whether this represents their own personal response to them, or one that they project on behalf of the child. However, this positive attitude would inevitably be tempered in the case of mothers of the handicapped because of problems attached to their efforts at mediation. The disruption of the mother's mediational role would impair the quality of cognitive stimulation available to the child. It would also deprive him of a satisfactory model for the development of intrinsic motivation. The latter factor could help to explain the inadequate motivation towards play materials and learning characteristic of the handicapped child.

Higher-Order Cognitive Processes

The present rationale assumes that constitutional factors in the handicapped can produce an aberrant developmental course, and that this will lead, in turn, to some degree of cognitive dysfunction. It is further posited that this dysfunction is concentrated in higher-order intellectual processes. Research support for this view is provided by House and Zeaman (1963), Luria (1963), and O'Connor and Hermelin (1963).

A further line of support for a special deficit in the higher-order process of the handicapped is provided by Jensen (1969). He hypothesized that children's abilities can be subdivided into lower-order associational ones (Level I), and more advanced higher-order ones (Level II). Based on an overview of relevant research, he concluded that both disadvantaged and retarded children perform as well as equal MA normals on Level I tasks, but lag behind them on more advanced Level II tasks.

A final reason for postulating a higher-order processing deficit in the handicapped is based on two studies conducted by Levitt. Both studies dealt with higher- and lower-order cognitive processes as inferred from behavioral responses. The first study (1972b) showed that when retardates and normals are equated for reading scores, normals make significantly more higher-order errors than do retardates. The inference was that normals would also use more higher-order processes in making correct responses. The second study (1972a) suggested that mediational processes used by middle-class normals were superior to those used by retarded, brain-injured, and disadvantaged subjects.

IMPLICATIONS FOR HOME-BASED PROGRAMS FOR THE HANDICAPPED CHILD

The foregoing review has highlighted a set of adverse factors that may hamper the development of the handicapped child and contribute to his cognitive dysfunction. It suggests that remediation of such dysfunction requires early intervention; the involvement of parents, particularly mothers; and extensive curricular organization. Various curricular models stressing such organization can be found in both the early childhood and special education literature.

A deficit in higher-order processing characteristic of handicapped children was previously noted. These processes evolve autonomously in normal children (Kagan & Wright, 1963). However, their development and application present special problems for the handicapped. Hence, a relevant program for handicapped children could be profitably conceptualized along an additional dimension, based on the developmental accomplishments of the normal child and the higher-order strategies that underly them. It should be helpful to review representative tasks that tap higher-order strategies in normal children, and then use them as a base for developing similar strategies in the handicapped.

The foregoing review also highlighted negative aspects of the affective interchange between the handicapped child and his mother. Amelioration of these negative aspects would facilitate the mother's assumption of the parent-teacher role. There are well-developed general guidelines available in the literature (e.g., Robinson & Robinson, 1965; Barsch, 1968) for working with parents in terms of their attitudes toward their handicapped children. A variety of formats is available, ranging from parent-teacher conferences and group meetings, to individual counseling and psychotherapy. These formats would need exploration to determine which are appropriate for particular home-based programs.

Another aspect of mother-child interaction that emerged from the previous review needs consideration here. This centers on a difficulty mothers may have in fulfilling their function as mediator of experience for their handicapped children. This, in turn, may have a negative effect on their children's cognitive functioning and motivation. One helpful approach here would be to formulate a method which helps the mother provide both a cognitive and affective model for her child in the exploration and use of materials. One program which does this with mothers of young disadvantaged children is the Mother-Child Home Program developed by Levenstein (1971).

While the full impact of home-based instruction is still unknown, initial results have been encouraging. It is a promising new avenue for the education of the handicapped that obviously warrants further exploration. It is also bound to stimulate interesting new ideas and approaches to the education of the handicapped.

In an age when more and more severely impaired children are being kept in the home and community rather than in institutions, it is not only desirable but almost imperative for the educational world to provide direction and aid to parents in the long-term, difficult task they have undertaken. If we are really dedicated to helping handicapped children achieve their maximum potential, we will do this. If we want to make our own work as teachers more fruitful we will do this.

REFERENCES

Anderson, C. M. *Jan, my brain-damaged daughter*. Portland, Oregon: The Durham Press, 1963.

Barsch, R. H. *The parent-teacher partnership*. Arlington, Virginia: The Council for Exceptional Children, 1968.

Bereiter, C., & Engelmann, S. *Teaching disadvantaged children in the preschool*. New York: Prentice-Hall, 1966.

Burlingham, D. Some notes on the development of the blind. *The Psychoanalytic Study of the Child*, Vol. 16. New York: International Universities Press, 1961. Pp. 121-145.

Caldwell, B. M. The usefulness of the critical period hypothesis in the study of filiative behavior. *Merrill-Palmer Quarterly*, 1962, *8*, 229-242.

Caldwell, B. M., & Hersher, L. Mother-infant interaction during the first year of life. Syracuse University, unpublished paper.

Caldwell, B. M., & Richmond, J. B. The Children's Center in Syracuse, New York. In L. L. Dittman (Ed.), *Early child care: The new perspectives*. New York: Atherton Press, 1968. Pp. 326-358.

Calvert, D. R. Dimensions of family involvement in early childhood education. *Exceptional Children*, 1971, *37*, 655-663.

DiLeo, J. H. Developmental evaluation of very young infants. In J. Hellmuth (Ed.), *Exceptional infants: The normal infant,* Vol. 1. Seattle, Washington: Special Child Publication, 1967.

Doernberg, N., Rosen, B., & Walker, T. T. *A home training program for young mentally ill children*. Brooklyn, New York: League School for Seriously Disturbed Children, 1968.

Escalona, S. K. *The roots of individuality*. Chicago: Aldine, 1968.

Ewing, A., & Ewing, E. C. *Teaching deaf children to talk*. Washington, D.C.: The Volta Bureau, 1964.

Fowler, W. Cognitive baselines in early childhood: Developmental learning and differentiation of competence rule systems. In J. Hellmuth (Ed.), *Cognitive studies 2: Deficits in cognition*. New York: Bruner/Mazel, 1971. Pp. 231-279.

Fuerstein, R. A dynamic approach to the causation, prevention, and alleviation of retarded performance. In H. C. Haywood (Ed.), *Social-cultural aspects of mental retardation*. New York: Appleton-Century-Croft, 1970. Pp. 341-377.

Fraiberg, S., Smith, M., & Adelson, E. An educational program for blind infants. *Journal of Special Education*, 1969, *3*, 121-139.

Gordon, I. J. *Early child stimulation through parent education*. Institute for Development of Human Resources, University of Florida. Final report to the Children's Bureau, Department of Health, Education and Welfare, 1969.

Headley, L., & Leler, H. A nursery school for cerebral palsied children. *Children*, 1961, *8*, 17-21.

Hebb, D. O. *The organization of behavior*. New York: Wiley, 1949.

Horton, K. B. Home demonstration teaching for parents of very young deaf children. *Volta Review*, 1968, *70*, 97-101, 104.

House, B. J., & Zeaman, D. The role of attention in retardate discrimination learning. In N. Ellis (Ed.), *Handbook of mental deficiency*. New York: McGraw-Hill, 1963. Pp. 159-223.

Hunt, J. McV. Motivation inherent in information processing and action. In O. J. Harvey (Ed.), *Motivation and social interaction: Cognitive determinants*. New York: The Ronald Press, 1961. Pp. 35-94.

Jensen, A. R. Intelligence, learning ability and socioeconomic status. *Journal of Special Education*, 1969, *3*, 23-33.

Kagan, J., & Wright, J. C. (Eds.) Basic cognitive processes in children. *Monographs of the Society for Research in Child Development*, 1963, *28*, No. 2, Serial No. 86.

Kahn, J. P. The emotional concomitants of brain-damaged children. *Journal of Learning Disabilities.* 1969, *2*, 644-651.

Kanner, L. *Child psychiatry*. Springfield, Illinois: Charles Thomas, 1957.

Karnes, M. B. Evaluation of two preschool programs. *Exceptional Children*. 1968, *34*, 667-676.

Kastein, S., & Trace, B. *The birth of language: The case history of a non-verbal child.* Springfield, Illinois: Charles Thomas, 1966.

Klaus, R. A., & Gray, S. W. The early training project for disadvantaged children: A report after five years. *Monographs of the Society for Research in Child Development*, 1968, *33*, No. 4, Serial No. 120.

Levenstein, P. Learning through (and from) mothers. *Childhood Education*, 1971, *48*, 130-134.

Levitt, E. The effect of labeling on concept-matching task performed by four preschool groups. Teachers College, Columbia University. Unpublished paper, 1972. (a)

Levitt, E. Higher-order and lower-order reading responses of mentally retarded and non-retarded children at the first-grade level. *American Journal of Mental Deficiency,* 1972, *77*, 13-20. (b)

Luria, A. R. (Ed.) *The mentally retarded child*. New York: Macmillan, 1963.

Luterman, D. M. A parent-oriented nursery program for preschool deaf children. *Volta Review*, 1967, *69*, 515-520.

Meadow, K. P., & Meadow, L. Changing role perceptions for parents of handicapped children. *Exceptional Children*, 1971, *38*, 21-28.

Meier, J. H., Segner, L. L., & Brueter, B. B. An educational system for high-risk infants: A preventive approach to developmental and learning disabilities. In J. Hellmuth (Ed.), *Disadvantaged child*, Vol. 3: *Compensatory education: A national debate*. New York: Bruner/Mazel, 1970. Pp. 405-444.

Miller, J. O. Cultural deprivation and its modification: Effects of intervention. In H. C. Haywood (Ed.), *Social-cultural aspects of mental retardation*. New York: Appleton-Century-Croft, 1970. Pp. 451-489.

O'Connor, N., & Hermelin, B. *Speech and thought in severe subnormality*. New York: Macmillan, 1963.

Provence, S., & Lipton, R. *Infants in institutions*. New York: International Universities Press, 1962.

Robinson, H. B., & Robinson, N. M. *The mentally retarded child: A psychological approach*. New York: McGraw-Hill, 1965.

Solnit, A. J., & Stark, M. H. Mourning and the birth of a defective child. *The psychoanalytic study of the child*, Vol. 16. New York: International Universities Press, 1961. Pp. 523-537.

Susser, P. Parents as partners. *The Exceptional Parent*, 1974, *4*, 41-47.

Thielman, V. B., & Meyer, S. *John Tracy Clinic correspondence learning program for parents of preschool deaf-blind children*. Los Angeles: John Tracy Clinic, 1973.

Thomas, A., Chess, S., & Birch, M. *Temperament and behavior disorders*. New York: New York Uiversity Press, 1968.

Tracy, S., & Thielman, V. B. *John Tracy Clinic correspondence course for parents of preschool deaf children*. Los Angeles: John Tracy Clinic, 1972.

Weider, D., & Hicks, J. *Evaluation of an early intervention program for neurologically impaired children and their families*. United Cerebral Palsy of Queens. Final Project Report, 1970.

Weikart, D. *Longitudinal results of the Ypsilanti Perry preschool project*. Ypsilanti, Michigan: High/Scope Educational Research Foundation, 1967.

Westinghouse Report. *The impact of Headstart: An evaluation of the effects of Headstart on children's cognitive and affective development.* New York: Westinghouse Learning Corporation of New York, 1969.

White, R. W. Motivation reconsidered: The concept of competence. *Psychological Review*. 1959, *66*, 297-333.

Yarrow, L. Conceptualizing the early environment. In L. L. Dittman (Ed.), *Early child care: The new perspectives.* New York: Atherton Press, 1968. Pp. 15-26.

Yavner, M. *The Portage Project: A home approach to the early education of multiply handicapped children in a rural area*. Portage, Wisconsin: Cooperative Educational Service Agency No. 12, 1972.

Zigler, E. Greetings to all participants, Home Start National Conference, In *Report of First National Home Start Conference*. St. Louis, Mo., April 1972.

9

Helping Young Children Cope with Death[1]

Joanne E. Bernstein

City University of New York

Today's children are often separated from their grandparents by hundreds of miles, and the deaths of these older relatives can appear as remote incidents. Even when there is a death in the immediate family, it rarely occurs at home. Children are deliberately and specifically excluded from hospitals. In addition, most children today live in urban areas and do not have the same opportunity to observe the life and death cycle of animals as do children who are raised in farm communities.

Death has come to be looked upon as an accident, or an unnatural event in our culture. We live in a society which can send people to the moon, yet it is upsetting for many of us to reflect that we cannot master disease, old age, and the final mystery of death. We hide our ill and aged in segregated facilities, and we hesitate to answer questions or speak of our embarrassment when we seem unable to conquer cancer, heart disease, and death. Death remains the final taboo.

Yet by the age of five, almost one child in 20 has lost a parent through death (Kliman, 1968). It is impossible to keep news of these losses from neighbors and schoolmates. In addition, children continue to experience the death of pets and insects. Overhearing the adult news shows, a child would have to be deaf not to absorb knowledge of crashes, killings, and wars. Children's programming on television, however, offers a confusing counterimpression. On cartoon shows, people and animals are put through ordeals which would appear to damage or kill, yet the characters get right up to do battle once more. It appears that we are

[1]The material in this publication was prepared pursuant to a contract with the National Institute of Education, U. S. Department of Health, Education, and Welfare.

not raising a deathless generation, but we might be raising one which suffers confusion about death.

CHILDREN'S CONCEPTS OF DEATH

Even if society were willing to confront death, it seems that children under the age of nine would be confused about its meaning. Death is a very difficult concept to integrate. Children's concepts of time are poor. They do not firmly grasp what being old or young really means. Based on Maurer's research, researchers now feel that children's concepts of death grow along with their concepts of time, beginning with their awareness of the alternate states of wakefulness and sleeping (Gullo, 1973). These alternating states are also the first introduction to temporary separation. The next development for children is their playful investigation (peek-a-boo) of the concept of absence and presence. Children's experiments with throwing toys from cribs and high chairs, and their curiosity about the functions of trash cans and toilets with flush systems, pave the way toward a concept about death. For example, in the toy-dropping game, the pleasure is in the reappearance of the toy (even 20 or 30 repetitions of this game do not tire the young investigators). Children's interest in depositing waste into receptacles reflects pondering of the "all-gone" phenomenon. Some things reappear, while others never do (Kastenbaum, 1967).

Marcia Nagy did pioneering research concerning children's concepts of death in Budapest during the 1940s. She studied 378 children of varying religions and social levels, gathering materials in several ways. Children from seven to ten years of age were asked to "write down everything that comes to your mind about death." Children from six to ten years of age made drawings about death, sometimes explaining them. Younger children (three through six) took part in general discussions, using a free form technique encouraging rapport, in which they were able to talk about their ideas and feelings concerning death. Nagy's (1959) research reveals that children of age five do usually see death as reversible. They see life in death and are unable to separate death from life. They often view the dead as living in some limited state, either within the grave or in another place. The psychological reason behind such perceptions is the fact that young children know that they themselves are alive. Their entire world is seen through egocentric glasses, so they cannot imagine anything that is so totally unlike themselves. Those children under five who are able to assimilate the idea of physical death may think that to be dead is to be asleep or on a journey. At this age children are likely to view death as temporary, gradual, and/or reversible.

Between the ages of five and nine, children begin to see death as a permanent state, and are likely to personify death, perhaps seeing it as an angel or as an old man. Children often feel that they cannot see the "death-man" but that the person carried off sees him for a brief moment. In this stage, the existence of death is accepted, but it must be externalized, so that one might escape the grasp of the death-carrier.

Finally, at about the age of nine, children acknowledge freely that death is permanent and universal. Moreover, they now know that one cannot escape the "death-man," for there is no such being. Death is a natural part of life, governed by laws (Nagy, 1959).

Gerald Koocher (1973) recently made a study of children's concepts of death with 75 middle class American children between the ages of six and fifteen as subjects. He tested their cognitive development, placed them in groups which would match each of Piaget's stages, and asked them four questions: "What makes things die?" "How do you make things come back to life?" "When will you die?" and "What happens then?" His findings revealed that children's responses are related to their levels of cognitive development rather than age, and he recommended classifying their concepts in this way.

When asked about the causes of death, children at the preoperational level responded with egocentric, often fantastic responses (for example, eating a dirty bug), very much in keeping with Piaget's accounts of the child's perception of the world. Koocher's findings led him to recommend that adults who deal with death in their work with young children take the time to explore and listen to the children's ideas, so that distorted misconceptions can come to light and be cleared up instead of being allowed to grow larger in the children's minds.

In addition, Koocher found that only preoperational children believe that dead things can come back to life. This result corroborates Piaget's findings concerning animism. Because of children's lack of ability to differentiate between themselves and the world at younger ages, they tend to give biological and psychological traits (such as life and will) to physical objects and events. As they grow older, they gradually restrict the kinds of objects they are willing to give life (Piaget, 1951).

When asked how long they will live, Koocher's subjects, not yet at the concrete operations stage, estimated wildly (for example, ten, three hundred).

Perhaps Koocher's most interesting finding, however, was in response to the question, "What will happen when you die?" Koocher's subjects did not explain causes of death in terms of personification but elaborated upon actual consequences, such as burial, funerals, and other tangible matters. On first examination, this finding appears to be a direct contradiction to Nagy's results with five- to nine-year-olds. Koocher did not link his final question to the Piagetian stages, regarding the question as broadly interpretive. Koocher felt that his subjects were telling him that specificity of detail might be as effective a means of control over death as personification. If so, there may be no contradiction between the findings of the two studies. Might the difference in results merely reflect cultural differences between nations? Or between generations, the present one being influenced by the media? Or are there important structural differences in research methodology which deserve examination? These and other possibilities bear further investigation, but it is nevertheless true that the reliance of Koocher's children upon concrete detail and the reliance of Nagy's children on a person both uphold Nagy's finding that, for those children, death is still something they cannot grasp. If children today are saying, as Koocher indicates, that if they know some of what will happen in death they need not worry, then as he recommends, it becomes of paramount importance that death be explained honestly and reassuringly to them.

EXPLAINING DEATH TO CHILDREN

Until children are old enough to view death as a part of the cycle of life, it is certainly a difficult task to explain death. Currently, psychologists recommend that death be treated in a matter-of-fact manner as early as possible. It is hoped that then children's views of death as a game of cops and robbers will be diminished. Levinson and Kinney (1969) have described this "game" attitude toward death as one in which the "participants are resurrected when the rules of the game require it [p. 271]." Young children will, in part, cling to their idea that death is temporary, but perhaps they will at least be able to understand that people are not replaceable, as they appear to be in cartoons. It is, after all, quite a feat to explain satisfactorily to a child how a dead person can appear in a dream and still be totally dead. Yet it is necessary to explain truthfully. If death is explained as sleep, some children become fearful when they go to sleep (Salk, 1972). If death is described as a trip to heaven to join God, some children will deeply desire to be invited, and will hold out for a reunion (Schowalter, 1974b).

Fantasies of reunion are especially intense if children feel guilty about their life with the deceased and/or about the death itself. The child, being egocentric, might see the death as an expression of the dead person's wish to abandon him/her. In the child's mind, the deceased did not like certain behavior patterns which the child demonstrated and chose this method of desertion. As the child most likely wished "nasty" things upon the deceased sometime before death, his difficulty in discerning wishes and words from deeds merely compounds his guilt. When death can be looked upon as a part of the cycle of life, adults naturally help to minimize the child's fears that someone (usually him/herself) is responsible for this unnatural, unlawful thing called death.

Children are curious about death. Both those who have been affected by a loss and those who have not are highly interested. They do not shy away until they are taught that death is an improper subject for investigation. Anthony (1974) did a study in which the word "dead" was added to a vocabulary test. The word was avoided by only two of the 91 children taking the test.

Children's dramatic play may reflect death and loss themes. They may want to look at and touch dead birds. They may kill insects. Such play, rather than being morbid preoccupation, is actually an effort to come to terms with the permanence and irreversibility which they sense. For this reason, when adults quickly remove a dead pet from view, they keep an experience in mastery away from children. If they go the next step, and swiftly replace the pet, they announce that loved ones are quickly replaceable, almost interchangeable. Again, children are cheated of opportunities to express and master their feelings. In addition, children sense and assimilate the dismay and/or shame of the adults. If parents and teachers can bear it, they will help children by allowing them their curiosity (Stein, 1974).

Children want to know about cemeteries: what they are, why we need them, and what happens there. Funerals for pets provide a good introduction to the cemetery and burials. In a pet funeral, children see the reality of burial. They have an opportunity to express sorrow, and they also can be introduced to the continuity of life concept: in returning to the earth, the dead contribute to the well-being of the living.

As children become more cognizant of the occurrence of death, they are naturally fearful that their parents will die. "Who will take care of me?" they ask. Both parents and teachers are asked "When will you die?" or "Will you die soon?" The adult can explain that most people do not die until they have had a chance to accomplish some important tasks of living: seeing children and grandchildren grow up, or learning to do a job well, or any number of other tasks. It can be explained that by the time these tasks are finished the body has aged and the person is likely to be very old. While some people are not fortunate enough to live until they have had a chance to accomplish their life's tasks, most people die when they are aged and ready to die. Underlying any explanation of death can be a focus on living and an emphasis on enjoying the time we are here. Incorporated into the explanation can be talk of the work of the many life-keepers: the parents who give children good food so that they may remain healthy, the doctors who give children inoculations and medicine, etc. Children might also be interested in knowing that while we all must die, we pass on life-giving materials: our children, our genes, our traditions, values, and approaches to life.

All children need support in their efforts to master the concept of death, but the children who need the most help are those who have experienced a death within the family.

ASPECTS OF CHILDREN'S MOURNING

Childhood mourning has been described by Kliman (1968). He speaks of three stages in the mourning process. The first is testing and accepting the reality of the loss. Examples: The child instinctively runs up to the bedroom, expecting to find the deceased father there, or absentmindedly sets a place for him at dinner. Stage two is the working over of memories related to the deceased. Examples: The child wants to see movies of the father, or wants to hear and re-hear certain stories about the times they had together. The third stage, according to Kliman, involves the cultivation of substitute object relationships. Examples: The child begins to want to sit next to a particular uncle at family dinners, or develops a warm rapport with a man at school.

Acute grief is accompanied by bodily symptoms which have recently been found to be rather consistent. Common manifestations of bereavement are shallowness of breath, fatigue accompanied by inability to sleep, and lack of appetite. There are many other possibilities. Children should be helped to understand that such physiological changes are not unusual.

Adults often wonder if young children should attend the funeral of a family member. The funeral service has several functions. It is a way of saying goodbye. It is also a way of reinforcing the reality of the death: at the funeral service, participants give up the lost person. The funeral is also an opportunity for release, and for sharing, among family and friends. In addition, the funeral has elements of ceremony and ritual. It can be an impressive and memorable event.

Psychologists have differed in their judgments concerning the age at which a child should be asked to participate in a funeral service. It is generally agreed, however, that a child of *any* age who wishes to attend should be allowed to do so. Many psychologists feel that the attendance of a young child can be far more beneficial than protecting the child. Burial is vivid, and subsequent fantasies of reunion will be less intense. The funeral takes place early in the mourning process and can set the tone for later stages of bereavement. The difference between deliberate exclusion and an invitation to share in family sorrow can mean the difference between a child who hides grief and one who is able to talk about feelings. John Schowalter (1974b), a psychiatrist at Yale University, recommends that certain steps be taken if a young child does choose to go to a family funeral. He recommends that someone explain the procedure beforehand, and that a relative or good friend be assigned to stay with the child constantly throughout the service. He advises that the young child may fall asleep or wish to leave the service and that these possibilities should be acceptable to the caretaker.

At times adults have difficulty understanding children's grief patterns as these are not identical to those of adults. Martha Wolfenstein (in Wolfenstein & Kliman, 1965) has elucidated a phenomenon which confounds and irritates those who observe it without understanding it. When young children experience a loss, they feel deeply sad for awhile, but then they quickly replace their distress with industrious, happy pursuits. The adult is often shocked at the child's seeming lack of feeling. Actually, according to Wolfenstein, the child becomes preoccupied with normal living only because the sadness is so huge that it would be overwhelming and intolerable to continue to experience it. She calls this the "short sadness span [p. 69]."

The short sadness span is not uncommon and can be considered normal. However, one should be on the lookout for an overlong period of denial, for delayed mourning, and for neurotic mourning. These conditions might require therapeutic intervention.

When children do not react at all to a death in the family, they often displace their feelings about the death onto another event. One might be surprised to see sudden and bitter tears over the death of a celebrity or over a death in a movie, for example. Mourning can be delayed if the significant adults in children's lives consciously or unconsciously indicate that death is shameful and that mourning must be limited. Schowalter (1974a) writes:

> Adults' reactions to death influence the response of their children. Death has been rightly recognized as a taboo topic, and adults usually encourage children's denial. Ignorance obviates understanding, and keeping the facts of death a mystery makes effective grief less possible. This situation is all the more confusing if the surviving parent then rebukes the child for his lack of feelings. Usually when a parent dies, the child really loses both parents–one to death and the other to mourning [p. 5].

The act of sharing grief and feelings with another person has several benefits, both for children and adults. Among the benefits is the clarification of life as it was with the deceased. The survivors work over memories, discussing both the good and bad times, and reach some sort of perspective about the person and their relationship with that person. During this process the person becomes less idealized and the survivors can go on with the business of life. A second benefit of sharing is that of release, and a third is the realization that one is not alone in one's feelings.

Paul Norman (1969) has made a clear distinction between sympathy and empathy which can be useful in a wide variety of instances.

> In sympathy . . . the subject is principally absorbed in his own feelings as projected into the object's special, separate experience. In sympathy, the subject is likely to use his own feelings as standards against which to measure the object's feelings and behavior. Sympathy, then, bypasses real understanding of the other person. . . . The empathic relationship is generous; the empathizer does not use the object as a means for gratifying his own sense of importance, but is himself principally concerned with encouraging the other person to sustain and express his feelings and fantasies [p. 187].

Thus, in empathy, an individual is allowed unique feelings and ideas. There are no feelings which one *should* feel, and no guilt when one does not feel them.

Accomplishing the work of mourning is extremely important. Kliman (1968) and Wolfenstein (1966) have studied and described several retrospective studies of adult mental illness. Wolfenstein cites the work of Brown (1961) and others who state that people who have lost a parent during childhood "more often succumb to mental illness in adulthood than those who have not suffered such a loss." Wolfenstein cautions that a cause and effect relationship does not exist. She feels that it is not childhood bereavement but, rather, suppressed grief which can create the later problems. Wolfenstein is concerned with children who, because they are not ready for the work of mourning, subconsciously deny the reality of the death. A child should have a continuing relationship with both parents. Occasionally, when one parent dies, a child may remain at the emotional stage he/she is in when the death occurred. Contributing to this possibility is the fear many children have of regressing totally if they let go and cry freely and often. Adults, who know that return to babyhood is not possible, can grieve more openly. Some children also wind up in trouble because they decide that their compact with fate has been broken by death. (Why do good deeds if there is no protection from events of chance?) The poor school achievement and home behavior problems which may result only serve to complicate a relationship with the surviving parent that has already been made more difficult because of the death (Neubauer, 1960).

If, as Kliman and Wolfenstein claim, death of a loved one creates a hazard to the survivors' mental well-being, then a list of factors which would serve to identify surviving children as high risks would be a helpful tool. Kliman has devised such a list. Among the high priority recommendations for preventive psychiatric care are cases when the death was a suicide, when either the deceased or remaining parent was mentally ill, and when a girl of less than eight years of age loses a mother.

OPPORTUNITIES TO HELP CHILDREN COPE WITH DEATH

The most important step one can take in helping children cope with death is to examine his/her own attitudes toward death and loss. It is difficult to offer guidance without coming to reasonable terms with one's own fears, distastes, and past experiences. Talking in small groups is one way to bring about confrontations with our own predispositions. Workshops on loss, held in schools and other settings where people work with children, will grow richer if a reading list is drawn up for members. *On Death and Dying*, by Elizabeth Kubler-Ross (1969), is an account of her hospital research with dying patients and their families. The book's ramifications are broad, and it has become a classic in its small but growing field. Another useful book which draws from many sources is David Hendin's (1974) *Death as a Fact of Life*. Also recommended is Anna Wolf's (1973) paperback, *Helping Your Child to Understand Death*, which was written for the Child Study Association and has been revised and reprinted several times. A relatively new organization has been formed specifically to study problems of death and grief. The Foundation of Thanatology, based at Columbia-Presbyterian Medical Center (630 West 168 Street, New York, N.Y. 10032), publishes many books on loss. *Death and Bereavement*, cited in this article, is one of its many publications. The Foundation is also responsible for the *Journal of Thanatology* and other journals concerned with loss.

Reading adult material is one avenue for exploring ideas. Another way to expand thought is to discuss children's picture books about death (see attached list). Reading these books in a workshop setting instantly provokes reflection, questions, and arguments. Basic questions must be considered: Is it the teacher's place to use these books? Do the books belong only at home? Might the teacher cause, rather than solve, problems? What is the proper timing for offering a book which treats death and loss? Should a teacher read the book to the entire class? Might the book step on the religious tenets of the children's families? Should the book be evaluated in literary terms, or merely in therapeutic terms? Should the book be graphic—how will children react to the descriptions of rigor mortis in *About Dying* and *The Dead Bird*? How do adults react?

These questions and many others have very individual responses. What is right for one person in one setting is not necessarily proper for another. If that principle is kept in mind, workshops can yield individual growth.

Additional opportunities exist for helping children grow in their mastery of concepts related to loss. Research findings concerning grief caused by death are applicable in differing degrees to loss and grief caused by divorce and short-term separations. Professionals at all levels can find out what services their communities provide for bereaved children and their parents. Programs such as Widow-to-Widow, begun in Boston by Phyllis Silverman, and Widows' Consultation Service in New York indirectly aid children. Therapeutic nursery schools exist in some areas. The Center for Preventive Psychiatry in White Plains, New York, is one; Rutgers (New Jersey) Medical School has another. Such programs are springing up elsewhere and can serve as models for other communities.

Research in the area of death has begun to spread. Stephan Gullo, for example, is working on a project in which children who have been identified as high risks in bereavement are spotted before their parents die. While the parents are in the terminal wards, such children are given preventive therapy. Data on this and other research programs can be obtained from the Foundation of Thanatology.

There is growing interest in helping children cope with death. An international conference focusing on death and the child is planned for early 1977. The conference will be held at Columbia-Presbyterian Hospital in New York and will bring together educators, psychologists, doctors, and others who work with children in schools, service organizations, and research programs.

Thanatology is one of the newest branches of scientific study. It is an interdisciplinary study which includes investigations into theology, medicine, psychology, education, nursing, social work and librarianship, and other fields. Because thanatology is in its infancy many questions remain to be answered. But with the increasing interest of many individuals in fostering knowledge and understanding about this basic factor in human life, it seems likely that the lifting of the death taboo may begin in this decade.

CHILDREN'S PICTURE BOOKS WHICH TREAT DEATH

Bernstein, Joanne, & Gullo, Stephan. *When People Die*. New York: Dutton, 1976.

Brown, Margaret Wise. *The Dead Bird*. Illustrated by Remy Charlip. New York: Young Scott Books, 1938 and 1965.

DePaola, Tomie. *Nana Upstairs and Nana Downstairs*. New York: Putnam, 1973.

Fassler, Joan. *My Grandpa Died Today*. Illustrated by Stewart Krans. New York: Behavioral Publications, Inc., 1971.

Kantrowitz, Mildred. *When Violet Died*. Illustrated by Emily A. McCully. New York: Parents' Magazine Press, 1973.

Miles, Miska. *Annie and the Old One*. Illustrated by Peter Parnall. Boston: Little, Brown, 1971.

Schecter, Ben. *Across the Meadow*. Garden City, N.Y.: Doubleday, 1973.

Stein, Sara Bonnett. *About Dying: An Open Family Book for Parents and Children Together*. Photographs by Dick Frank. New York: Walker, 1974.

Tresselt, Alvin. *The Dead Tree*. Illustrated by Charles Robinson. New York: Parents' Magazine Press, 1972.

Viorst, Judith. *The Tenth Good Thing About Barney*. Illustrated by Erik Blegvad. New York: Atheneum Press, 1972.

Zolotow, Charlotte. *My Grandson Lew*. Illustrated by William Pene DuBois. New York: Harper and Row, 1974.

REFERENCES

Anthony, In D. Hendin, *Death as a fact of life*. New York: Warner Paperback Library, 1974.

Bernstein, J. & Gullo. S. *When people die*. New York: Dutton, 1976.

Brown, F. Depression and childhood bereavement. *Journal of Mental Science*, 1961, *107*, 754-777.

Gullo, S. Games children play . . . when they are dying. *Medical Dimensions*, November 1973, 26-29.

Hendin, D. *Death as a fact of life*. New York: Warner Paperback Library, 1974.

Kastenbaum, R. The child's understanding of death: How does it develop? In E. Grollman (Ed.), *Explaining death to children*. Boston: Beacon Press, 1967. Pp. 95-96.

Kliman, G. *Psychological emergencies of childhood*. New York: Grune and Stratton, 1968.

Koocher, G. P. Childhood, death, and cognitive development. *Developmental Psychology*, 1973, *9* (3), 369-375.

Kubler-Ross, E. *On death and dying*. New York: Macmillan, 1969.

Kutscher, A. H. (Ed.) *Death and bereavement*. Springfield, Ill.: Charles C. Thomas, 1969.

Levinson, B. M., & Kinney, J. R. The pet and bereavement. In A. H. Kutscher (Ed.), *Death and bereavement*. Springfield, Ill.: Charles C. Thomas, 1969. P. 271.

Nagy, M. The child's view of death. In H. Feifel (Ed.), *The meaning of death*. New York: McGraw-Hill, 1959. Pp. 79-98.

Neubauer, P. B. The one-parent child and his Oedipal development. *The Psychoanalytic Study of the Child*, 1960, *16*, 471-480.

Norman, P. Psychiatry: Its role in the resolution of grief. In A. H. Kutscher (Ed.), *Death and bereavement*. Springfield, Ill.: Charles C. Thomas, 1969. P. 187.

Piaget, J. *The child's conception of the world*. London: Kegan Paul, 1951.

Salk, L. *What every child would like his parent to know*. New York: David McKay, 1972.

Schowalter, J. Parent death and child bereavement. Paper presented at the Workshop, Spring Conference, Foundation of Thanatology, Columbia-Presbyterian Medical Center, New York City, March 1974. (a)

Schowalter, J. Workshop comments at the Spring Conference, Foundation of Thanatology, Columbia-Presbyterian Medical Center, New York City, March 1974. (b)

Stein, S. B. *About dying: An open family book for parents and children together*. New York: Walker, 1974.

Wolf, A. W. M. *Helping your child to understand death* (rev. ed.). New York: Child Study Press, 1973.

Wolfenstein, M. Death of a parent and death of a president: Children's reactions to two kinds of loss. In M. Wolfenstein & G. Kliman (Eds.), *Children and the death of a president*. Garden City, N.Y.: Doubleday, 1965. Pp. 68-69.

Wolfenstein, M. How is mourning possible? *The Psychoanalytic Study of the Child*, 1966, *21*, 93-123.

Wolfenstein, M., & Kliman, G. (Eds.) *Children and the death of a president*. Garden City, N.Y.: Doubleday, 1965.